Mission to the Head-Hunters

HARPER & BROTHERS, PUBLISHERS
New York

FRANK and MARIE DROWN

MISSION
to the
HEAD-
HUNTERS

Special acknowledgment is made to the following persons for the photographs
reproduced on the pages indicated: Dan Derr (Missionary Aviation Fellowship),
pp. 88 (top), 89, and 93; Kenneth Gosney (Radio Station HCJB), pp. 86-7,
88 (bottom), and 92 (top, right); and Frank Drown, p. 83. All other photographs are by Cornell Capa and are used by courtesy of Magnum Photos, Inc.

To 94-year-old MRS. MARY OLSON,
pioneer missionary of the Gospel Missionary Union
to the Jivaro Indians of Ecuador

Contents

Foreword

by RUSSELL T. HITT
EDITOR OF *Eternity*; AUTHOR OF *Jungle Pilot*

BACK IN THEIR BIBLE SCHOOL DAYS IN MINNEAPOLIS AND Chicago, two young missionaries-to-be—Frank Drown, an Iowa farm boy, and Marie Page, a small-town girl from Berkley, Michigan —caught the vision of planting an indigenous church in a primitive tribe: a church that would be self-supporting, self-governing, and self-propagating.

This book is the moving, heart-wrenching story of how this young couple, against the most incredible odds, saw such a church born in one of the most unlikely places on earth—among the savage Jivaro head-shrinkers whose wanton intertribal warfare has become a legend of the jungles of eastern Ecuador.

The world knows well by now the heroic story of the five young missionaries, fellow workers of the Drowns, who gave up their lives in an effort to reach another primitive tribe. Here is a chronicle of a different kind: the day-to-day struggle of two people, inspired by God, to prevail against the long-entrenched evils of superstition and bloody fighting. In their own simple but forceful words, the Drowns recount the recurring experiences of pioneer missionaries— the dangers of taking the gospel to hostile Indians, the hardships of plodding over muddy, thorn-entangled jungle trails, the unending fight against loneliness, disease, pestiferous insects, and poisonous snakes.

By steadfast faith, willingness to put up with privation, and back-breaking work, they have seen their mission station at Macuma grow during fifteen years from a rough clearing in the heart of the jungle to an efficient gospel nerve center, including "God's House" where the Indians conduct their own services and experimental farm, and schools for boys and girls. Their story shines with the sheer joy of serving God and loving their Indian "neighbors," thereby bridging the gulf between abject heathen bondage and the life of liberty in Jesus Christ.

"In all that fifteen years," Marie once said to me, "there was hardly a moment when there wasn't a crisis of some kind, involving either ourselves or the Jivaros. But even at the time our situation never seemed to us totally grim. We could always see the funny side. We never faltered in our belief that no matter how dark the outlook the Lord would bring us through somehow. And He always did."

When I visited Frank and Marie Drown at Macuma station in 1958, while I was doing research for *Jungle Pilot*, the biography of the twentieth-century martyr, Nate Saint, I saw with my own eyes the fruits of their remarkable accomplishment.

I brought with me some preconceived ideas about the nature of missionary compounds. I thought I would find the missionaries living in isolation from the the "natives," the mission station itself an island reserve of a cherished foreign culture.

This notion was dispelled the moment I stepped from the Missionary Aviation Fellowship plane which brought me to Macuma.

The station was swarming with Jivaros who obviously felt right at home. Most of the men were decked out in ornate headdress of bright feathers, their faces garishly painted. In contrast, the women were drably dressed.

Many of the men carried guns as protection against attack by pagan Jivaros, although in the Christian circle around Macuma, feud killings were becoming a thing of the past. But in spite of their shotguns or occasional blowguns, all were relaxed and outgoing in their friendliness.

A knot of Jivaros were gathered like loafers at a country store on the steps of the plain little building that housed the mission dispensary. The Indians were waiting their turn for the pills or injections that Marie and her fellow workers would provide to help cure their jungle ulcers, worms, wounds, or ordinary common colds. Marie did more than dispense medicine; she gave them kindness and compassion. Through such treatments many came to know the Lord.

Though the Drowns tried to maintain a degree of privacy in their home, I soon discovered that they spent most of their waking hours with the Jivaros. They had learned the greatest of all missionary lessons—identification with those they had come to serve. This couple were demonstrating that their lives were, as Oswald Chambers puts it, "broken bread and poured-out wine."

The very day I arrived I found Frank struggling with one of the many problems that daily tested the reality of Christian witness in the little Jivaro church. One of the young husbands wanted to discard his "old" wife of seventeen for a slight girl of thirteen who before long would bear his child. Frank's tired eyes gave a clue to the emotional intensity of the ordeal in which he was involved. He well knew the long history of polygamy in the tribe, the tension between the entrenched animistic jungle culture and the demands of a new life in Jesus Christ. Here was an issue that involved the happiness of many lives and, indeed, the future course of the church itself. It was a matter that had to be handled by the Christian Indians themselves without too much coaching from the missionary. Yet it required from Frank the utmost in patience, tact, and love to see that the rights not only of the principals but of all the relatives involved were properly safeguarded.

"I feel as though I had been battling Satan himself," Frank said with a sigh when he had done his best.

I saw more evidence of the self-effacement of the Drowns when the Jivaro believers gathered for church worship on Sunday morning. "God's House" was built by the Indians themselves. In architecture it was pure Jivaro, rather like one of their own leaf-thatched palm-pole communal homes, but larger. There was one important difference. "God's House" had a wooden floor rather than the plain earth of their own dwellings. A Jivaro elder conducted the service in his native tongue. Marie accompanied the hymn singing on the accordion. That instrument was the only mark of an outside culture.

How the Drowns found time for their other manifold accomplishments—the scholarly and painstaking preservation of one of the most difficult languages, the establishment of schools for girls as well as for boys, the battle to win a food supply from the reluctant jungle soil—all of these things are excitingly told in their book.

Not the least of their accomplishments has been to bring about, as the basis for an enduring Christian church, a fundamental change in the way of life for this tribal people at a criticial juncture in their history, a change rooted in the introduction of scientific farming methods.

It is my own belief that in years to come many visitors will go to Macuma, as indeed they are doing today, to study it as a shining example of what can be accomplished both in establishing an indigenous church and in bringing enlightenment, physical as well as spiritual, to an underprivileged people.

The Drowns' achievements can be truly evaluated only in terms of the struggle and self-sacrifice required to bring them about. This is the warp and woof of their book, a fascinating narrative rich with incident, compassion, and inspiration.

As for the Drowns themselves, they take it all as a matter of course. They view themselves not as exceptional people but as instruments of the Lord.

They are one link in a long line of missionaries who have faithfully given themselves as "living sacrifices" to make Christ known in the dark places of the earth.

Preface

"THE JIVAROS ARE SUCH A LIVELY, FASCINATING PEOPLE we ought to write a book about them," we said to each other when we first moved to Ecuador's jungles in 1946. But as our days with the Indians became busier each year, we put aside the idea indefinitely.

When Roger and Barbara Youderian came to Macuma in 1954, we found Roj had started writing a history of evangelical work among the Jivaros. After his martyrdom in 1956, Barbara gave us a copy of the material he had compiled. We hoped that someday we might finish the project.

Then in 1959 Melvin Arnold of Harper & Brothers encouraged us to write of our own experiences as missionaries. His undying enthusiasm and co-operation have made this book possible.

For fifteen years we have had a firsthand view of the never-ending drama of the lives of the Jivaro Indians. It has been our special thrill and joy to see the power of the Gospel come on the scene and transform many of the "actors." Of these and their contemporaries we have written.

The persons and places mentioned in the following pages are all factual. Only when two Indians bore the same name has one of them been changed to avoid confusion.

We, Frank and Marie Drown, have worked together writing this story. However, to simplify our presentation, we have written it from Frank's viewpoint except where otherwise indicated.

We are deeply indebted to many persons who have helped in the production of this book:

First, to Mrs. Barbara Youderian, our understanding and faithful co-worker, for typing the original manuscript and for taking over many of Marie's station responsibilities in order to free her to write.

To our mothers, Mrs. Earl Page and Mrs. Mary Drown, who had preserved all our letters since we first traveled to Ecuador.

To Dan and Elsie Derr for providing us with a quiet room in their home in Shell Mera for several months.

To Miss Margaret Nordvedt for copying hundreds of pages of missionary letters originally written by Mr. and Mrs. Charles Olson.

To a host of missionaries and friends in Ecuador who gave of their time to read the manuscript and offer suggestions: Mr. and Mrs. Ernest Johnson, Mrs. Marjorie Saint, Miss Dorothy Bucher, Miss Mardelle Senseney, Mrs. George Gibbs, and others.

To Mr. and Mrs. Michael Ficke for staying in Macuma with Mrs. Barbara Youderian while we flew to New York to be near the publishers during the last stages of work.

To our churches and friends in the United States for continuing their support and prayers and considering this book a vital part of our missionary work.

To Cornell Capa for his superb job as picture editor.

And especially to Mr. Edward Sammis, who worked with us during the final months of revising the manuscript. We are grateful for his innate understanding and skillful handling of our problems.

Our story differs little from the stories of many other missionary couples; the hardships and dangers described are no greater than those they have faced. We would like this book to be regarded as a typical account of missionary work on the Christian front in any primitive part of the world. It should be clear that we view ourselves neither as heroes nor as martyrs, nor are we gifted with special strength or talent. We are just ordinary folk filled with joy, energy, and enthusiasm for carrying on the Lord's work. It is our hope that through this book many others will be enlisted to join us with their prayers, faith, and lives.

Ours has been, and still is, a rich and rewarding life, full of happiness in our family circle and in our daily contacts with the Indians.

We would not have it any other way.

FRANK AND MARIE DROWN

April, 1961

Mission to the Head-Hunters

CHAPTER 1

Preparation for a Mission

Repentance and remission of sins should be preached in His name among all nations.   LUKE 24:47

· As the plane droned over the jungle of the Oriente in eastern Ecuador, taking me back to rejoin Marie in Guayaquil, my mind was a tumbling kaleidescope of vivid new impressions.

I had just had my first glimpse of the lonely, fly-infested outpost where Marie and I would soon be stationed to carry on the Lord's work. In a few days' visit, I had sampled the life that would be ours.

I had seen for myself how hard was the daily existence of the missionary couple now living there, how much it took out of them just to survive, to feed themselves, to fight against ill-health, to communicate with a strange race that had no written language.

I had learned something of the primeval customs that held the Jivaro Indians in their spell—of the dark ways of witchcraft, of the murderous and constant warfare, of the grisly practice of hunting and shrinking heads.

Looking down, I was awed by the vastness of that great ocean of trees. The rivers cut so clearly through the beautiful map below. But I knew that the smooth carpet of leaves was only a camouflage that hid the tangled and turning trails beneath, the steep ascents and descents, the swamps and seas of mud.

It also hid the forces of evil at work in the hearts of the Jivaros. Would we ever be able to prevail against these long-entrenched powers of darkness?

I tried to get it all into perspective. I thought of the ant and what he has to overcome to crawl half a mile with his load of leaves. The big log he climbs must seem like a mountain. He climbs, he falls, he climbs again. But he never gives up.

Then I thought of the hummingbird and how he sees both obstacles and strugglers from high up, in proper proportion.

The plane ride gave me the chance to see the problems that lay ahead of us from the viewpoint of the hummingbird.

I was on my way to tell Marie that in spite of the obstacles and the hardships ahead, this was the place to which God had called us, the place where we would find happiness and satisfaction in serving Him. I had no doubt that she shared my faith.

It was only four months ago that we received the final indication that God wanted us to serve Him in the jungle of Ecuador. It came on a snowy November morning in the year 1945, back in Kansas City. Marie and I, not long married, had been spending several months as young candidates at 1841 East 7th Street, the headquarters of the Gospel Missionary Union. We had no funds of our own—only the promise from the Berkley Community Church in Berkley, Michigan, that if we were accepted as missionaries the church would pay our minimum monthly support. This was a real encouragement to us; but there still remained one question: How was the plane fare of five hundred and ninety-eight dollars to be paid? Time was running out. An older, experienced missionary was returning to Ecuador in December and we hoped to travel with her. But only God knew how the plane fare would be supplied.

Marie and I stood in the hallway with several other missionary appointees watching the mailman unload his pack. We were hoping for letters from our families, but looked in vain for the familiar handwriting. Only one businesslike, impersonal envelope was handed to us. We took it to our room, feeling neglected and forgotten. Sitting on the edge of our bed, we opened it without much interest, expecting some bit of advertising or a printed brochure. Imagine our surprise and delight when out dropped a check for six hundred dollars! With it was a note from a casual acquaintance who knew of our situation, instructing us to use the money for our plane fare to Ecuador. We dropped to our knees and gave praise to the Lord.

We could see then that through all our lives God had been preparing us for missionary service.

I was a country boy, born and raised on a small farm just outside Curlew, Iowa. Next to the youngest in a large family, I learned from growing up with my two brothers and four sisters to live in love and respect with my fellows.

My father, Jay R. Drown, though of sound Christian principles, was no great one to preach or even to talk about the Lord. Not until I was older did I hear him pray aloud in the family circle. But he lived by the standards of the Bible, which he instilled in us by the force of his example, and on occasion, his big right hand. He believed that children should respect their elders and that hard work and sweat were necessary to life. We were never allowed to make fun of anyone less fortunate than we. If any of us broke this rule, his heavy hand came down quickly. To this day I am thankful to my father for also teaching us, by not giving us much spending money, what a nickel was worth.

From early childhood, we all had to do our part to earn a living from our eighty acres. But father saw to it that we had our good times, too. He loved to take us hunting or fishing. Before I was old enough to hold a pole, I'd dig myself a few worms and go out with my brothers to the old dredge ditch along the road. We usually came home with a few bony bullheads which we'd throw into the livestock tank to watch them swim around. I can still hear my father's deep voice when he took us hunting, reminding us always to be careful, take no chances, obey the game laws, and consider the rights of others.

Mother was a devout Christian who knew the Lord as her personal friend and Savior. She taught us all to love Him and His Word. It was she who instilled in me the urge to preach. She led us in prayer, and in the singing of hymns. In snow or rain, mother took all seven of us half a mile down the road to every service that opened the doors of the little white Baptist church. Through sermons heard there and my mother's teachings and prayers, we were all converted before we were twenty-one. Today all of my brothers and sisters are active in their churches.

From boyhood, I had a real love for Iowa's rich black soil and for the work it took to make it produce the best in corn, hay, and oats. I would have been perfectly happy to spend the rest of my life on the farm. But God's call to preach had first claim on my life and before I was eighteen I was practicing sermons out loud, while guiding the plow down the straight rows of the cornfield. I started going to neighboring towns to take part in street meetings with other young folks. This strengthened my faith and also my desire to take the Gospel to others. Before long, I was given an occasional opportunity to preach in a nearby church which was too small to support a regular pastor.

Each of my older brothers and sisters had gone on to Bible School after high school; and I knew the Lord would want me to go too.

But all I had was the conviction. I had almost no money when I landed up north at Minneapolis to attend Northwestern Bible School (now Northwestern College). Minneapolis seemed like a huge city to me. I was homesick; I was lost. But I didn't have much time to brood about it. I had to get busy and find something to do to pay for my board and room and school expenses.

I took all kinds of jobs during my three-year course. I washed dishes in a big hotel; I cleaned rugs in the middle of the night. It took a lot of my energy. But I'm not sorry for it. I learned many lessons in practical Christian relationships with my many employers.

In spite of my broken schedule, I concentrated on the Bible, taking as many courses as were offered. I studied its doctrines, its arrangement, its history, its application to daily living. I also learned homiletics—the way in which Bible truths should be preached. But I was often thankful for those preparatory lessons I had received sitting in the front row at the Curlew Baptist Church.

All through school I had planned to preach. Then, in my senior year, in January, 1944, a zealous young missionary named Paul Fleming came to Northwestern. He was one of many special visitors who addressed us, but through him the Lord really spoke to me. I no longer remember Mr. Fleming's words. But I do remember that, sitting alone at the back of the church, I heard God commanding me, "I want you to go." For the first time I stood up and went forward. I felt great joy. From that moment on I never questioned God's call to me. I promised I would go anywhere in the world to serve Him. I would judge my every decision in terms of preparing myself to be a missionary.

I began making plans. The lands to the southward had always appealed to me. Although there were not many Latins in Minneapolis, a fellow student and I found a little Mexican mission where we started taking Spanish lessons. I got up early every morning to attend 7:00 A.M. student prayer meeting for missionaries.

Now that my direction was clear, I thought of finding a wife to share my calling. I'd had a number of girl friends during my time in school. But now I needed much more than a friend. There was no rule as to whether missionaries should marry; but for myself I felt the need of a partner.

Several girls in my class were going to be missionaries; but only one attracted me. She was a pretty, lively girl from a small town in Michigan. Her name was Marie Page.

I had watched her with keen interest for many months. But I was too bashful to approach her, partly because I had the idea she liked somebody else, partly because I felt she was far beyond the reach of a country boy like myself.

With the unexpected help of our roommates and in answer to prayer, wonderful things began to happen.

In March, when we had a heavy late winter's snowstorm, the senior class got up a sleigh ride. I always enjoyed a good time. But I didn't have the nerve to ask Marie and I didn't want to ask any other girl. I told my roommate all about it. Teasing and encouraging, he kept at me until I called Marie on the phone. She wasn't in her room. I was ready to give up—but not my roommate. He dashed out, calling, "I'll find her for you!" He checked both girls' dormitories until he learned where she was. Then he wrote an invitation, signed my name to it, and gave it to one of the girls to take to Marie. Soon there came back a reply with Marie's name signed to it. She would love to go with me. O joy! O delight!

A long time later Marie told me her side of the story. After a day of wearying work and study she was definitely not planning to go on the sleigh ride that cold and snowy night, particularly since she had no suitable clothes. But *her* roommate had made up her mind for her. She wrote out an acceptance note, and signed Marie's name to it, after insisting on loaning Marie her own snow suit. In spite of ourselves we were brought together by the determined plotting of roommates.

Lumbering along under the frosty stars, sometimes singing with the group, sometimes rolling in a snowdrift and running again to catch the sleigh, I soon found my fears that Marie would prove remote and unfriendly were without foundation. From the first moment, we felt as though we had known each other all our lives. That night when I left Marie at her dormitory I found it easy and natural to ask her for another date. I invited her to go with me to a missionary meeting our class was sponsoring at the YWCA. But even when she said "Yes" I still wasn't sure whether she had accepted because she enjoyed my company, or whether she just wanted to encourage my interest in missionary work.

That meeting brought me my first real understanding of what a missionary's life would be. The speaker was a veteran from the China Inland Mission, the Reverend George Kraft. As he told us of his work and answered our questions, what impressed me most was the sheer happiness which he radiated. He did not talk about the snakes or the hardships; he just told us how much he enjoyed serving the Lord as a missionary.

As the meeting broke up and I bent to help Marie with her boots, to my surprise I heard myself blurt out in a clumsy, half-joking way, "There's nothing I wouldn't do for you—even zip up your snow boots." As soon as the words were out I knew that was how I really felt.

The rest of the year went by in a happy hurry. Marie and I were together often and I was beginning to hope that I might one day win her.

The great night of the senior banquet came and of course I asked Marie to go with me. As we led the line of our classmates into the dining hall, I could hardly take my eyes off her. I had always thought she was nice-looking. But tonight I saw that she was beautiful.

In the past months I had come to know and appreciate her character and personality. I knew now she would be an ideal missionary wife. She had been converted at thirteen. Since that time she had always looked forward to going to Bible School. Back in Berkley, Marie had been one of a small group who did not take part in the school dances and parties. Her own life was full enough as it was. Marie was a girl of good humor, spirit, and energy. She played the flute both in the high school orchestra and the high school band. After school she worked behind the counter in a nearby drugstore. Her evenings she devoted to church work.

Bible School gave her all she had hoped for. She loved, as I did, to listen to speakers from the foreign field. She was an avid reader of missionary biographies. As the year came to an end, she understood that nothing less than a lifetime spent in God's service would be satisfying to her.

I was very much in love. But I refrained from making my feelings known because I wanted to be sure. She, too, seemed fearful of mistaking our attraction for each other for more than God wanted it to be.

June came, and graduation. Marie was to spend the summer in the pine country of northern Minnesota, near Park Rapids, teaching in the same daily vacation Bible Schools as the summer before. I, too, was going to northern Minnesota to do evangelistic work. We discovered we would be only thirty miles apart. But there was no direct highway between the two towns and strict gas rationing was in force, so we had little chance of seeing each other. We said good-by with only the promise to answer any letters each might receive from the other.

In spite of a busy schedule, I couldn't let a day go by without writing. And what was even more surprising, she answered every one of my letters.

By the last of July Marie's Bible Schools were over and she was going home to Michigan. But I could not let her leave without seeing her once more, so I arranged for her to come visit me in the camp where I was working.

On the night she arrived we went for a walk along the lake. I knew that the moment had come. I asked Marie if she would be my wife and go with me to South America. What joy when she accepted! I was now as certain that this sweet girl was the right one to be my partner as I was that God had called me to the mission field. Our love was truly from the Lord.

Once again we parted as Marie boarded a bus for her home in Michigan. Soon I went back to Iowa. It looked now as if we might be separated for some time. Marie had already arranged to go to a missionary training center in Chicago. I had made my plans to return for another year of seminary at Northwestern. All we could do was hope and pray that the Lord would bring us together somewhere.

In August I made a hurried trip to Michigan to get better acquainted with her family. On my way home I decided to stop in Chicago and visit the training center to learn more about it. As a result I realized that God wanted me to go there too. It was a happy decision. I could profit from the training course and also be near

Marie. Now that we were to be together, we saw no reason for not planning a fall wedding.

Wise friends urged us not to marry until we had been in the mission field for at least two years. They pointed out that this would give Marie a chance to get her basic language study before taking up the responsibilities of married life. But after talking it over we decided that we would rather share all our experiences—getting ready, going to the field and learning the language. Also, we both felt we needed the stability that marriage would give to our lives. And so, on November 11, 1944, with our dear friends and roommates from Northwestern joining in the wedding party, we became man and wife. Within a few days we returned to Chicago to finish the first part of the missionary course.

In this training period we were particularly instructed in what a missionary's main task should be. This was more than learning a strange language and holding Bible classes; more than winning souls for Christ. A missionary's chief goal should be to establish churches—indigenous churches that would be self-governing, self-supporting, and self-propagating. "If your work as a missionary does not result in strong native churches that can carry on without you," our leader pointed out, "you will have failed as a missionary." This had been the Apostle Paul's method, we realized, and with God's help, this would be ours.

The following January we went to northern California to complete the second half of this missionary training course at "boot camp." Here we learned the practical side of missionary work—everything from the principles of linguistics to basic medicine, carpentry, butchering, bread-baking, barbering, etc. We were glad to learn these skills which would be useful in helping a primitive jungle people. My own life would one day be saved by what Marie learned here of treating tropical diseases.

What a wonderful six months that was: an education, a challenge, and a delayed honeymoon all rolled into one. We relished it all, the overnight hikes, sleeping out-of-doors, the hymn-singing, the lessons, the comradeship.

Then it was over and we had no plans. We had no affiliation with any mission board and were no closer to getting to the field.

But we did not pass the summer in idleness. Responding to an invitation from friends, we returned to northern Minnesota. This was another link in the chain of events leading us to Ecuador.

One evening the guest speaker at a special missionary service was Rev. G. Christian Weiss, then president of the Gospel Missionary Union. He was a short, jolly man with graying hair and dark expressive eyes. Although we had heard him speak before in Minneapolis, we had never met him personally. But knowing he had served as a young missionary in Morocco, we felt he would understand and direct our ambitions.

After the service we introduced ourselves. We talked with him at length about our desire to go to a needy field. In our innocence we asked if he knew of any tribe of Indians that were without knowledge of the Savior. To our delight he began telling us at once of the Jivaros, a wild and reputedly ferocious tribe, who lived in southeastern Ecuador and the jungle flatlands of northern Peru. This was the first time we had heard the name of those primitive people among whom so much of our future work was to be carried on. Then Mr. Weiss, his dark eyes mirroring our own enthusiasm, drew from his pocket some application blanks and handed them to us. We were excited, for this was our first definite indication of any future prospect. But we were still not sure anything would come of it.

The summer schools ended. We were broke. I had to earn some money right away. The threshing season was at hand. I knew that threshing paid well and it was something I could do. So I took Marie home with me to my family's farm in Curlew, Iowa.

By then I knew our own family would soon number three and I had to take seriously the responsibilities of coming parenthood.

The outlook for Marie and myself was not exactly bright. We had no home, not a stick of household furniture, no money, and no steady job. All of these problems should have given us great concern. But they didn't. Our hearts' wish to get to work in the mission field was further intensified by our desire to get there before the baby was born. The idea of establishing a State-side home to wait for the birth of our little one seemed only a hindrance to our missionary calling. We were missionary parents; he—or she—would be a missionary baby, born on the foreign field.

One night after a hard day's threshing, I sat with Marie at our dining-room table and we began to fill out the blanks Mr. Weiss had given us for the Gospel Missionary Union. But we were in a hurry. Because Marie was pregnant the board might not want to

send us for another year. We decided to go in person to the GMU
headquarters. Halfway through the forms Marie went to the telephone, called the Curlew depot, and inquired about train connec-
tions to Kansas City.

We spent the weeks that followed in getting acquainted with
the organization's sound Biblical policies and godly leadership, and
in learning about the Jivaros and the country where we hoped to
go. We searched the atlas to find out where Ecuador was located,
looked at many pictures of the Indians among whom we would be
working, and listened by the hour to the stories of returned missionaries. In response to our questioning they told us of the dangers
and discomforts, the heat, the heavy rains, the poisonous snakes,
the vampire bats, the stinging gnats, and the strange diseases. Only
through experience would we learn what grace and patience the
Lord would give us to put up with them.

The stories of the Jivaros themselves were enough to daunt the
most daring adventure seekers. We wondered if we would be able
to make friends with, and live among, such Indians as these. Though
outsiders called them "Jivaros" we read that they called themselves
"Shuaras," a term meaning *the* people." They must have been
among the most primitive and savage tribes left on earth. They must
have been among the last, too, to follow the practice of head-hunt-
ing and head-shrinking. The blackened, shrunken head of an enemy,
hung inside the door of the conqueror, was a valued talisman called
a *tsantsa*. We tried to picture how it would be to live with Indians
who had taken part in shrinking an enemy's head.

We discovered that the Shuaras in Ecuador had once lived mostly
on the eastern slopes of the Andes called the Cutucu Mountains.
But as white colonists entered their territory, many of the Indians
pressed steadily farther eastward and southward toward the jungle
flatlands. Here they encountered their most hated enemies, the
Atshuaras. Although Jivaros are subdivided into many hostile groups,
the two principal tribes called themselves the Mura Shuaras (hill
people) and the Atshuaras (lowland people), a contraction of Atshu
Shuaras, so-called because the *atshu* palm grew in the jungles where
they lived.

For generations the Mura Shuaras and the Atshuaras have been
destroying each other with their ceaseless feuds. As the Mura Shuaras
moved eastward and southward from the Cutucu Mountains, armed

with muzzle-loaders obtained from white colonists, they drove the spear-carrying Atshuaras ahead of them. But as the Atshuaras made contact with other soldiers, they also came into possession of guns—big repeating Winchester .44's. With such deadly weapons, they resumed the conflict on more equal terms. Warfare increased until there grew between the two tribes a kind of jungle no-man's land in which members of neither group dared settle for fear of being murdered by the other. Within the larger tribes there were also smaller factions which hated and killed one another. Each killing brought in its wake many more. According to their code, every death was attributed to an enemy's curse, and had to be avenged. This was true even of death from natural causes.

We shuddered to realize that their revenge killings, witchcraft, and related customs were leading to the extinction of the tribe. Unless their basic attitudes could be changed—unless they could become born again children of God—they would be eternally separated from Him.

The Indians' whole way of life was dictated by the tribe's unwritten laws which they called *shuartica*. They did everything according to *shuartica*: the building of their homes, the weaving of cloth, the planting of food, the giving of child brides in marriage, the communing with evil spirits, and the killing of their enemies. Jivaros were unable to change any of their ways because *shuartica* does not change. It admits of no element of progress. Its strength and pride lie in its immutability. We thought again of our goal to plant Christian churches in the jungles—churches whose ministers, evangelists, and supporters would be jungle Shuaras. How could illiterate, revengeful, demon-controlled Indians ever become propagators of the Gospel of Jesus Christ?

One custom in particular of the savage Shuaras haunted us. When an Indian goes to avenge a death he never goes alone. Using the words of an age-old ceremony, he challenges another. These two in turn may challenge two others. The object is to whip up a large raiding party to attack the enemy. Marching toward each other and then back, they repeat the words of the challenge, sometimes antiphonally and sometimes in unison. The emphatic syllables of the challenge are synchronized with the first of the forward and the first of the backward steps, while the guns in their hands are thrust upward on the same beat. For a full half-hour the ceremony may continue. Although the exact words of the challenge are in an archaic form of the language, no longer fully understood by either challengers or listeners, the chant, with its accompanying dance, has the power to carry the performers to a peak of malevolent hypnotism. When their frenzy has reached its height they start out after the enemy.

None of these things which we heard dampened our ardor. These people, too, were loved of God. Who, on this earth, could benefit more from learning the way of salvation from sin and death?

Work of the Gospel Missionary Union among the Jivaros had had a very long and lonely history, dating back to 1903.

At that time, a solitary couple, Mr. and Mrs. L. Freeland, began the work in Ecuador first in a frontier jungle settlement called Macas. In time they were joined by Charles Olson. Not long thereafter Mr. Freeland died, Mrs. Freeland returned to the States, and Mr. Olson carried on the work alone. Then in 1919, Charles Olson married the widowed Mary Freeland. Together they established the still existing mission station at Sucúa, south of Macas in a valley on the eastern side of the Andes, at that time deep in Jivaro territory. For years they served alone until, in 1936, a single missionary, Ernest Johnson, joined them. In the meantime, Mr. and Mrs. George Moffat, working under the Christian and Missionary Alliance, had set up a station two days' walk to the south of Sucúa. But throughout the years right up till 1945, these were the only two places where the Gospel was being preached regularly to the Jivaros in their own language.

Mr. Olson had since died, but Mary Olson was with us in Kansas City. Fellowship with her was one of the highlights of our candidacy. She was an inspiration. She had been widowed twice, had undergone every imaginable hardship and ordeal. Yet there she was, with her wrinkled, dimply smile and her bright eyes, lively as a cricket, radiating joy and love, a living testimonial to the satisfaction of a life spent in the service of the Lord.

Hour after hour she held us spellbound with her tales of riding over the Andes on horseback, traveling on foot along jungle trails, or crossing swift rivers on rope bridges or in dugout canoes.

Every weekday morning she would begin the day with an hour's instruction in Spanish grammar and the customs of Ecuador.

"You know," she said to encourage us when we faltered, "I was thirty-three years old when I first went to Ecuador. And yet, with the Lord's help, I learned not only Spanish but Jivaro. Why, you young people ought to pick up a language or two a whole lot easier than I did and learn to speak it much better." We agreed all too readily, without any idea of how difficult it would be to learn an unwritten Indian tongue.

Then came welcome news. Every evening at the dinner table, letters from missionaries on the fields were read aloud. One of them had special meaning for us. It was from Mr. and Mrs. Ernest Johnson who were trying to get a mission station started among the Jivaros along the Macuma River. They very much wanted a young couple to come and help them. Daring to hope we might be that couple, we filled out our application blanks and set our sights on arriving in Ecuador by the first of the year.

The one remaining problem, how we were going to pay for our transportion, was solved by the arrival of the letter with the six-hundred-dollar check.

Things then began to happen fast. We applied for passports and visas, took health examinations, received our shots, and started packing our belongings. These didn't amount to much, for we had never kept house. We had blankets and sheets, books, a few tools, and a highly prized aluminum double-boiler which some friends had sent as a wedding present from Canada; this was wartime and aluminum was unobtainable at home.

In high spirits we left the mission headquarters for last brief visits with our families and friends in Michigan and Iowa.

But we did not accomplish our good-bys without some tears and sadness. Our parents felt the sharpest pangs at our parting. We were young and had our minds on the intriguing jungle. They understood far better than we what five years or more of separation would mean.

It was six days before Christmas and our last evening in Kansas City. Seven of us were about to leave these homey and familiar walls for foreign lands. The Gospel Missionary Union held a farewell service for us in the chapel room. There were hymns and messages of special comfort.

The words of Mr. Weiss, the president, on the subject of "The Complete Man of God," were so full of wisdom and sound counsel that we were to recall them long after:

"As each of you goes out to the mission field, four men must go with you: the spiritual man, the intellectual man, the social man, and the physical man. You dare not forget any of them on pain of failing as a missionary. You must have robust physical health; consecrated practical intelligence; the ability to make genuine friendships out of casual social contacts; you must build a strong spiritual life maintained by regular and consistent prayer and Bible study habits. The latter is of the most importance, for we are waging a spiritual battle against spiritual powers with spiritual weapons."

The next day we left Kansas City for New Orleans where we would board the plane for Guayaquil, Ecuador. We were glad that everything was ready in time for us to go with the returning missionary, Mrs. Julia Woodward. She knew a great deal about Ecuador, having spent forty-five years of her life there, twenty-five of them without coming home. She was going back to work among the Quichua Indians of the Andes, for what was to be her last term.

Seventy-eight-year-old Mrs. Olson not only went to the train with us, but insisted on carrying Mrs. Woodward's suitcase because our arms were loaded. There in our seats, between laughter and tears, we said good-by. Mrs. Olson's parting words were to tell us how happy it made her that we were going out to work among her beloved Jivaros and to assure us that she would be praying for us.

The first lap of our long journey had begun. We were on our way.

CHAPTER 2

Scorpions and Vampire Bats

*The Lord . . . is not willing that any should perish but that
all should come to repentance.*   II PETER 3:9

SHORTLY AFTER NOON ON SUNDAY, DECEMBER 23, 1945,
our plane touched down at Guayaquil. Our hearts sank as we
stepped into the smothering heat and saw no one on hand to meet
us. Evidently our attempt to get word to the local missionaries who
were expecting us had failed.

All around us quick, smartly dressed Latins greeted one another
in rapid Spanish. How glad we were that Mrs. Woodward was
familiar with the confusing routine in this airport. We followed
her about in the noisy, crowded office while she calmly addressed
the uniformed officials in Spanish, helped us clear our passports,
pursued our baggage through customs, and guided us to a waiting
taxi. She easily directed the driver to the home of our hosts, Mr.
and Mrs. Cornelius Klaassen, the leaders of our Ecuador mission.

With keen interest we looked out the windows at this foreign
city. The first streets through which we passed were lined with lovely
Spanish villas, their gardens bright with hibiscus and roses, surrounded by bougainvillaea-covered walls.

When we reached the poorer districts where low ramshackle buildings crowded against the sidewalk and burros and barefooted cart
pushers nearly filled the narrow streets, we felt even more strange
and far from home. People in dark doorways stopped their jabber-
ing to stare and point at us as we went by.

We saw little to remind us that this was only two days before
Christmas. There were no snow-covered streets, gaily decorated
store windows, carols or tinkling bells such as we had left behind
in Kansas City. Here, it was hot—as hot as the Fourth of July—and

just as noisy. Raucous music blared loudly from sidewalk cafes and firecrackers burst in our ears. A wave of homesickness swept over us.

Our taxi drew up at a two-story frame building protected from the street by a whitewashed mud-and-stone wall. The only entrance was a locked wooden double door. We stood on the sidewalk feeling lost as the taxi went off down the street. Mrs. Woodward gave three sharp raps. We could hear the sound of footsteps scurrying about on the cement inside. Then the doors opened and everything changed. We were engulfed by warm embraces. The Klaassens had been awaiting our arrival and expressed their delight that we had come to share in spreading the Gospel.

Unfamiliar sounds, sights, and smells surrounded us in those first days.

The sounds began early in the morning with the running, shuffling footsteps of those who sold the daily papers. The resident of Guayaquil had only to reach out his window to get his breakfast from passing vendors who loudly advertised their commodities, and, in the process, taught us not a little useful Spanish.

The man who sold butter in little three-cent paper-wrapped pats proclaimed his product in a high-pitched wail, *"Mantequi-i-i-i-illa! Mantequi-i-i-i-illa!"* Hot rolls came by in baskets balanced on the heads of boy runners; oranges in two-wheeled carts pushed by barefoot men; milk in metal containers swung over the sides of braying donkeys.

Life in Guayaquil was one long succession of loud noises. A roaring motor, squealing brakes, the dispatcher's whistle, constant cries of *"Vamos!"* ("Let's go!") announced the passing of the always overcrowded bus. Blaring of taxi horns, grinding and grating trolley wheels, added to the din.

The commanding *"Basura!"* of the street sweeper made us drop whatever we were doing to dump our day's trash and garbage into his cart. Then there was the broom man shouting *"Escobas y escobas!"*—brooms of every description, from ten-foot ones for sweeping cobwebs and scorpions from the ceiling down to kitchen brushes, making him look like a walking corner of a United States hardware store. And there was the deep baritone, *"A uno cincuenta los vasos,"* telling us that drinking glasses could be bought for six cents each. *"Hay que soldar"* proclaimed the coming of a stooped, soot-covered fellow with his soldering iron and bucket of glowing embers, ready to mend any pot in need of fixing. Fruits and vegetables in season, tables and chairs, undergarments, charcoal in gunny sacks, pencils, shoestrings, tinware, glasses of fruitades or Coca Cola —these were some of the items that could be bought from vendors who passed our house in unending stream.

All the life of the neighborhood spilled out onto the street, as people escaped from their suffocating dark rooms to the slightly cooler air outside. Children played with their hoops, kites, or marbles, or practiced soccer; lovers strolled hand-in-hand; office workers and teachers peddled by on bicycles; whole families spent hours in nonstop animated conversation.

And the smells! The air of this port city was not so fresh as its ocean breeze promised. A nearby coffee factory produced its own strong burnt odor. The smells of onion and garlic from our neighbors' soup kettles were constant and overpowering.

But we had our quiet pleasures. One was walking along the Malecón or river drive.

Downtown we saw the formal side of Guayaquil. There was no such thing as casual streetwear. The men wore suit coats and neckties in spite of the heat; the women, the highest heels and latest fashions. Introductions, salutations, and farewells, though businesslike, were courteous, complete, and friendly, and took a great deal of time.

Guayaquil was to be our home for nearly a year while we studied Spanish under the tutelage of senior missionaries and helpful nationals. Having the intricacies of the grammar drilled into us every day turned out to be tedious work.

Those who have never struggled to master a foreign tongue do not know what it is to open one's mouth, hopeful of relieving the pressures of thought and feeling, only to bring forth a few feeble stammerings. But we took it as a challenge and learned to express ourselves little by little. Spanish is such a beautiful language that we wished we had more time to give it deeper study.

We had been in Guayaquil about six weeks when our friend Mr. Weiss arrived from the States. He had invited me to accompany him on an inspection tour of the jungle mission stations of Sucúa and Macuma. With the enthusiasm of youth—I was then twenty-three years old—I could hardly wait to get started. It seemed a long time that I had been looking forward to seeing these stations out among the jungle Jivaros.

Early one morning I reluctantly kissed Marie good-by—this was our first separation since we had been married—and left Guayaquil with Mr. Weiss by train. All day we jolted over the coastal flats, then through the twists and turns of the mountain gorges, up, up, up. By evening we reached the mountain town of Cuenca where we spent the night with missionary friends. The next morning we continued our journey by bus until the road ended high up in the cold, barren, windswept Andes. There we switched to horseback, jogged up and over the divide and started down the eastern slope.

Then the fun began. I had been leading a sedentary life studying Spanish and my muscles were soft. It was about a four-day trip to Sucúa through mountain wilderness. We were on the trail all day, the only resting places, the so-called hostels along the route which were nothing more than open, chilly, lice-infested shacks.

The eastern slopes of the Andes, rocky above, green with jungle below, are like the folds of a skirt. Gushing torrents cut deep ravines in the steep mountain sides. The trail criss-crosses back and forth, now going down in a descent so sheer we had to clutch at branches to keep from falling; now climbing back up. In some places the trail was so faint we had to trust to the instinct of the horses. And there were torrential rivers to be forded. Some of them we waded, up to our armpits. Others we went over on shaky bridges or fallen logs, dismounting while the horse driver went ahead with the animals. Just when we thought we were making progress down the mountainside, the trail led back up again. We were never quite sure where we were.

It was a relief to hit the warm jungle air and tropical foliage. But the trail was still up and down: more hills to climb, more rivers to cross, and the added interest of mud.

Back in Kansas City when Mrs. Olson had tried to describe such trails to me, I could hardly believe her. Now I knew she had understated them. Yet, the missionaries stationed in Sucúa and Macuma had traveled this way with their babies. Maybe I was soft.

When Mr. Weiss disclosed his plans to set up a missionary aviation program that would make such an ordeal unnecessary, I found myself a hearty enthusiast for it.

That night, trying to get to sleep in one of the damp, chilly hostels, I could not help praying,

"O Lord, don't ever let Marie have to go through this. Please bring a missionary plane before the time comes for Marie and our baby to go into the jungle."

On the last day on the horse trail, I came down with dysentery and had to spend a week in bed at Sucúa. For the first time I met Michael Ficke, a big, warmhearted ex-woodsman, and Ella, his generous wife, who were running this mission station. During the time I spent with them I had a chance to reflect on what we had learned about the pioneer missionary effort which had its springboard in this valley town.

When the Olsons first came to the Oriente, Macas was the last settlement along the horse trail. After living there several years Mr. Olson bought land from the Indians at Sucúa and eventually moved his family here. At that time the country around Sucúa was mostly jungle, inhabited by Indians. For over thirty years Mr. and Mrs. Olson had worked to gain a few converts. The difficulties of maintaining their health and food supplies, of reaching the roving, sparse population of Indians hidden over thousands of miles of jungle, of learning the complicated Jivaro language, of traveling the trail, sapped their strength and vitality until they had little left for direct evangelism. They had established no Christian Jivaro churches. But their faithful work had laid the foundation for those who succeeded them.

Through the years, white settlers followed the Olsons along the road to Sucúa. By the time I first saw Sucúa, much of the jungle had been cut down and the land taken from the Indians. The town itself was a white settlement of about a hundred inhabitants with a courthouse, a jail, a slaughterhouse, and a Catholic mission. Many of the Jivaros who had lived around here were moving to the eastward.

That was why Ernest Johnson, who had lived at Sucúa for several years, first as a single missionary and then with his bride Jean, was establishing a new station deeper in the jungle at Macuma.

Even though I was weak and shaky, the moment came to take to the road again, and this time on foot. I was glad to hear from Mike Ficke that he was going with us and was bringing some of his Indians. There were four more wearying days on the trail. Then, at the end, as darkness was closing in and I did not see how I could walk another step, I saw a clearing ahead. We had reached the mission station where Ernest and Jean Johnson lived.

The cleared space wasn't very big. In the middle of it was a low thatch-roofed hut with palm-pole walls. But to me it spelled shelter, warmth, and friendship. After our nights in the hostels or sleeping on the damp ground, no palace could have looked more inviting.

While shaking our hands and pounding our backs in enthusiastic welcome, the lean blue-eyed missionary and his slender dark-haired wife took us right into the kitchen, helped us get off our mud-caked shoes, and brought us warm water in tin pails to wash up. When dinnertime came we all sat down to the best they had to offer—roasted green plantains and smoked monkey meat.

Dinner was a festive occasion. We all talked at once. The Johnsons were starved for news of other missionaries and of the outside world. We compared experiences on the jungle trails. Looking back, we could all laugh at our close calls and discomforts.

But being tired, we didn't talk long before Jean showed us our sleeping quarters. We noticed then that less than half the house was floored. A portion of this served as a bedroom for the Johnsons with their two baby sons, one thirty months old, the other fifteen. The rest was used as a storeroom. There, Mr. Weiss, Mike Ficke, and I were put down for the night.

Weary as I was, I could not doze off, but tossed restlessly in my sleeping bag on the split-bamboo floor. When I turned one way I faced an oval room where visiting Jivaros lay around their fires. When I turned the other way I could see the blackness of the jungle through cracks in the bamboo wall. The night was filled with weird sounds. From the forest came a strange symphony of insects, punctuated by the croaking of a frog. From the other side came the stirrings and grunts of the Indians. And the snoring around me threatened to drown out all else. I thought of the story Ernest had been telling at dinner of the latest killings between the Jivaros and the Atshuaras. If an Atshuara were to creep up on this house, might he not think we were all Jivaros and kill us in our sleep before he knew the difference?

I groaned aloud, trying to find some new position that would relieve my aching hipbones. My mind flashed back to California and those first missionary boot-camp hikes. What fun we had thought jungle travel was going to be! I had not foreseen that fatigue would take away any thrill at hitting the trail. The glamour had worn off completely since I said good-by to Marie. This was reality.

An Indian in the adjoining room sat up, coughed, and stirred his fire. This roused another. The two began a lively and, to me, altogether unintelligible conversation.

But if I couldn't sleep at least I could pray. So I prayed for the Johnsons and for their mission until, through the cracks in the wall, I saw the first pale glow of dawn above the black treetops, and the chorus of insects gave way to morning trills of jungle birds.

Rubbing my eyes, I stumbled from our makeshift bedroom into the dirt-floored kitchen to be greeted by a cheery good morning from Jean. Then I noticed she was staring ruefully at a dead chicken lying on the ground.

"Look at what the vampire bats did last night," Jean said. "And she was my best layer, too." She looked up and smiled. "Anyway, it's a good thing it happened while you were here. Now we can have stewed chicken for supper."

We sat down to breakfast of cooked tropical wheat. I did not enjoy it because it was full of chaff, even though Jean told us she had spent hours washing and cleaning it.

The mission layout seemed primitive to me. The Johnsons had only such basic utensils as they were able to bring in with them. They had made rough furniture from what the jungle offered. The table was built of bumpy split-bamboo boards. Stumps served as chairs. Two wooden crates had reached them out of the many they packed in Sucúa to be brought in by Indian carriers. One was now a shelf in the storeroom; the other a playpen for the baby.

That morning, to save the remaining chickens and two goats from the vampire bats, Mr. Weiss and I helped line with leaves a small shack where they were housed.

In the course of our three-day stay, I came to appreciate these missionary pioneers. On first acquaintance one would think them both almost too frail for jungle living. But though slight in build, Ernest had a determined stubbornness that drove him to remarkable accomplishments, such as mastery of the complicated Jivaro language. Both were single when they came to Ecuador, Ernest a number of years before Jean. They met in a mountain town and were later married. Ernest had been seven years in Sucúa. From that base he had gone with Indian guides up and down the Upano River

Valley to take the Gospel to isolated groups of Indians. He had trained himself to live like a Shuara, to eat their diet of plantain and cassava, to sleep on their hard bamboo-rack beds. His leg muscles were as strong as any Indian's and he could withstand the hardships of the trail as well as they.

In January, 1944, Ernest walked to Macuma to make final arrangements with the Indians who lived there for establishing the new mission station. This location, at a crossroads of jungle travel, was four days' walk from Sucúa. Since he had been here before, he was already decided on the piece of land he wanted to buy: a stretch of virgin jungle on the south side of the Macuma River, several hours east of the Cutucu Mountains.

This land was a piece of neutral territory which he needed so he could be friends with all the Indians. For it Ernest paid the Indians with axes, machetes, cloth, and other trade goods.

"In a year I will come back with my family to live on this land," said Ernest to the Jivaros as he left. "You will have to plant the gardens, so there will be food for us when I return; and you will build us a small house right on this spot. When I come to live I will bring medicines, clothing, and other items that you will want. I'll have plenty of work, so you will be able to earn these things. I will also bring God's Book to help you Shuaras. You will hear about God's love."

Both Ernest and the Indians had kept their bargain.

After repairing the chicken house I went to watch while Ernest directed an Indian man and his wife who were clearing a space for a garden. As a tree crashed to the ground, the bare-backed Indian rested on a fallen log and passed his hand before his face to discourage the swarming gnats. He motioned to his old witchy-looking wife to bring him something to drink.

Noticing he was much younger than I, I asked the missionary how the young man happened to marry such an old woman.

"Because so many of the older men have taken three or four women that there are not enough for the younger ones. They are forced to marry either a little girl six or seven years old or an old widow like Chingasu, as this man, Chumpi, has done. He knows he won't always be contented with her and will later want a younger woman to bear him children. Chingasu is already suspiciously accusing him of looking for a second wife."

Chingasu poured a thick white liquid from a hole in the side of a curved-necked gourd into a small half-gourd. Then she added water from a second gourd and stirred the contents with her fingers. As she brought it to Chumpi, she picked out bits of stringy root, licked her fingers, and continued stirring the mixture. I wondered how the man could possibly drink the stuff, but he held his hand out eagerly toward the bowl. Shutting his eyes, he quickly emptied it. Then handing it back to the dirty, unkempt woman with the drab, ragged piece of cloth only partly covering her body, he picked up the ax. His wife set the gourd on the ground and bent to a squatting position to blow into her neglected fire.

Ernest then called them over to meet me. He introduced me as "Panchu" (the Spanish nickname for Frank). And "Panchu" I have been to the Jivaros since that day.

When the sun began to drop toward the hills in the west, the Indian workers joined others in the visiting room, sitting around on log stumps while Ernest taught them of God. These Jivaros were hearing for the first time the only message that could free them from their fears of witchcraft, wars, and death. The Indians around me gripped their guns in their hands or held them across their knees, mute testimony to their terror of enemy attack. This sense of fear I had seen in the Indians who came with us over the trail. Our guides and carriers had often stopped to examine the remains of a leaf shelter and fire, or strange footprints in the mud. Although I couldn't understand their dramatic-sounding talk, I had guessed that unless they could find out who made the fires and left the footprints, they suspected enemies were nearby. In the Jivaro houses too, where we stayed along the way, the men had not slept through a single night without rising to cock their guns and prowl around the clearing.

I watched the Indian men as they repeated in singsong fashion most of what Ernest was saying. They appeared to agree with him. What actors they were!

The women sat inattentively at their husbands' feet, nursing babies, swatting flies, or killing gnats. Many were much younger than their men, and were the burden-bearers and the slaves. I knew that most of them unhappily shared their husbands with other wives. They did not recognize that the message of God's love was for them, too.

When the service was over all the women arranged their belongings in heavy loads. Chingasu placed her cooking pots, gourds, and a head of bananas in a woven basket which she lifted to her back and supported from her forehead by a strap of supple bark. Holding sticks of glowing fire in one hand and a machete in the other, she walked away from the house. Chumpi shouldered his gun and followed her. The picture of the burdened, stooped women leading the way for their straight-backed arrogant men stayed in my mind.

In the middle of the next afternoon a large party of Indians arrived. Each carried a box on his back. These were the supplies the Johnsons had paid them to bring over the trail months before. The missionaries, according to Jivaro custom, had to spend an hour greeting the newcomers before they could open their packages. We felt for the Johnsons in their disappointment at finding their long-awaited foodstuffs and clothing ruined by jungle dampness. It was plain that supplying the station by Indian carrier wasn't working out.

This incident, in addition to the hardships Mr. Weiss had undergone on the long hike, strengthened his conviction that plane service for missionary stations in the jungle was urgently needed.

Just before leaving he suggested to Ernest Johnson that he start building an airstrip. He had already urged Mike Ficke to begin one at Sucúa. It pleased me to hear Mr. Weiss say that an old classmate of mine, Bob Hart, had volunteered to come down and serve as pilot to help get the program going.

Ernest welcomed the idea, but he couldn't promise when he would be able to finish the job. The labor of clearing land, planting gardens, preparing lumber for a new house, and the daily cares of providing for his family were already putting a serious strain on his rather frail health.

To Ernest the jungle was a living, evil force that he had to fight day by day to keep it from swallowing the clearing with its choking growth. Now, on top of this job, he, with his Indians would have to chop out of virgin forest a strip long enough and wide enough to accommodate a plane. For implements he had not so much as a wheelbarrow—only machetes, axes, baskets on Shuara backs, and fire—to aid him in this difficult task.

We left that lonely outpost not by the trail over which we had come, but by a shorter one. This led in the opposite direction to a

recently established Shell Oil Company camp at a place called
Ayuy, some six hours' hike away. Ernest and Mike Ficke came
along. At Ayuy, Mr. Weiss and I were flown by Shell Company
plane to their main base at Shell Mera where we would find trans-
portation back to Guayaquil.

I felt sorry for my missionary brothers, as I looked out the
plane window and waved to them on the ground. I thought of the
hikes they had ahead of them—Ernest back to Macuma, and Mike
Ficke all the way back over that hard trail to Sucúa.

I was returning to tell Marie all that I had seen and felt about
these crowded days, and what the missionary plane would mean
to us when we, too, came to live at Macuma.

With the compass a little east of north, we winged over those
formidable jungles toward Shell Mera. Off to the left, I could see
the Cutucu Mountains looming up behind the Macuma station.
There, standing out against the sky, was the saddle-shaped silhouette, I had seen from the trail. Already, in some strange way, it had
become a symbol to me of home.

CHAPTER 3

Fallen Hope

All things work together for good to them that love God.
ROMANS 8:28

AFTER I RETURNED TO MARIE IN GUAYAQUIL, WE SETTLED
down to continue our language study.

On the morning of the 19th of April, 1946, the first of God's gifts
to us, Linda Faith Drown, began her life in a dingy downtown clinic
in Guayaquil. I stood by while Marie struggled through nausea
to consciousness after her first experience with ether. In a white
screened crib beside her lay a perfectly-formed baby girl, our own
daughter. Marie wept tears of joy and hugged the trim dark-haired
young nurse, who cautiously held a kidney-shaped dish under her
chin. Not until we had named her did we know that "Linda"
meant "beautiful" in Spanish. It became our hearts' prayer that her
life would be an expression of beautiful faith.

Then, within a few days came a letter from the Gospel Missionary Union in Kansas City, saying that funds were available to buy
a missionary plane for Ecuador, and that there would be no delay
in obtaining the necessary entry permit. When this news reached
the missionaries at their outposts in the jungle, it stimulated both
Mike Ficke at Sucúa and Ernest Johnson at Macuma to hasten the
completion of their airstrips.

Now there was a change in our plans. We had hoped to go
straight from Guayaquil to Macuma. Instead, we were asked to
spend a year in Sucúa, replacing Mike Ficke and his family who
were due to go home on furlough.

Although it meant a definite departure from our personal desires,
we knew it was what God wanted us to do and we were happy to
obey. God was teaching us that to follow Him often meant chang-

26

ing our ideas of what the future would hold. To look ahead one day at a time and trust Him with tomorrow was a lesson we thought we had learned. But it was one we had to relearn—again and again.

Seven months after Linda's birth we completed our basic language studies and Bob Hart arrived in Guayaquil with the missionary plane called "El Evangelista." First he made his initial flights to Sucúa and the Shell camp, Ayuy. He left the plane in Shell Mera, gateway to the jungle, and returned to the coast city. Bob had to play everything by ear in those days; he was doing a real pioneering job. There were no radio communications to guide him. He was not a licensed mechanic himself and had no one to help him, except for one of the Oil Company mechanics at Shell Mera who offered to work on the "Little Cucaracha" in his spare time. Bob's first tasks were to get us and his family to Sucúa.

We were ready to move. Our household goods—baby bed, washing machine, books, tools, and utensils—were packed in large trunks and crates. We had arranged for two Christian Ecuadorian girls to go with us—Ester, a schoolteacher, and Raquel, who was to help with the housework.

Together with Bob, we boarded Ecuador's narrow gauge railroad train and spent all day bouncing and swaying over coastal flatlands past banana and sugar-cane plantations, then up the mountainsides covered with a patchwork quilt of neatly-pieced fields. In the bright whitewashed town of Ambato, Marie and I parted company. She and the girls stayed there with missionary friends for a few days while Bob and I transferred the baggage to a bus and accompanied it down the eastern side of the mountains to Shell Mera. Here the Shell Oil Company had built its main base and airstrip to service the several camps it had throughout the jungle. The company had kindly granted us permission to use the airstrip and store our goods in a nearby shack. Bob and I had to open up the large crates and trunks and repack our household goods into smaller boxes, which could be flown out, a few at a time, in the four-place Stinson plane.

On the appointed day, while Bob and I were still sweating over the repacking in drizzling Shell Mera, Marie, Linda, and the girls took a taxi from the center of Ambato to the town's seldom-used airstrip on a high plateau about twenty minutes away. They reached there at ten o'clock in the morning to await Bob's arrival with the plane which would fly them to Shell Mera and then on to Sucúa.

Marie sat down beside the strip and made the baby comfortable on a bed of long, tough, dry grass blown by the mountain breezes and warmed by the sun. Several inquisitive workers from a nearby hacienda drifted by. The many questions they asked were far from reassuring: Did Marie know there had been no regular flights here for months? Did she know they were not expecting any plane? Did she have any idea what the weather was like at Shell Mera? Had she been in radio contact with the pilot?

All Marie could tell them was that she had arranged to meet the plane there that day.

When noon came, they ate the little lunch of sandwiches and fruit they had brought along. Still no sign of the plane. The weather was beautiful at Ambato and she did not know what could be delaying Bob. Marie passed the hours walking up and down the airstrip, carrying Linda, chatting with the girls and the ever-curious passersby. Never once did she doubt that the plane would come. Her faith was so strong that she did not give any thought as to how she would get back to town in case Bob didn't show up by nightfall.

But the Lord in His faithfulness did not forget us. Back at Shell Mera, around three o'clock that afternoon, the weather suddenly cleared. Bob was able to start out, flying up between rugged mountain ridges to Ambato.

The workers from the hacienda, clustering around the airstrip, were even more astonished to see the plane come in and fly off with Marie and the girls than they had been to see them there in the first place.

Marie's trip—her first experience in flying through narrow, twisting mountain passes—was a thrill to her, but to me it was the definite answer to my prayer. She and the baby would not have to undergo the dangers and sufferings of that horseback-and-foot trek. The flight from Ambato to Shell Mera took twenty-five minutes; from Shell Mera to Sucúa, forty-five. One hour and ten minutes of comfortable—though sometimes awesome—flight had replaced between five and ten days of miserable trail-slogging. My heart lifted in praise to God for this great blessing.

On our second wedding anniversary we moved into the large frame house in Sucúa which Mr. and Mrs. Olson had built so many years before. Our household was growing.

Besides Ester and Raquel, a young medical missionary, Señor José Andrade, who had been converted through the ministry of the Fickes, stayed on to help us. He continued to run the small medical dispensary for both white colonists and Jivaro Indians. A couple of weeks later Bob Hart brought his wife Ivy and nine-month-old son Bobby to live with us. Our "family" now numbered nine.

This was the first time in our married lives that we were not living in a dormitory or someone else's home. The full responsibility for running the house—as well as the mission—was ours. We began to get some idea of what our parents had gone through for us.

We had not been in Sucúa very long when we were visited by a senior fellow worker, George Moffat, who with his wife had established a station far to the southward for the Christian and Missionary Alliance. He had undertaken a long journey on horseback to look in on the young missionaries and give us the benefit of his wise and kindly counsel. Among the many helpful things he said was that the tool the Devil used most successfully in keeping missionaries from winning souls was just plain hard work.

We came to understand how right he was. There were meals to prepare and the families to care for. Even with Raquel to help with the dishes, the washing and ironing, our wives seemed to spend most of every day cooking, baking, cleaning house, or minding babies.

All these tasks took much time and effort since we had no such conveniences as are enjoyed at home, to say nothing of prepared foods. There was no electricity. We studied at night by gasoline lantern. Our wives and Raquel used a gasoline iron. They cooked on a slow clumsy range for which wood had to be chopped and carried. They did their own canning, and baked all the bread, cakes, and cookies. Water had to be carried in buckets and boiled. I butchered our own meat. There was no refrigeration and no way to keep things. But how we blessed the late Charles Olson for the lovely fresh oranges and grapefruit from the groves he had planted in the front yard so many years ago.

I had to give most of my time to chores outside: overseeing the large fields of corn, pasture grass, banana, plantain, and cassava; looking after the chickens, horses, and cattle; and keeping the buildings in repair. There was also the supervision of those who came to work for wages—improving the airstrip, clearing ground, gathering and chopping firewood, and erecting a hangar for Bob's plane.

There were petty annoyances—as with the gasoline-powered washing machine. On many a washday, Marie and Ivy would be ready with the hot water and dirty clothes, only to find that the cranky little engine wouldn't run. Then there was nothing to do but wash the clothes by hand or wait till I got the engine going. I spent hours taking it apart, cleaning it, and putting it together again. The Indians were fascinated by the wringer and by the fact that the motor drank gasoline. I let them smell the stuff just to watch them wrinkle up their noses.

Most of our missionary activities were with the white population. Even the fifteen Jivaro boys who attended the mission's boarding school spoke Spanish. It was good training for me. I preached my first sermons in Spanish at the regular Sunday services while Marie taught both a Sunday School class for the settlers' children and a singing class in the Jivaro school. With Señor Andrade's able help we held open-air services in the town square on Sunday evenings. We all sang; Andrade preached; I gave my testimony; Marie played the accordion. On weekdays we visited the townspeople. Señor Andrade helped us improve our Spanish grammar and study the books assigned to us as new missionaries.

Bob Hart's plane was an attraction to both white settlers and Indians. The yard around our house was usually filled with people waiting to see him land or leave. In one way or another, they all wanted to take advantage of it. Bob used to fly the sick from Sucúa, Macas, or other nearby settlements to Shell Mera from where they could go by bus to get medical help. Aside from his missionary trips, Bob had to limit his services to emergency cases, because the insistent colonists asked for more flights than he could handle. Running such a flight program was a first-time experience for us, and there were no rules to go by.

Bob began making regular flights to Camp Ayuy with supplies and mail for the Johnsons. He would detour over Macuma on his way back, both to signal Ernest that his supplies were in Ayuy and to check on the progress of the new airstrip. Early in March Bob found a note from Ernest at Ayuy saying the strip would be ready in two weeks. When Bob returned to Sucúa with the news I decided to go with him on that maiden flight. I hadn't been back to

Macuma since my visit and I wanted to see how the station had developed since that time.

We came in for the landing. Bob lowered the flaps and shouted, "This is it, Frank! Watch that log at the other end!" I couldn't take my eyes off it. That log seemed to come up and fill the whole windshield before Bob slowed the plane to a stop.

From a maze of fallen trees at the side of the strip, Ernest and Jean, followed by several Indians, came running to greet us. We saw the new house he had begun and marveled at all the land he had been able to clear, not only for the airstrip but for gardens as well. Some of the Indians remembered me and called me "Panchu."

It was nearly noon and the air was hot and oppressive as we prepared to leave. Bob turned the tail of the plane to the big log and revved up for the take-off. I felt the wheels leave the ground. But as we whizzed by the end of the short rough strip itself, our wings were still below treetop level. Only a few hundred feet of jungle had been cut down for the approach and we were using these up fast. "Will we make it?" I shouted above the motor noise. The plane seemed to have no lift, which we realized could happen in this still, moist, midday jungle air. High treetops were racing toward us. Bob turned slightly and missed one tall jungle giant, but others were coming at us. Then the wings caught a slight air current and we were up and over. It left me slightly weak, but thankful to be aloft. This experience convinced us that more work would have to be done on the strip to make it safer. But the main thing was that air service for Macuma had begun. This meant much to Marie and me since we were still looking forward to going there to work with the Johnsons.

At Sucúa our dependence on plane service grew from month to month as Bob flew regularly to Shell Mera and back for supplies and mail. Then one day in August this blessing came to an end.

I was out in the yard preparing some duck feed when I thought I heard the sound of a plane motor. Although I couldn't see any plane I set the feed down and listened more carefully. For several days we had been expecting Bob to return from a series of flights to Shell Mera and Macuma. But when he failed to come we supposed, since we had no radio communications, that it was because of bad weather.

I heard the sound again and ran through the yard to the airstrip to make sure there were no wandering cows on the field. Then the noise of the motor faded.

"Why doesn't he come in?" I thought to myself. "The sky is plenty clear."

I heard it again. But this time it didn't have the familiar pitch. Suddenly I could see the plane. It was not the little gray-and-maroon Stinson, but a black-and-yellow Grumman Goose, which I recognized as belonging to the Shell Oil Company. What could be bringing it this way? Our airfield wasn't big enough for that plane. I watched it turn toward the ridge at the south, lose altitude and disappear behind the trees. Then I heard the noise of the motor again. It grew louder; it was coming back. Surely he did not expect to try for a landing. This time it whisked by no more than fifteen feet above the ground. Marie and Ivy ran with the children from the house and stood beside me, watching. Again it came back. This time I saw a man standing in the open doorway of the plane. He looked steadily out—but beyond us—and all around. A sinking feeling hit me in the pit of my stomach. He was looking for the little Stinson.

That meant Bob must have left Macuma—or some other point—on schedule. Now I understood why he had not returned. He had not reached Shell Mera. He was down somewhere in the trackless jungle—I had no way of knowing where. I looked at Ivy and Marie. From the drawn expressions on their faces I knew they must be thinking the same thoughts. They took little Linda and Bobby and walked slowly back into the house.

My heart was troubled. Bob's work meant so much to him, and to those of us who had come to depend on the plane. By this time he was not only serving Sucúa and Macuma, but a neighboring station to the south and another far to the north.

To all of us the plane meant regular mail and supplies of staple foods and fresh vegetables; and even more important, that sense of security when anyone became ill. Medical help was now only a forty-five-minute flight and a day's bus ride away, instead of a week or more by trail. There was Bobby Hart. He might have died, in spite of all Señor Andrade could do for him, from diarrhea and vomiting if it had not been for the plane. Bob and Ivy had flown him out to Shell Mera, and then taken him by bus to Quito where they were able to get expert medical care before it was too late.

What a relief to us all when they finally returned with a well, happy baby!

Now Marie and I were up against a grim situation. We were expecting our second child. I knew that Marie should be under a doctor's care, and we had planned to go to Guayaquil where Marie would stay until she had her baby, delaying our departure so that our visit would coincide with a missionary conference. Our plans were to leave this very week. We had allowed our sugar and flour to dwindle to almost nothing, thinking we would be away. We had come to depend so on the plane. And now—

But Bob's fate was our immediate concern. Was he alive or dead? It didn't seem right that he had come all the way to Ecuador to rot in the jungle with no one to help him.

I stood alone for a long time, thinking, forming a plan, then went inside to the others. Marie and Ivy and I sat around the table, first praying, then talking about what steps we could take to find Bob. We wondered if I should organize a search party to comb the jungles along the flight routes. We decided I would first go to the army base at Macas, the provincial capital, to see if I could learn anything there. Several Jivaro boys offered to go with me.

The day began with rain and fog. But I knew I faced greater odds than the weather in hoping to find Bob. I said good-by to Marie, Ivy, and Linda, with tears in my eyes. I took Ivy's hand. Trying to keep my voice from breaking, I said, "We'll do our best to find him." Then I started out on foot.

The much-traveled road to Macas had always been one of the worst of the horse trails. Spurred on by fear for Bob's safety and the urgency of my errand, impatient with the clinging mud that slowed my speed, those twelve miles over hills and through swamps seemed endless.

At the army base, I went straight to see the major in charge. He told me that at seven-thirty that evening he would be in radio contact with his headquarters in Quito and might have some word. He invited me to listen with him.

Seven-thirty came. The operator leaned forward. He could receive by voice, but had to transmit by key. He tapped out his message, then settled back. We all stood with our eyes glued to the radio receiver, fearful of what it might have to tell us. Then the message came through. Yes, the plane, pilot, and one passenger, a fellow missionary named George Poole, had been missing now for eight days. Missionary Radio station HCJB, at Quito, had dispatched a sound truck to Shell Mera and were setting up a field communications base there. A search party was being organized at Shell Mera. We were asked to form another at Macas. I hastily scribbled the news and sent it by horse runner to Ivy and Marie, knowing they were waiting anxiously in Sucúa.

The word spread quickly through Macas. Tension mounted. This was a loss in which many shared. The first plane which had come to break the isolation of jungle life was missing. There was no lack of volunteers to help find it, both among local residents and army personnel.

Some time that afternoon, a Saturday, an Indian who lived near Shell Mera arrived in Macas. He reported that on the day of the disappearance he had seen a plane flying very low over a river at what we guessed would be about ten minutes away from the old camp. All sorts of rumors started to circulate. But there was nothing trustworthy to be learned until we could make contact with Quito again at seven-thirty that evening. I was watching the clock. The minutes seemed hours: seven-fifteen; seven-eighteen; seven-twenty; seven-twenty-two; seven-twenty-five; at last, seven-thirty.

The operator sent his message and waited. The receiver began to crackle. Straining our ears while the operator fiddled with the knob to cut down the static, at last we heard it:

"Stay in Macas . . . Stay in Macas . . . George Poole has just been brought into Shell Mera by Indians. He says that on a flight from Macuma engine failure forced a landing only five minutes away from Shell Mera. The pilot suffered a leg injury in the crash. Mr. Poole left him by the plane to go for help. But he found none, lost his way, and wandered alone for two days. When he finally circled back to the plane the pilot was gone. He thinks that Indians must have taken him away. A rescue party is leaving from Shell Mera."

Again I wrote out the news to be sent back to Sucúa by horse runner.

But our fears were not all quieted. We still did not know whether Bob was alive. No further word was radioed to Macas Sunday night; nor yet on Monday. Then, on Tuesday morning we heard that Bob had been found! The missionary search party was taking him back to Shell Mera. With vast relief and a lighter step I hurried off for Sucúa to take the tidings to Ivy and Marie.

But now, with all plane communication cut off for the foreseeable future, a new ordeal loomed ahead of us. I had been advised to take Marie and Linda, Ivy and Bobby, out to civilization at once. This would mean traveling by horseback over the Andes. Aside from the hardship on the children, Marie was now five months' pregnant and could hardly stand such a trip. Ivy's heart had been weakened by rheumatic fever in childhood and the journey would be even riskier for her.

We talked this over for several days and were still undecided, when one morning a Shell plane roared by overhead to drop us our first direct communication from Bob.

His note read:

"In spite of having spent eleven days in the jungle with nothing to eat but one raw squash, I'm all right. My leg was broken near the ankle, but it is getting better. The Shell directors have decided to send a company plane to Sucúa for our families. Try to lengthen the airstrip."

Here was new hope. But to stretch out the airfield would require hired labor, and hired labor cost money. Where was it to come from?

I couldn't help thinking of the hundred dollars Marie and I had set aside, a little at a time, to buy a radio which we so badly needed to keep in touch with the plane. We had it tucked away, all in Ecuadorian sucres, in an envelope in a drawer. It didn't take us long to decide to use it.

We rounded up all the men we could find—both colonists and Indians—and put them to work. Each day's payroll ate alarmingly into our fast-dwindling radio fund.

On September 16, Marie wrote in her diary:

"Spent the day washing and packing our clothes. We expect the arrival of the Shell plane any time. It is hard not knowing at what hour to be ready to leave. But we are experiencing more of the Lord's grace in teaching us patience. Frank works hard—too hard—every day on the airstrip. The field has been lengthened to 2,300 feet. But now we have spent all the money we had."

We finished the prescribed length in a remarkably short time. One day after another went by—then a week—still no plane.

Finally we decided I would have to walk to civilization to see what I could do.

On my way I stopped in the village, hoping there might be mail. There was—a letter from Bob, telling us that the Shell Company had finally decided it would be too much of a risk to try to land one of their big planes on such a small airfield.

I went back to the house to deliver this sad news to Ivy and Marie. Again we talked it all over and concluded that it would be best for me to continue my journey as planned. I had no definite objective in mind. In my desperation, my head was full of all sorts of wild schemes. Perhaps I could persuade a commercial airline to fly in for them. Perhaps I could organize a group to help me get them out over the jungle trails instead of having to climb the Andes. In any event, I would walk to Macuma, then to Camp Ayuy, and from there try to get on to civilization.

The trail to Macuma was no easier to travel than I remembered it from my first trip. Heavy rains had made the mud deeper than usual. On the morning of the third day our party reached the headwaters of the Macuma River and found it almost too heavily flooded to cross on foot. The four Indians and I joined hands to make the crossing, in true Jivaro fashion. In this way, if one slipped the others would keep him from being washed downstream. What a beautiful lesson for the Christian walk through life, I thought. Just in this way should we hold each other up through prayer. We hiked long hours every day in order to make time.

When we reached Macuma, after traveling that up-and-down trail, I was exhausted.

I had known for some time that the Johnsons had gone to Guayaquil, since Jean was expecting a baby. Their work was being carried on in their absence by our old friends from California boot-camp days, Keith and Doris Austin.

Doris wrote a note to Marie, describing my arrival in Macuma, which she sent by the Indians who were returning to Sucúa:

"Frank got here just before dark on Thursday. Imagine my surprise when I looked out the door and saw him! He had been running for over an hour and needless to say, was all in. He was unshaven, of course, and completely covered with mud. With a bath and some supper he looked a little more like himself. After not having eaten anything all day, he must have eaten too heartily, because the next morning he was sick to his stomach. However, he went on to Ayuy, even though he didn't feel like it. Two of our Indians went with him.

"Frank seems to think that if you girls must walk out, it will be easier for you to come this way, rather than by horseback over the Andes. I'm sure you could make it if you took your time. You could stay here and rest as long as you wanted before going the last day to Ayuy.

"In a note he sent back Frank said he was leaving Ayuy by plane that same day. He found the last part of the trail the worst of all, because it was so hilly. I think he noticed it more because he didn't feel like himself."

I reached Guayaquil just in time for the missionary conference, thinking sadly that Marie and I had planned to attend it together.

I went first thing to see Bob Hart, who had been in the hospital there. He still had his leg in a cast and had lost twenty pounds. He told me the story of his eleven days in the jungle.

Bob had not been taken away by Indians, as George Poole had thought. When George did not come back, Bob decided to try to make his way through the jungle toward Shell Mera. He picked up a stick to use as a cane because he had to drag one leg. Two things he took from the plane: an expensive camera belonging to a fellow missionary, and a yellow, crooknecked squash Jean Johnson had given him to take to us. He got his bearings every morning from the distant zoom of the planes taking off from Shell Mera, and from the course of the little streams which he knew flowed into the Pastaza lying between him and the oil camp. He could not handle the squash, the camera, and the cane; so he would throw the camera and the squash ahead of him into the underbrush and hobble along until he caught up with them. Before the first day ended, he found he had to choose between the camera and the squash. He chose the squash. That was all he had to eat for eleven days.

When the search party found Bob, he had come out on the bank of the Pastaza. He was sitting there, chin in hand, trying to figure out some way to build a raft to float him to the other side.

Bob's testimony of God's care thrilled us all at the conference. He said that each day he had prayed it would not rain. But every night he would lay on the bare ground, shivering and soaked with torrential downpours. God had reminded him: "My grace is sufficient for thee: for my strength is made perfect in weakness" (II Cor. 12:9). In spite of the great danger of contracting fever from exposure, God had kept him free from illness and given him strength to walk a little farther each day until he reached the Pastaza.

When the meetings were over, a group of us including Ernest Johnson and Keith Austin went back to Shell Mera. We were anxious to find the fallen plane. We wanted to see for ourselves how badly it had been damaged and whether there were any parts that might be salvaged. Not one of us considered this accident as the end of missionary air service in the jungle. We knew that others were coming to carry on the work Bob had begun. We remembered the words of Isaiah 40:31: "But they that wait upon the Lord shall renew their strength; they shall mount up with wings as eagles; they shall run, and not be weary; and they shall walk, and not faint." Those words seemed a literal promise to us then—a promise which sustained us.

The place where the plane fell was only a day's walk from Shell Mera. We had no trouble finding it. When we parted the branches and saw with our own eyes the miraculous way in which the plane had fallen, we praised the Lord anew. The little Stinson, it seemed, first struck a palm tree, turned over in midair, and came down on its back. The wings straddled a gully, leaving the cabin suspended and the occupants unharmed. Fearing the plane might burn, Bob had tried to get out in a hurry. But his foot had caught in the twisted rudder pedal. In the effort to wrench it free he broke his ankle. The motor was resting solidly on a log. One had to see it to believe it could be possible.

We set to work stripping the parts that might be useful. We removed the wheels, front seats, parts of the motor and instrument board and strapped them on our backs to pack them out.

As we turned away, we gave a last look at the remains of the plane that had meant so much to us. It was destined to lie there forgotten, the home of rats and cockroaches. The myriads of umbrella ants using it as a handy bridge across the ravine would never know it had once been a proud bird soaring above the skies, the sound of its approach eagerly awaited wherever it went.

CHAPTER *4*

Back to Civilization

*I press toward the mark for the prize of the high calling of
God in Christ Jesus.*   PHILIPPIANS 2:14

WHILE I WAS STILL IN SHELL MERA IT BELAME CLEAR TO
me that whether I liked it or not, I had no choice but to take Marie,
Ivy, the children, and also Raquel out over the eighty-five miles of
jungle trail. I discussed this with Keith and he offered to help
me on this trip.

A month had gone by since I left Marie and Ivy in Sucúa. As
they had no more flour to make bread, they had been living on
corn, corn, corn—corn-on-the-cob, creamed corn, fried corn.

We made plans to leave Sucúa for Macuma. Our sojourn here
was coming to an end. From Macuma we would go to Guayaquil
for Marie to have her baby. Ester would remain with a woman missionary who came to take our place until the Fickes should return
from furlough.

In spite of all that had happened we were sorry that our year
at Sucúa was ending. Our experiences here had begun to give us
a love for the jungle and its people. We packed our household
goods into fifty- or sixty-pound loads, and arranged for a number
of Indian carriers to take them to Macuma. Even though we knew
the journey ahead would not be easy, there was nothing to do
but go.

Early on the morning of October 27, 1947, our curious caravan
set forth, some on horseback, some on foot, for the first stretch
to Macas. I had Linda up in the saddle with me; Señor Andrade,
who would go with us as far as Macas, held Bobby Hart. Neither
Marie, Ivy, nor Raquel had done much horseback riding. Although
their first attempts to guide the horses were frightening, they managed to hang on.

It was muddy most of the way. The horses plunged and lurched. Their legs often sank deep in the muck, and made loud sucking and popping noises as the beasts struggled to pull them out. About noontime we came to a place that was so bad we had to ride with our legs sticking straight out to keep them from dragging and gathering more mud. At last Marie dismounted and walked along the outer edge. It was easier for her to plow on by herself than to struggle to keep her balance in the swaying, pitching, uncomfortable saddle.

At Macas we were hospitably received by the major who had helped us many times during our stay in Sucúa. He even opened a can of artichoke hearts—a rare delicacy in that part of the world—to give the typical meal of rice and meat a luxurious touch. Our beds that night were only bare boards, but we rolled in our blankets and slept soundly.

Next day we left the horses and continued on foot. We tied the children into wooden chairs we had made out of packing boxes and strapped them to the backs of the Indian carriers. Tramping down, down the long steep descent to the Upano River, the Jivaros would nearly double over to balance their heavy loads.

The only way to cross the swift, wide river was by dugout canoe. The ferryman who was to be there with his boats was nowhere in sight. We sat on the bank and waited. Marie freed the children from their chairs and let them run up and down the rocky shore.

A sudden drenching shower came up. We all ran together and made a leaky shelter by throwing our raincoats over some bushes. As we sat huddled in there, Marie recalled that this was Ivy's birthday. We all sang, which delighted the children and made us laugh to think of having a party in such strange surroundings.

The ferryman came at last. The Indians went over first with the boxes and baskets. Our wives and babies went next. They all crouched as low as possible to avoid upsetting the unsteady canoe. With my heart in my mouth, I watched the precious load being swept downstream and out onto the rushing waters. I lived a lifetime before I saw them wave to me from the other side. The rest of us were finally ferried over. We then hurried as fast as possible to make up for the long delay. That night we slept at the house of some Jivaros who lived by the side of the road.

Next morning, when we turned off the road onto the jungle

trail, it was rather like leaving a glaring city street for a dim high-vaulted cathedral. The Indians went ahead noiselessly; even the insects and birds were hushed in this awesome forest. But we soon found there was another side to the jungle besides its beauty. Our wives' feet and legs were quite unaccustomed to such abuse as they encountered here. The way was a kind of Pilgrim's Progress —climbing over fallen logs, slipping in the mud, snatching for a steadying branch, being scratched by thorns or tripped by vines, and alternately panting up steep ascents or through oozing swamps. Marie remarked that the United States Army could probably never devise a better obstacle course for the toughening of its recruits.

Mud, mud, mud—always ankle deep and sometimes up to our knees. It stuck to the women's trousers and boots, making them as heavy as lead. Marie had put on a pair of my overalls when we left Sucúa, which served very well while riding horseback. But on the footpath they were more troublesome than helpful. Being much too long, they collected mud all the faster. And since bending down to roll them up was hard for a woman six months' pregnant, I had to stop again and again to do this for her. When they still refused to stay rolled, I cut them off just below the knee. Later, when she got wet up to the hips, the overalls began to bind on her knees and make it hard for her to climb. She asked for another fitting, and I had to cut them even shorter. The next day she discarded them altogether and continued the trip in comfort, wearing a wrap-around rose print maternity dress.

The days were long and hard for the mothers and Raquel, but the nights were even longer. As they tramped along the trail, they would wish for night to come so they could stop and rest. Then, after lying down a while on leaves spread out on the hard ground, their strained muscles twitched and jumped, their bones ached, and they would wish for daylight to come so they could start walking again.

Ivy, Marie, and Raquel were usually so tired by the time we made camp that it took all their strength just to eat and get themselves and the babies ready for the night. Keith and I did most of the cooking, dishwashing, packing and repacking of bedding, clothing, and food, besides making the leaf shelters and building the fires.

Our feet were wet every day, all day long. We had two changes of clothing, one for day, one for night. After picking out our campsite, we would go to the nearest stream and rinse the mud from our boots, socks, and trousers. It was always wonderful to change into dry things for the night. But in the morning it took a lot of grit seasoned with good-natured banter to get back into those wet clothes.

I pitied the children most, jogging along as they did in their chairs, sometimes awake and crying, sometimes asleep, their heads swaying and jerking on the Indians' backs. Although heavily loaded, the carriers would go faster than the women, so Keith usually ran along with them while the rest of us followed. We always caught up with them by noon. Often Keith would already have fed the children some powdered milk mixed with warm sterile water he carried in his thermos bottle.

They gave us a number of scares, one of which particularly sticks in my mind. We had stopped to have our lunch together as usual, this time in a clearing on top of a knoll. Keith had trampled down a spot of brush and weeds and untied the children so they would have a chance to move around a bit. After enjoying our lunch on the spread-out leaves, the girls and the Indians had started ahead, while I finished packing my knapsack. I stooped to pick up a can of cookies on the ground, but stopped with my hand on the can. A shiver ran up my spine as I saw the bright hues of a deadly coral snake slither away into the bushes around the clearing where the youngsters had been playing.

I could only conclude that God had kept the poisonous reptile dormant. It was only one example of the way the Lord took care of us, protecting us not only from fevers and diarrhea, but also from serious accident.

As we went along, the girls got their second wind. They made a game of counting the number of streams they crossed and the number of times they fell. We came to the last day. Keith and the Indians thought that if they hurried ahead with the children they could make it to Macuma before nightfall, and were soon far in the distance. But the worst climb of all lay just before us; because of Ivy's heart we had to take it very slowly.

At the top of the ridge the view out over the valley was breath-taking. But the way down was so steep that the girls' leg muscles kept knotting in pain, so we had to stop often to rub and relax them.

We were at the bottom; the sun was sinking toward the Cutucus behind us. We would have to push hard to reach Macuma before night closed in. This was a flat level stretch and we almost ran. It was now getting so dark we could hardly see the trail. We were quite close to Macuma—I urged the girls to go faster. But the strain was too much for them. Ivy dropped down on a log and sobbed, "I'm not going to take another step. I don't care how close we are. I'll just have to stay here all night."

Our blankets and dry clothing were ahead with the other Indians. We could not possibly sleep in the forest. Somehow, the Lord helped Ivy to get up and stumble on. The blackness closed in. I pulled a flashlight out of my pack, but the batteries were almost gone. One of our two Indians lit a bit of tree resin he had found in his basket, thus giving us a flickering beacon.

We left the trail and found ourselves in the maze of logs and brush that still covered the approach to the airstrip. The Indians and I began to call "*Tu-u-u-u-u-u-u-u-u-u-!*" in the hope that someone in the house would hear. Nothing but the sounds of the jungle ... We called again. "*Tu-u-u-u-u-u-u-u-u-u-!*" came an answering call at last. A few minutes later the flare of a gasoline lantern assured us that Keith was coming to show us the way. Oh, what a moment that was! We saw clearly that the end of the airstrip was only a few yards ahead. Swinging down its wide grassy length was pure joy after all the logs and mud we had left behind.

Inside the house were hot water ready for our baths and hot soup for our supper. Doris Austin had already fed Bobby and Linda and then put them to bed between clean sheets and blankets. After chatting a while with Keith and Doris, we retired for the night. How grateful we were that we could look forward to a week's rest in Macuma and that the worst of our trip was behind us.

By comparison, the remaining day's walk to the Shell Camp at Ayuy seemed easy. From there we were soon on our way by Shell Company plane to Shell Mera, then on to Guayaquil where Ivy and Bobby were happily reunited with Bob. Raquel returned to her family, and Marie and I helped with missionary work here while awaiting the birth of our next child.

CHAPTER 5

Beginning Life in Macuma

Lo, I am with you always.   MATTHEW 28:20

ONE DAY TOWARD THE END OF JANUARY, 1948, WHILE WE were still in Guayaquil, a letter came from Ernest Johnson that caused us much concern.

We knew that he was anxious for us to join him in Macuma soon and that he was doing all in his power to arrange for us to fly from Shell Mera to Ayuy in a Shell Company plane. From Ayuy it would be only a day's walk to Macuma. Without this help we would have to travel over that dangerous horse trail from Cuenca to Sucúa to Macas, then by foot to Macuma through days of that seemingly endless jungle mud.

Now Ernest had learned that the Shell Company was quitting Ecuador. It had found no oil and was closing down its jungle camps including Ayuy.

"If you were here now," he wrote, "you could fly in one of the empty cargo planes that go to Ayuy every day, returning to Shell Mera with personnel and equipment. It will not be long before this camp is abandoned completely and the flights will stop. You must not delay."

This meant we ought to leave Guayaquil immediately. But our baby was not yet born. We could only trust God to keep those planes flying.

In mid-February, baby Ross was born. But shortly afterward we were told he had a heart defect. Doctors advised us that he must be kept in Guayaquil for at least three months' medical care.

Another letter from Ernest told us that the Shell Company definitely would not be flying after the middle of April—two weeks away. By then Ross was nearly two months old and we could wait no longer. Although it was entirely against the doctors' advice, we felt led of the Lord to go ahead.

We hurried our preparations. Arrangements had been made with the Johnsons to engage a Christian Ecuadorian family named Lopez to go with us to the jungle to help with the material work.

We left by train with them, traveling to the mountain town of Riobamba. There we had to stay a few days to buy supplies. We were counting every hour, because we had no way of finding out on what day the Shell Company would stop its plane flights. Finally one morning in the cutting cold of 4:00 A.M. we boarded a *mixto*, a vehicle that was half-bus, half-truck, in the hope of reaching Shell Mera by nightfall. The only route was a narrow, twisting, one-way road that wound round the edge of steep precipices down the eastern slopes of the Andes to the jungle. Marie, our two little ones, the Lopez family, and I all squeezed onto the hard benches, while our baggage was piled in the back along with gunny sacks of vegetables and assorted boxes. We were thankful for every foot of descent, since we were worried about the effect the high altitude might have on baby Ross. But so far he seemed all right.

Halfway to Shell Mera, our *mixto* ground to a halt. We saw in front of us another *mixto* stopped before a pile of mud and rocks that covered the narrow mountain road. People standing alongside informed us there had been a landslide. Stepping out, we saw that the road ahead was blocked. Someone said it might well take days before it could be repaired. A delay of a few hours could make us miss the last plane to Ayuy.

But since others around us took the disaster as a matter of course, we did, too. We unloaded our belongings, paid the driver, and, carrying babies, sacks, and boxes, picked our way over the muddy debris.

On the other side similar confusion reigned. Here were trucks, buses, and *mixtos*, headed in the opposite direction, unable to carry their passengers and cargo any farther from Shell Mera. The drivers on both sides of the washed-out road were dickering with stranded passengers and switching loads. Marie and I bargained with a driver on the Shell Mera side, and finally settled ourselves, children, and baggage in another *mixto* for the rest of the trip. Although we were assured we would be leaving immediately, we sat for over an hour until every inch of space—inside and outside—was packed with impatient mud-stained passengers and their gear. By this time it was raining and getting dark. It was cold outside; the air within reeked of damp clothes, perspiration, and human breath.

At last we started to move, first going backward down the narrow road until the driver found a place where he could turn around. We forgot our discomfort as we enjoyed the changing scene from barren mountain grasses to rich jungle growth. Now and then the incongruous sight of a lovely lavender orchid bending over from the clay banks gladdened our eyes. In the last moments of daylight as we rounded a turn we saw the familiar saddle-shaped silhouette in the Cutucu Range that marked the headwaters of the Macuma. Our destination seemed so tantalizingly near.

It was quite dark now and we could see nothing. But the change from the cool mountain breezes to the humid air of the jungle indicated we were not far from Shell Mera.

By the time we arrived it was quite late and the Shell offices had long since been closed. We would have to wait patiently till morning before learning if the planes were still flying.

Now for a place to sleep; we were all dog-tired. In the town's only boardinghouse there was but one room to be had—four bleak walls with one bare bed and no windows. Here our party of five adults and three children passed the night.

I went first thing in the morning to the Shell office. Bad news: Camp Ayuy had already been stripped; the planes were no longer flying there.

Downhearted, I went over to the hangar to see the pilots in the hope I would find one who was a friend of Ernest. A quiet, reserved young Englishman listened impassively while I told my story.

"You know, I've got a mother back in England," he said when I had finished. "It would make her happy to know I'd helped a missionary. I'll fly you to Ayuy."

I ran all the way to the boardinghouse with the glad tidings. We had to wait three more days for the pilot to schedule the flight. But it didn't matter. We were going to make it.

Ayuy was a dismal ghost town. On my last visit, its buildings and yards had been filled with the cheerful sounds of men at work. Now they were silent and overgrown with weeds. Some structures had burned down. Termites and cockroaches had done their destructive damage on others. But barracks and cookhouse were still intact. We slept in one and cooked our meals on the big range in the other.

On his return flight, the pilot had dipped his wings over Macuma as a prearranged signal to Ernest to send Indians to help us. Although it was noon on the day they came, we left with them at once, in spite of the fact that it would mean spending the night with the babies in a Jivaro house on the way. Once more we strapped Linda into the box chair. One of the women carried baby Ross in a sling around her shoulder, just as she would have done with her own child.

Climbing the steep trail up from the Macuma River, we had our first glimpse of the Johnsons' new large bamboo house at the top of the rise.

To move into this house with the Johnsons was like coming home. Our room was light and airy with bright curtains at the windows. There was a bed with a mattress on a palm-board base, with two smaller ones for Ross and Linda.

It didn't matter that we would have to sleep under stuffy nets to protect us from the biting vampire bats, that there was no electricity, no fresh milk, and only rarely any meat. This was the place to which the Lord had called us and we loved it.

To watch Ernest and Jean using daily opportunities to make friends with and help the Indians who were always coming and going, was an inspiration to us. We wanted to be like these missionaries—to talk with the Indians and gain their confidence. We were aware this would take a long, long time, for we could catch only a few phrases out of the Jivaro jabberings. We were eager to have a part in everything they had to do—clear the jungles, build a combined church and schoolhouse, help relieve the sick, visit among the Indians, and teach them the Word of Life.

In the evenings, after putting the children to bed, we sat around the kitchen table and talked of our great dreams. By the light of the gasoline lantern, we drank in all the Johnsons had to tell us about their life among the Jivaros and what we might accomplish together.

The biggest job was to lengthen the airstrip. We would have to get this done in time for the arrival of the first Missionary

Aviation Fellowship plane, which we hoped would be no later than July or August. We wondered if our staple food supplies would last till then.

On one of these nights, Ernest, his blue eyes shining, told me of his vision of training Jivaro boys to be preachers and evangelists. My mind flashed back to our missionary training course. This was what we were here for—to establish indigenous churches that would go on long after we were gone—and here was a man, a veteran in the field, who shared our goal. I felt inspired.

After building the schoolhouse, we were ready to start classes. Jean would teach most of the Spanish secular subjects; Ernest would give the Bible lessons in Jivaro; Marie would lead the hymn singing; and I would take care of the lessons in arithmetic. The next step was to enlist the students. I offered to go along with Ernest to remind the Indians that it was time to send the boys to school again. But Ernest, from his experience, understood better than I that getting the co-operation of the Indians was not going to be easy. At best they were indifferent; most were openly antagonistic.

We went first to call on a patriarch named Washicta, who had nine sons. Charles Olson had sometimes stayed at his house during his itinerating through Macuma. Washicta had consistently opposed Bible teaching and the idea of a missionary school. But Ernest accorded him the respect due a Jivaro chief by paying him the first visit. Also, Ernest understood that visiting a Jivaro home would be a real treat for me.

After a two-hour walk we came to the clearing surrounding the low oval-roofed house. As we stepped into the dim, smoky interior it took several minutes before our eyes could distinguish anything but the bare outlines of the room.

Around the wall was a series of bamboo racks. These were the Jivaros' beds. At the end of the beds were forked sticks to support the sleepers' feet. Underneath were the embers of smouldering fires that kept their feet warm during the night. There were no windows, only two very narrow doors, one through which we had entered, one leading to a room beyond. This, Ernest explained to me, was the *tangamash*, or men's quarters. The *ekenta*, or space for the women and children, lay beyond the farther door.

The head of the house, Washicta himself, sat stolidly in the center of the room on a *cutanga*. This was a very important piece of furniture, a two-legged stool without back or arm rest, its curved seat rubbed shiny from constant use.

Ernest and Washicta began to talk. As they did so, other Indians came and went. I began to get my first clear impression of the Jivaros in their native surroundings. They were mostly small in stature, with Mongolian features. The indolence of their movements was in contrast to the alertness of their eyes. It took only a few words to change them from apathy to excitability. Most of them wore long straggly hair and the wrap-around *itipi*. I was also impressed by the designs on their faces, which were either for decoration or, in the case of hunters, for camouflage, to simulate the shadows of the forest. They always kept their guns at hand, laid across their knees or standing between their legs as though in readiness for attack. These were old-fashioned muzzle-loaders that they obtained from white traders.

While the men talked a woman entered from the *ekenta*, bringing clay bowls of *chicha*. This milky-white liquid brewed from the cassava root is the Jivaro household drink. The root is cooked, then masticated by the women to speed its fermenting and spewed back into the pot. It is then left to ferment and becomes a slightly alcoholic beverage, not unlike a strong beer. At times it is a mild social drink, at times the basis for their orgiastic feasts and revelries. The women served Washicta and the other men. We waited quietly while they drank. Not to drink with them, I found, was not considered an offense against their hospitality.

Ernest and Washicta soon picked up their conversation. Although I could not understand anything they said, I was fascinated by the rhythmical, explosive sounds of the language and the dramatic gestures accompanying their conversation. I could have listened for hours. Talking seemed to be the particular pride of the Jivaros, their art and form of self-expression. They did nothing else nearly so often nor so well. Each individual Jivaro is a talking repository, not merely of news of the day, but of history, folklore, superstition, tradition, and vital statistics. What people elsewhere in the world get from their television, radio, newspapers, books, and magazines, these Indians get from one another. And they give it out with flair and style. I felt sure no cast of actors on television or the movie screen could be so dramatically arresting as this group of Jivaros recounting their simple everyday experiences. As I listened to the two men they appeared to be competing, trying to outtalk each other. Evidently one really had to be able to speak the language in order to gain the respect of these Indians. I determined to learn it as fast as I could.

My first impressions of these Jivaros and others I had met, were that they were like friendly, uninhibited children. Also, they were not a downtrodden beaten people like the Quichua Indians I had seen in Ecuador's mountains, but were independent, self-centered, and arrogant. But although their liveliness attracted me, I was repelled by their filth and personal habits. They always smelled of perspiration, smoke, and rotten food, and scratched themselves like monkeys. Most of these men and women had worn their garments until they were unsightly with stains, then dyed them a deep purple. They regarded soap as a medicine to be used only for skin diseases.

Outwardly they were an easygoing, laughing, careless lot. I could hardly believe that Washicta, now looking like a gentle grandpa with one arm around his naked son, was also a drunkard, wife-beater, polygamist, and a murderer.

Now the old man and Ernest rose to their feet as a sign the visit was almost ended. I couldn't tell whether Washicta had consented to send his boys to school or not. I stood with them and recited the two words I knew of Jivaro good-byes before following Ernest out the door.

Washicta still did not want his sons to come to school. He believed like all Jivaro men that it was more important for his boys to become strong warriors and skilled hunters than it was to read and write. The year before, three of them had run away from home to attend the missionaries' school. If they came this year they would probably do the same thing. I could see it would not be easy to establish schools for these jungle children.

A week later when the classes began with fifteen boys (including four sons of Washicta who had come to us against their father's orders), I understood more of the problems involved. Most of the students were far less civilized than the ones we had known in Sucúa. Few came to us fully clothed or with any conversational knowledge of Spanish, which was the language we were to teach. They were completely undisciplined and had little respect for rules. They attended when they felt like it and ran away at the slightest feeling of boredom or resentment. They complained about the food Ernest cooked for them, the clothes we gave them, and about the two hours of weed cutting required of them daily.

But like children anywhere, they loved to sing and play. I helped fashion for them a long seesaw by fastening a pole to a stump. Sometimes I went to the river with them to fish. Although I couldn't talk much of their language, it wasn't hard to make friends with these responsive Jivaro boys.

The schoolhouse was a thatched palm-pole hut. The boys sat on long board benches with a high bench in front of them to write on. Although they were very intelligent, they had to learn everything from scratch. They had never before tried to understand pictures, and didn't always recognize when they were wrong-side up. It took days of practice before they succeeded in writing neat rows of a letter of the alphabet on the restricting blue lines of their notebooks. Jean taught them Spanish, using Ecuadorian primers. They received their first wondering glimpses of the outside world from colored illustrations Jean had cut out of the *National Geographic*. They had not known that any world existed outside their own.

The boys took naturally to arithmetic and liked learning to count. When we got up to numbers beyond their fingers and toes we used beans or corn kernels. They enjoyed naming the months and days of the week.

Some were quicker to learn than others. We wished there were more like Wampiu. His mind was a sponge. Even after school hours he kept asking questions and practiced writing with charred sticks of wood on trees whose bark he had skinned with a machete.

Besides helping with the school, we drew plans and began building our house. For the first time in our married lives we would be living by ourselves in our own home. Working with bamboo, jungle thatch, and long-haired Jivaro helpers was an exciting challenge to me. It was great fun to try to imitate these men skilled in picking up vines with their toes and folding and tying leaves on the roof.

When the house was ready and we moved in, we felt as though we were living in a bushel basket. The bamboo walls and springy floors of the same material were filled with cracks. These had both advantages and disadvantages: dust and dirt could easily be swept through them and onto the ground; any spilled liquid quickly disappeared. But very often a table, bed, or chair leg would go crashing through, leaving the occupant surprised and somewhat shaken.

The cracks in the walls also made convenient peepholes for the Indians. Our back porch often overflowed with brown-skinned visitors come to satisfy their curiosity about our strange ways and customs. When they couldn't see enough through the windows they walked around the walls to peek through the cracks.

And as they looked they laughed with amusement. They thought their own ways were far superior to ours. They were fascinated by the white diapers hanging in the sun to dry, but wondered why we needed those things. Any Jivaro woman knew enough to hold her baby away from her at the proper time and leaves were always handy for cleaning up. As for washing dishes and tableware three times a day with soap and hot water—that seemed to the jungle dwellers definitely pointless. How much more sensible to eat with one's fingers from disposable plates of leaves as they did, afterward rinsing only the few gourds or clay pots in a nearby stream. Indian mothers could not understand why Marie needed so much paraphernalia just to give Linda and Ross-boy their baths. All they had to do was take a mouthful of water, hold it until it reached body temperature, spew it slowly onto their babies, then rub and wipe them dry with their hands.

No wonder the Jivaros did not share our high opinion of our own hard-working missionary wives. To them, Marie was a rather useless creature. She could not walk the trail with a load on her back, nor plant the garden, nor peel the barklike skin from the cassava root without cutting herself. She did not even nurse her own babies. She spent most of her time cleaning her house or making strange marks on sheets of paper. But those marks produced neither food nor clothing, so what good were they to anyone? What good was she?

The Jivaro's world is a man's world. Once he has cleared his land of the trees and brush and built his house he is free of family responsibilities. He may then weave himself a new *itipi* or fashion crowns and ornaments of feathers for his hair. Aside from such duties, he has nothing to do but hunt and fish, loaf and talk about his exploits. As Keith Austin put it, the Jivaro is master of the three S's—sitting, sleeping, and spitting.

His multiple wives do all the cultivating and harvesting of food and carrying of heavy loads, besides cooking and caring for the children. To a Jivaro mother, her children are her chief delight. She never likes to be without a little one in her arms and nurses her babies until they are three years old. As we learned more about them we understood why they felt our way of life ridiculous.

Now that we were in our new house, we began serious study of the Jivaro language. Ernest gave us regular lessons from a small grammar he had compiled. Marie spent long hours copying it in longhand and memorizing its conjugations. But I learned more by always being at Earnest's side when the Indians came to work in the morning or when he paid them in the afternoon, and as I listened and watched I would try talking with them myself.

Ernest warned us that the Indians were accustomed to communicating with the white man in a kind of trade language, a highly simplified form of Jivaro. This was what he had learned during his first year in Sucúa; but when he went on the trail he found he could understand only a part of what the Indians were saying. He determined to forget the trade language and master the true Jivaro. He also set before us the same goal.

However, we did not gain facility in this language as quickly as we had done in Spanish. That had been simple compared to the complications of learning Jivaro. There were not even words to express the spiritual concepts we had come to teach the Indians. Their language is rich in terms which describe their jungle surroundings, family life, adventures in the forest, wars, and witchcraft. It would be years before we would learn all their varied and eloquent expressions associated with evil, hatred, killing, lust, witchcraft, and filth.

But finding phrases to expound the truths of the Bible would be something else. There were no words for salvation, grace, belief, or peace. After long and patient work Ernest had discovered only a few which approximated thoughts of joy, comfort, patience, gentleness, goodness, and the many other virtues named in the Bible. When we spoke of the righteousness of God we had to employ the same word the Indians used to describe a well-cleared garden patch. We had to face the fact that since the Jivaros did not know these things they felt no need to talk about them.

But the more we studied the more we loved this strange jungle tongue.

Besides helping us with the language, conducting school and Sunday services, our senior missionaries also offered medical care to the disease-ridden Indians. Nearly every day someone would come to the mission in need of medicines. Although they always went first to their witch doctors in times of illness, they were slowly learning that some of their ailments could be better cured by the white man's remedies.

One such case was a Jivaro baby, brought to Jean by his mother in serious condition. Jungle people generally suffer from intestinal parasites and this child was evidently another victim. Jean administered a shot for dysentery and waited—but without much hope.

About ten minutes later, the mother, moaning with grief, called frantically to Jean. He had begun to roll his eyes and breathe spasmodically. His feet and hands were already cold. Jean applied a hot-water bottle, rubbed him, and gave him a heart stimulant. But it was to no avail. The child died in his mother's arms.

Tearfully, Jean then did her best to comfort the woman by telling her that her baby was safe with the Lord and that she would surely see him again someday if she would just put her trust in Him.

We could only hope the woman understood, as we watched her go wailing down the path, her dead baby clutched to her heart. We clung to the hope that someday there would be Christians among them who would trust in the Lord in time of sickness, even in the face of death.

There were other cases, though, that had a happier outcome. One day we saw Jean approaching our house running and crying. She wanted Marie's help in treating a baby who had rolled off a bed rack into an open fire and was badly burned. Five days had gone by since the accident before the child's parents, a Jivaro named Pitur and his wife, could make up their minds to bring the baby to Jean.

Upon examination, Jean and Marie found one side of his head was literally cooked and smelled putrid. There did not seem to be much that they could do. They had to wipe away so much of the rotted flesh that the bone showed through. Jean dressed the wound and made the parents understand that they must bring the baby every day to have the dressing changed. For nearly a month Pitur and his wife complied faithfully. Marie sewed caps for his head and helped the mother wash and change them. Slowly, new flesh grew over the scalp until finally the baby recovered completely. But he would always have to wear a cap to cover the bald ugly scars.

Another day, about three months after school had opened, old Washicta came for medicine. He had become somewhat reconciled to his sons' being in school but was too proud to admit it was good for them. Truculently, he demanded that since four of his boys were in school and working in our gardens, he ought to get medicine free. He wanted more sons and asked Jean for some pills that would give him strength so he could have more children. "If I have another son won't he come to your school?" he reasoned insistently. I don't know what she gave him, but it must have had the desired effect, because within a year he did have another boy.

During these months with the Johnson's, Sunday preaching services were held in the schoolhouse instead of in the missionaries' home as when I first visited Macuma. Ernest always gave simple Bible lessons with an evangelistic emphasis. Whenever he asked how many wanted to become Christians there would be an enthusiastic response among the thirty to fifty Indians in attendance. But there was more real understanding of the Way of Salvation manifested by the schoolboys who heard Bible teaching each day than by the older ones who came only occasionally. Even though there was growing interest in knowing God we saw as yet little evidence of changed lives.

But Ernest kept on preaching, visiting, praying, and planning for the salvation of the Jivaros. And often we talked of establishing another mission station among the tribe to the southeast, known to the Jivaros as their fiercest enemies, the Atshuaras. Some of them had lived along the Macuma years before Ernest had moved here. One afternoon while I was building my house, some pieces of broken pottery were brought to me by Indians who had been grubbing stumps from our new yard. "These were made by Atshuaras," they had said as they rubbed fresh dirt from the primitive-looking bits of clay. "Some of them used to live right where you are building your house in the days before our grandfathers drove them away.

Now we never see them anymore. They live many days downstream hidden in the deep forests like wild animals. It is impossible to get at them, they are so fierce."

And I had heard stories, too, of the wars between the two tribes. Although the Atshuaras did not shrink the heads of enemies they killed, they were hated and feared by all the Jivaros. Only a few years before we came, Big Saantu and a young witch doctor named Catani had led a war party against the Atshuaras and shrank one of their heads.

It was with these Indians that we hoped to make a friendly contact. We prayed that we would be able to win not only Jivaros for Christ but Atshuaras, too. We knew that the power of the Gospel could change their lives and break down the barriers of hatred and warfare that stood between them.

One Saturday afternoon while Ernest and I were working with a group of Indians lengthening the airstrip, one of our schoolboys named Tiwi emerged from the brush. His new shirt and trousers were tattered and dirty. We leaned on our shovels, brushing the stinging gnats away from our perspiring faces, to rest a minute and visit with him. He laughed as Ernest told him we were doing the job the lazy schoolboys should have finished the day before. Looking out to the hills, Tiwi said he was thinking of going monkey hunting and would like to buy some gunpowder.

"Come along," said Ernest, shouldering his shovel. "Let's quit for today and give the fellow what he wants." His blue eyes twinkled as he said in Jivaro, for Tiwi's benefit, "Next week after Tiwi becomes strong from eating his monkey meat, he'll level that pile of dirt in no time."

One afternoon a few days later we heard Indians shouting, "*Shuar maayi! Shuar maayi!*"

The boys poured out of the schoolhouse at the sound of the piercing voices.

"What are they saying?" we asked.

"Men have killed! Men have killed!" Jean translated quietly so as not to disturb our children playing nearby.

It was not until later that evening while sitting around the kitchen table that we heard the whole story from Ernest:

"Tiwi did not go monkey hunting after he bought that powder and shot from us last Saturday. Instead he went straight to the house of his uncle named Nawich." Ernest's normally genial face grew angry as he realized how he had been deceived. "This is what happened:

"A few months ago Nawich gave his oldest daughter to a young witch doctor who lived downstream in Catani's territory. Soon afterward the girl got sick and died. Nawich thought the witch doctor had cursed her. He plotted his revenge. Nawich sent for Tiwi, and promised him his youngest daughter if Tiwi would help him kill the son-in-law."

Marie broke in, exclaiming,

"To think that our Tiwi who sang the hymns so happily should get caught in that evil trap!"

"Tiwi accompanied Nawich to the son-in-law's house," Ernest continued. "They asked him to go fishing with them and he went, not suspecting anything. After fishing for two or three days they visited the house of a relative of Nawich near the Cusutca River. They all sat down to drink *chicha*. As the son-in-law lifted the bowl to his lips, Nawich shot him in the stomach. He did not die, but lay on the ground screaming and begging the Shuaras to end his agony. But Nawich would not allow anyone to shoot again.

"'Let him lie there and think a while,' he said. 'Did he not kill my daughter? Let him suffer. Let him feel pain.'

"Tiwi finally picked up a spear and drove it into the heart of the tormented man, thus earning his bride. Then the other men in the house went wild, threw spears into the son-in-law's body, and tore out his hair.'

"But where are Nawich and Tiwi now?" I asked.

"Oh," Ernest answered in a matter-of-fact tone, "they're still living with relatives near the Cusutca River."

As newcomers, we were shocked that the murderers were so well known, yet nobody was doing anything about it. There were no authorities close at hand to call on. We considered sending a letter to our friend, the major in Macas, but Ernest pointed out there weren't enough soldiers to arrest all the Jivaros who had taken a part in revenge killings. So Nawich and Tiwi would go free—at least until some member of the young witch doctor's family avenged his death.

"There is no end to this slaughter," observed Ernest sadly. "And no hope for the Jivaros, except in God."

We four were the only missionaries in thousands of square miles of Jivaro territory this side of the Cutucu Mountains. That night, as we prayed together, we felt completely unequal to the task of changing the Jivaros in this vast area. Yet we knew that God's power is, and always had been, unlimited. We would faithfully continue our Sunday services, and take daily opportunities to teach the Bible to all. His Word—not force—would someday change their hearts.

Tiwi never returned to school. He and Nawich remained in hiding, fearing revenge from their enemies.

Our days, filled as they were with language study and contacts with the Indians, passed quickly. It soon was the middle of August in that year 1948, and no plane had appeared. Our salt, sugar, rice, and flour were running low. Still more disturbing, our supply of powdered milk which we needed so badly for our babies was nearly exhausted.

We had been so certain that the MAF plane service would be in operation by now, that we had lengthened the airstrip to twelve hundred feet.

But shut off in our jungle clearing, we had no way of knowing what was going on. For several months we'd had no contact with the outside world by radio, plane, or foot messenger.

Ernest and I decided to walk to Shell Mera. We would take a party of Indians to help bring back needed foodstuffs, including the indispensable powdered milk.

Just as we were leaving we heard from the Indians that a white man had appeared at one of their houses. Upon investigation we found that he was a Shell Company employee who had flown out to Camp Ayuy and then walked to Macuma to check on some cement markers the company had left behind. I quickly took advantage of the chance to fly with him to Shell Mera.

As we circled for a landing and looked down, I could hardly believe my eyes. There on the long Shell airstrip was a new yellow Stinson. The MAF's long-awaited plane had arrived. God had answered our desperate need.

I sought out the pilot. He was a slim, sandy-haired, engaging young fellow named Nate Saint. He was all sympathy when I told him of our plight at Macuma.

A few days later, Nate made the first of several trips to our isolated station. That MAF plane changed our lives. He brought us mail and food on regular flights. Once he flew in with our washing machine, bed, and other household items which we had left behind in Sucúa. On another trip he brought a small light plant and a generator. At last we would have not only light by which to study, but some radio communication with the outside. Shortly before Christmas, Nate came with a welcome visitor, Mr. Don P. Shidler, new president of the Gospel Missionary Union.

Christmas had always been a happy time for us. Now we hoped to bring something of its joy and significance to the Jivaros, who, for the most part, knew nothing of it. We planned three days of special services, games, and feasting. To our surprise, nearly a hundred and twenty Jivaros showed up. With so many there wouldn't be nearly enough meat to go around. Ernest decided to kill some of his precious chickens and ducks to make up the deficit.

Conducting the services and preparing meals for so many people kept us busy. The Indians listened respectfully while Ernest preached; many agreed that God's Word was good to know. But aside from a few schoolboys there were no real Christians. There was no joyous spirit, no loving exchange, no singing of carols such as we were used to at home. Instead, we noted among the Jivaros a strong feeling of fear. They had come here in groups for protection, armed with guns or spears. Their talk was all of murder and threats of killings. For us it was a Christmas that left much to be desired.

But now there loomed another event to which we could look forward. Shortly before New Year's we were all planning to fly to Shell Mera, a few at a time, to go on to Guayaquil for the G.M.U. conference, after which the Johnsons would go on to the States for their furlough.

Nate Saint was coming for us on the Friday after Christmas. But although the weather was clear, the plane did not arrive as scheduled. Saturday—Sunday—Monday went by. The weather stayed clear. Still no sign of Nate.

On the first Monday evening of every month, the missionaries of radio station HCJB broadcast an off-the-record program of personal greetings to friends. This might be our chance to get some word.

We started the light plant and tuned our radio to the station. An announcer came on with startling news. Nate Saint's plane had been caught by a downdraft while taking off from Quito and crashed. Although we were relieved to hear he had not been killed, we learned that his back was injured seriously. The brand-new Stinson was a wreck.

Marie and I looked at each other.

Now what would happen to our lifeline? Our main concern was for Mr. Shidler who was scheduled to speak at the conference. How would he get to Shell Mera? There was no way except on foot; Mr. Shidler himself didn't mind the idea. He wanted to leave the very next day.

Marie and Jean would have to stay in Macuma. This was the second time Marie had looked forward to going to a conference only to be prevented by a plane crash. But she and Jean soon forgot their disappointment in the rush of getting things ready for our departure.

Early next morning, Mr. Shidler, Ernest, and I left for Shell Mera with eight Indians. What a surprise was in store for us when, after six hard days on the trail, we found Jean Johnson there ahead of us. She had an amazing story to tell:

The MAF had not let us down. Hobey Lowrance, a new pilot, had arrived in Shell Mera just two days before Nate crashed in Quito. He too was concerned about getting Mr. Shidler to the conference, so he had enlisted the help of the Shell Oil Company.

The day after we had left Macuma, a large Shell plane flew over the house and circled the strip. A man stood in the doorway and parachuted down a large box. Marie and Jean, thinking it must contain food supplies, sent Indian boys to get it. For twenty minutes they watched the plane fly back and forth over the strip, and wondered why it lingered. Finally it went away. Back in the house, when they opened the box, they found a note from Hobey to Mr. Shidler, saying, "If you so desire, I can hire a commercial plane to land at Ayuy and take you and two others out to Shell Mera. If none of you can be at Ayuy within three days, stand on the airstrip with arms extended."

Not having seen the note, they had not signaled the plane. Therefore, the commercial plane would be landing in Ayuy after three days. Marie and Jean decided that one or the other of them ought to take advantage of this chance to fly to Shell Mera. Marie was reluctant to go because she was pregnant with our third child. If she went outside now she would not be able to get back until after our baby was born. Jean thought this was a reason for Marie's going. But Marie and I were just beginning to win the confidence of the Indians and she knew I would not want to be away from our chosen place of service for the seven months or more. As soon as Jean saw Marie was bent on staying, she made up her mind to go.

Marie was left alone with the Lopez family. She was not feeling very well, but she went about caring for our home and children as usual. She knew the Lord would take care of us somehow, plane or no plane.

Meanwhile, I attended the conference in Guayaquil and after about a month again covered the jungle trail to return to Marie in Macuma.

Now our jungle outpost was a very quiet place.

I had plenty of work: adding on to our house, building a storage shed for the gasoline, improving the airstrip, digging drainage ditches, harvesting the tropical wheat, planting more gardens. I worked with the Indians from daybreak to nightfall.

Within a week I was flat on my back with malaria contracted on the trail. I couldn't keep down the bitter quinine pills, so my fever rose higher and higher while I tossed and rolled and wondered why I had to be sick. Marie slept on the floor to give me more room on the bed. She got up every little while to bring me a drink or rub the ache out of my bones.

Marie knew she had to do something further. She thought she remembered having seen a few ampules of injectable quinine on a shelf in the Johnsons' house. She found them and also a hypodermic needle and syringe which she put on to boil. In California boot-camp days we had both had thorough practice, first in shooting a hypo filled with sterile water into an orange, then into each other. But neither of us had given a shot since then. Praying to God for strength, she rolled me over and stuck in the needle. Within twenty-four hours I began to recover, although it was a long time before I could leave the bed.

I had to fight hard not to give way to discouragement. But I had more time to think, pray, and read the Bible than I had had for months. Finally I realized God was teaching me a lesson. I had been neglecting what was most important of all to Him—more important than all the hard work I could offer—time spent in fellowship with Him, praying and meditating on His Word. I thought of the words of instruction given by Mr. Weiss in the farewell message just before we left Kansas City:

"You must build a strong spiritual life maintained by regular and consistent prayer and Bible study habits."

I did not want to fail as a missionary. I knew why God had put me on my back, and cried to Him for forgiveness and help to do better in the future. God wanted my heart's devotion and my worship and communion with Him more than anything else I might be able to do. Could God ever use such a person as I was, weakened in body and wavering in spirit, to win Jivaros for Christ?

A passage from the Bible sustained me: "He which hath begun a good work in you will perform it until the day of Jesus Christ" (Phil. 1:6).

A battle had been won. I slept peacefully that night.

CHAPTER 6

Alone on the Station

He that abideth in me and I in him the same bringeth forth much fruit.   JOHN 15:5

THIS WAS THE TIME OF OUR TESTING. IT WAS FEBRUARY, 1949. Before I left Guayaquil to return to Macuma, Ernest had told me that he and Jean could not continue in the Jivaro work. The rigors of the jungle had so impaired their health that they were planning, upon their return from furlough, to live in Guayaquil and itinerate to surrounding towns to hold evangelistic campaigns. This meant that we would be without missionary companions until the resumption of plane service could bring Keith and Doris Austin, along with a new worker, Miss Dorothy Walker.

There was no longer the plane to bring us supplies and mail, and there would not be one until another could be flown down from the States. We hoped that would be soon because once again our food staples were getting alarmingly low. We had not expected such an abrupt end to the service. The boys' school had been closed since November, as there was not enough in the gardens to feed the youngsters. Few Indians appeared to work, visit, or attend our weekly Sunday service.

We realized how much we had depended on the Johnsons. Up to this time, they had taken the responsibility; we were only learners. Ernest understood how the Indians thought, as well as what they said. He was always there to listen to their woes, give them counsel, and teach them God's way. Jean, although not a registered nurse, had skillfully and lovingly cared for the sick. Now the responsibilities were ours and only ours. There was no one to turn to but God. But as He promised, He never forsook us. On one of those rare days when we could get a letter out by an Indian who was going on a visit to Sucúa, Marie wrote to her folks:

"Without the Johnsons, our spiritual work among the Jivaros is somewhat at a standstill. Aside from our prayers and the witness of our daily lives we cannot do much. We cannot open school again until we have a Christian national schoolteacher. Frank cannot hold preaching services until he knows the language better.

"But we are neither discouraged nor longing to leave this place. We hope folks are praying for us but that no one wastes any time feeling sorry for us because we do not have the same ease of living that we could have in the States. We have all that is necessary for complete happiness—the love and fellowship of our Lord, and a real goal in life that keeps material things in proper perspective. I need not mention the blessings we share of unbroken harmony between Frank and me, and of the laughter and tears of two babies to make each day interesting and different. . . ."

We never had time to feel lonely or sorry for ourselves, even if we'd been so inclined. Rot and decay necessitated continual repair and reconstruction of the thatch and bamboo buildings. Before we finished harvesting one garden of plantains and bananas two more needed planting.

I had planned a full work program and needed all the help I could get. But the Indians didn't see things the same way. Those who walked back in with me from Shell Mera and knew I had brought some store goods spread the word around. At first they were all eager to earn new clothes, machetes, and fishhooks. But when I wouldn't give them the coveted goods on credit, many lost interest. Only a few returned to work in the days following.

We held a service on Sundays for any Jivaros who would come. We were pleased that enough usually turned up to fill our back porch. Marie played her accordion and we all sang hymns. Then with the help of pictures in a Sunday School paper, I related to them, in my limping Jivaro, stories about Jonah and the whale, and Jesus healing the sick. I learned more from *their* comments than they did from mine.

My bout with malaria stopped the work program and even the Sunday services. Some Indians came every day to sit with me on the back porch. I couldn't understand nearly all they said, and therefore could not be of much help to them. But I was glad they were beginning to bring me their problems, just as they had done with Ernest. As my strength returned, I went with them to their homes and so learned more of their everyday lives. Slowly they accepted me and invited me to go on hunting and fishing trips with them.

One such trip stands out in my mind. I had gone on a monkey hunt with two Indians and their wives.

Late the second night as we sat around the fire after eating the stringy chunks of monkey meat, a squat, hook-nosed, heavy-browed Shuara named Jeencham ("the bat") hunched forward and began to tell me how the Jivaro seeks help from the spirit world. His object is to make contact with his dead warrior ancestors. In the Jivaro's belief, they have become demons who may appear in the shape of certain beasts, birds, or reptiles.

Having induced a cataleptic state by drinking a brew of *tsaangu* (tobacco leaves) or *maicua* (belladonna), his mind is free to communicate with the spirits of departed loved ones to gain strength or ask questions which will later be confirmed by the witch doctor.

But in serious matters, as when a relative is very ill or when a group is deciding whether to go to war, Jivaros summon the witch doctor who has the strongest contact with the spirit world.

Before the witch doctor arrives, the family will have cooked up for him in a big black pot a narcotic of simmered vines. This is called *natema* (Banisteriopsis caapi). The witch doctor drinks the liquid until he attains a state of delirium.

Now the ancestors appear to him, in the guise of water boa, fer-de-lance, toucan, deer, owl, jaguar, or ocelot. As the witch doctor sings his chant, he waves before him a handful of leaves to protect himself from the demons who are writhing toward him. They advance and retreat and advance again, drawing ever closer. They are a hideous, nightmarish sight, a fact which the witch doctor makes clear as he describes to his audience what he is seeing. Gradually, he surrenders his own will power and gives himself up to the power of the demons. They, in turn, will reward him by revealing the cause of the illness and the name of the enemy witch who has sent the curse.

The witch doctor loudly and dramatically sucks on the afflicted part of the body, then proudly spits out the "arrow" that caused it all, which may be a stone, a bone, a bug, or a bit of glass.

To prepare young boys for manhood, or older warriors for battle, the patriarchs will take a group up into the mountains, where they will bathe in clear streams at the foot of certain waterfalls. There they drink the *tsaangu* or *maicua* and talk with the spirts of their dead, distinguished ancestors. This communing with the spirits gives special power to the supplicant. A strong contact produces such a conviction of invincibility that a Jivaro will unhesitatingly go to war in the face of the greatest odds, certain that he cannot be killed.

The firelight flickered eerily as Jeencham, in his excited voice, described these rites. I thought how intoxicating with power, yet how hard, short, and dangerous, is the life of a witch doctor. Of the many killings among Jivaros in our neighborhood, most of them happened to witch doctors. Jeencham's accounts aroused in me a lasting desire to learn all that I could about their strange religion and folklore.

As I look back on my convalescence, I can see that what appeared to be an affliction was really the working of God's will. Those apparently wasted hours spent visiting, talking, and wandering through the jungle when I could not work brought nearer by many months the day I would be able to stand up and preach the Word to the Jivaros. It helped me to learn the language in the easiest way possible for me; it helped me to understand their true natures. Above all, it paved the way as nothing else could have done, for them to accept *us*.

In time I was able to do more work each day building the house and improving the airstrip. Still using our radio and generator, we listened weekly to radio station HCJB. We had been notified to tune in every Friday night for a special broadcast, for there might be news about the replacement plane. The Friday night broadcasts were bright spots during those long weeks. We didn't have much gasoline, so we rationed it, denying ourselves other uses of power so we could go on listening to these weekly newscasts.

Finally, one Friday evening came a message we knew was especially for us. Robert Savage, one of the station directors, was speaking from Quito: "Now a special announcement for all our colleagues working in the Oriente. The new MAF plane is on its way. It should be seen over these towers within two weeks . . ."

This filled us with great rejoicing. Now we had something definite to look forward to. The plane's arrival could not be too far in the future.

Then we both faced emergencies that drove all thoughts of the plane from our minds. Marie was about to perform her first delivery of a baby. I was called upon to deal at firsthand with the murderous feuding of the Jivaros. These things happened almost at the same time.

It was early in the afternoon when Graciela, our Ecuadorian helper, came running breathlessly to our door. Her mother, Señora Rosa, who lived in her own house nearby, was about to give birth to her long-expected baby. This daylight delivery was an answer to our prayers, for there was no light in Señora Rosa's house by which to manage a night delivery.

"It's really happening!" exclaimed Marie. She began to make ready according to Jean Johnson's instructions. This birth had to be a success. Señora Rosa had suffered sad misfortunes in childbirth. She had lost three babies. One had been dropped; two had died from infection of the umbilicus. In her great faith, Señora Rosa looked on Marie as God's instrument to bring her safely through this one.

But Marie's only experience had been the birth of our own two children. She was outwardly calm as she moved about efficiently, but I knew how she must be feeling inside. Graciela built the fire in the stove and put water on to boil. Marie gathered some old magazines which she had sterilized in the oven to serve as bed pads. She got out a pan with scissors and tape to cut and tie the umbilical cord, and a syringe with which to give the ergotrate after the delivery. As a last-minute refresher between all of these operations, she frantically consulted the obstetrical book Jean Johnson had given her.

The children, Linda and Ross, were clamoring to go with her. They wanted so much to see the new baby. But Marie said no. She persuaded them to stay with me on the promise that they could come the next day and watch the baby being bathed.

Marie gathered all her paraphernalia together and set out. My heart went with her, and my prayers, as I stood in the doorway with the children, watching her go.

I had barely sat down on the log bench on the porch when I saw a crowd of Indians coming up the hill from the river. They were all shouting at once, hoarsely and out of breath, as though they had been running for some distance. At the head of the band was Nawich, a tall, gaunt Jivaro, his black eyes blazing, his hair flying. He had a gun in his hands.

At first all I could get from their rapid-fire conversation were few familiar phrases: "You'll see! You'll see! He'll pay! He'll pay!" Then I heard them shout, *"Shuar maayi! Shuar maayi!"* which I remembered meant "Indians have killed!"

I directed them to sit down on the porch in the hope this would calm them. Ross crawled into my lap; Linda sat down beside me. First we hurried through the familiar, usually long-drawn-out salutations.

Slowly I drew out their story, which I had them repeat many times before I could understand what they were saying. Juang, a witch doctor who was Nawich's brother, had just been killed by a Jivaro named Uyungara and his band from the Upper Macuma. They had attacked at night, under cover of a rainstorm, shooting through the walls of the house into Juang's sleeping form.

As soon as I could get a word in I asked,

"But why did Uyungara want to kill your brother?"

I learned that Nawich and Juang and the Cusutca River Jivaros had long been enemies of Uyungara and his Upper Macuma gang. A relative of Uyungara's had died of an illness. Uyungara blamed Juang, the witch doctor, for having caused his death by putting a curse on him. Uyungara had sworn never to rest until he got his revenge on Juang. Now, in turn, Nawich was bent on avenging himself on Uyungara.

At this point, the purpose of the visit became clear. In his peculiar, twisted Jivaro way, Nawich had come to enlist my help in his war against Uyungara. He fixed me with his burning eyes.

"You're against the Shuaras killing each other, aren't you?"

I admitted that I was.

"All right. Then you mustn't let Uyungara go free. If you do, he will finish us all off."

I asked him what he wanted me to do.

"Send for the soldiers. Get them to come and put Uyungara in jail. Ah, they'll make him suffer there! Then he can think about the evil he has done!"

"You hypocrite!" I thought to myself.

The distraught Indian was pacing up and down the porch, wildly waving his arms as he talked. The split palm-wood floor bounced under his step. Linda, looking at him wide-eyed, was afraid, since she was unable to understand a word he was saying. She cuddled closer to me. "He naughty, Daddy?" she said, "He naughty?" I gave her a gentle squeeze.

"Yes," I answered, "He very naughty. He needs the Lord Jesus to change his wicked heart."

This seemed to satisfy her enough for her to slide down and run to play in the kitchen with Ross tagging at her heels.

I had to do some hard thinking. Nawich's demand, on the face of it, wasn't altogether unreasonable. But there was a trap here. If I wasn't careful I would find myself siding with one group of Indians against another. I had reason to thank God then for my recent outings with the Jivaros which at least enabled me in Jivaro style to ask a few questions and deliver a few imperatives.

Turning to Nawich, I told him to sit down and be quiet. Then I asked him, "Many moons past, did you not go with young Tiwi and kill your son-in-law? Did you want the soldiers to come then?"

He had no answer for that one. I began to gain some confidence.

"You go on back to your home. Perhaps I will send for the soldiers and tell them about Uyungara. When they come, shall I tell them about you, too?"

Seeing in Nawich's uncertain look that my words were having their effect, I jumped to my feet and shouted,

"You want others to quit warring with you? Then you quit warring, too. Maybe you can't do it by yourself. But God can help you. Listen to Him. Obey His Word."

The Indians' response was to cover their mouths with their hands and laugh noisily. I knew by now that they did this to cover their embarrassment at having been outtalked by a white man. I had won their respect.

As they got up and shuffled away, I resolved that I would never take sides in these Indian wars, but treat everyone the same. I would try to teach them all to learn the love of God and give up their bloodthirsty ways.

Just then Marie appeared. I was so flushed with my triumph, I had to tell her all about it. She took me right down to size.

"Oh, you're just like the Jivaros," she said, "full of hot air. You know good and well you won't send for those soldiers."

Now it was my turn to listen to her experience.

"I found Señora Rosa lying on her bed," she recounted. "She was trembling and breathing irregularly in her pain. She didn't think it would be long before the little one would be born, so I quickly opened the bundle of clean papers and spread them over the foot of the bed and a table. Graciela brought the water, scissors, tape, and baby clothes, then left the room. I bathed the mother, tried to soothe her, and got everything ready. Having a few minutes left, I hurriedly consulted the instruction book to see if I was forgetting anything.

"I was deep in the book when I heard Señora Rosa calling my name very softly. She said the baby's head was through. I hurried to the bedside, hardly believing it was happening as easily as that. There on the paper at the foot of the bed lay a tiny mucous-covered baby girl, gasping for breath. I could scarcely see for the tears that filled my eyes. But somehow I managed to find the cord, cut it, and with shaking hands lift the little life to the table for its first bath. Graciela came back in then to help me care for her mother. Soon both Señora Rosa and her child were resting comfortably."

We recognized that the Lord had helped us in these situations.

Once more our thoughts centered on the plane. The day on which it was supposed to reach Quito was drawing near. The plane's coming would change everything. The hour came when we were to receive final word. We sat by the radio, straining our ears through the squeakings and squawkings for the news. Then we heard Robert Savage's familiar voice. The plane had not arrived. He didn't know what had gone wrong. It just wasn't there.

This was a blow. We had built up to such a terrible letdown. Up till now our faith that the plane would come remained so unshaken that we had not made any alternate plans. Our situation was getting worse. Our rationed gasoline was running out and we did not know how much longer we would be able to operate the radio. Our staple foods were just about finished. Soon there would be no more powdered milk for the babies. We kept all our staples in tight tin cans to protect them from the insects. When we bumped them together, oh the dismal effect of their hollow sound! Heavy rains further depressed us. Everything we touched was soggy and damp. For ten days it was either darkly overcast or streaming with rain. We resented the bad weather the more because we thought it was keeping the plane from coming.

Alternatives had to be considered now. I paced the porch, trying to make up my mind what to do. I thought of hiking out over the trails to bring back fresh supplies. But if the plane should come while I was gone, I would not be on hand to receive it. Every avenue was blocked. There was nothing to do but sweat it out, and put our trust in the Lord. It cheered us a bit to remember that April 19, two days away, would be Linda's third birthday. We made up our minds that whatever our troubles, nothing would spoil the day for her. She would have the best birthday party we could manage.

With the very last of our flour, Graciela baked her a big three-layer banana birthday cake. Marie, rummaging among the forgotten belongings left by the Johnsons, produced three fat candles. Linda would have some presents to open: six marbles wrapped in tissue paper from Ross-boy; an outfit of doll clothes for her favorite doll Larry, which Marie had sewed; and a set of wooden tinker toys. The final touch was added when, as we were sitting down to the table, in came Señora Rosa, her arms loaded with flowers. Graciela's little brother ran along beside her, bringing Linda his pet baby rooster with a gay red ribbon tied around its neck.

Linda's eyes were big and round as the birthday cake was brought in glowing with its three candles and we all sang "Happy Birthday." For a few precious moments, losing ourselves in her joy, we forgot the empty food tins and the silence in the sky.

The next day the weather lifted and the sun came out, bright and clear. Now, I thought, the plane will surely come. But it didn't. The day passed and there was no sign of it. The following afternoon I was working outside when I heard a faint sound overhead. Could it be the plane? Yes, I said to myself, it is a plane. Without waiting to hear any more, I took off in one leap, like a wild deer, for the airfield. My heart was pounding for joy to think the plane was coming at last, after so long a wait. I shaded my eyes and stared upward, eager for my first look. But I could see nothing. Even what I had thought to be the hum of the motor faded. I began to think it was all an illusion, that in my overanxiety I had been hearing things. I turned away from the airfield. Then, like the strains of sweet music, I heard the plane again, far in the distance. Only this time it was coming from a different direction. It grew louder. It might be a military plane, I thought, or even a Shell Company plane. Could it be just passing over? No, it was coming closer now, headed right for our mission station. It *must* be our plane. Before I could get back out on the airfield, I saw the little craft, bright yellow against the blue and white of the sky. It circled the field several times to have a good look, then lowered and came in for a landing.

I shouted to all within earshot. Marie and the children were already running, and also a number of Indians. We greeted those MAF pilots, who were strangers to us, as the dearest friends on earth.

The strain was off. There followed one of the happiest occasions of our lives.

The MAF pilots staggered into the house under loads of such delicacies as we had forgotten ever existed. They piled on the kitchen table hams, cheese, cocoa, raisins, potatoes, and fresh vegetables. We just stood and looked at them.

Thoughtful Marj Saint, Nate's wife, had even sent us trays of ice cubes from her kerosene refrigerator at Shell Mera. Tepid lemonade we drank almost every day—we had lemons in abundance at Macuma from trees Ernest Johnson and the Indians had planted years before—but lemonade with ice cubes was something out of this world.

As in a dream, we walked into the front room with our guests to sit and drink lemonade and talk, talk. It was so good to hear other voices again and the news of the outside world.

Our mood of celebration did not last long. In the stack of mail the pilots had brought was an urgent letter for me. I went off to one side, opened and read it. The letter was a reminder that I was to attend a session of our missionary field council which was meeting in Riobamba. The plane was to leave again within the hour. My instructions were to fly back in it. Our happy social hour came to an end all too soon, as I packed my bag for leaving. Marie made it easier for me by being such a good sport about it. In a few minutes I was walking out to the plane with the pilots, suitcase in my hand, having tasted no more of the goodies than my delicious glass of ice-cold lemonade.

Within a week I was back again. This time I brought with me

Keith and Doris Austin, our close friends from Bible school days in Minneapolis. With us also was Dorothy Walker. Sparkling-eyed, witty, and friendly as well as talented and trained, she was coming to work with us at Bible translation and language analysis.

The plane was on regular service now. On successive trips it brought in one-hundred-pound sacks of flour and sugar, cans of powdered milk and gasoline, and even plastic pants for Ross-boy.

A happy time of working with friends—new and old—was ahead. As soon as Keith and Doris Austin and Dorothy Walker were established in Macuma, Marie and I left for Guayaquil to await the birth of our third child.

Hobey Lowrance flew us to Shell Mera where we stopped to spend a few days with Nate and Marj Saint. Nate greeted us with his characteristic grin, wanting to know how the "yardbirds" were doing in the backwoods. Marie and Marj met for the first time but were soon chattering like old friends.

They were all busy people. The MAF had established headquarters here. Hobey did the flying, Nate the building, repairing and odd jobs, although his back was in a cast and he could not stoop. Marj operated the radio with which they maintained contact with the plane. No receiving sets had yet been installed in the mission stations.

Their house was almost always filled with guests. When Marj was swamped with tracking the plane flights by radio, or doing the bookkeeping, bread-baking, washing, or entertaining, Nate often gave her a hand with the housework or tending the baby.

Shell Mera was a new experience for our children, who had no memory of anything beyond our settlement in the green jungle. Reluctantly, we all left the warm oasis of hospitality and traveled to Guayaquil. On August 10, 1949, Irene Marie Drown was born. Within three weeks we were on our way back to Macuma.

During our absence, Hobey Lowrence with the help of HCJB radio technicians had placed short-wave radio sets in each of the jungle stations. Regular morning contacts were maintained between Shell Mera MAF and each of the isolated outposts serviced by the plane. This was an invaluable addition to MAF's operation. Now we could relay weather reports before scheduled flights and keep in constant touch with the plane. Never again would a plane go down without its position being known.

The Austins and Dorothy had moved into the Johnsons' house which they had remodeled. We all began working with the Indians in an earnest effort to learn the language, recording long lists of words and phrases and discussing better ways of writing down the strange sounds. The vowels gave us particular trouble. We discovered that under certain circumstances they were nasalized and under others they were whispered. Such minute variations could change the entire meaning of a word. "Oh," Keith would say upon hearing a Jivaro word ending in a voiceless vowel, "there is one of those things you don't hear and you don't say, but you have to write."

Keith and I carried out the manual work of the station, clearing more land and building a schoolhouse for Jivaro girls. Dorothy ran the dispensary, worked on language analysis, and helped with the routine housework. Marie and Doris looked after the little ones and helped sew clothing for the Jivaro school children.

Ever since I had been shown the pieces of pottery I longed to take the Gospel to the Atshuaras. Now I had a companion who would go with me. Keith and I had many talks and prayed for the day to come. But any mention of this plan to the Jivaros was met with dismay and fear. None in our area had friendly relations with the Atshuaras; in fact, they regarded them as their most hated enemies. We heard repeated references to the head-shrinking of an Atshuara named Chiriapa by Big Saantu and his gang.

One day Pitur, the Jivaro whose baby had been so severely burned, came to see us after having been away on a long trip. He had cautiously traveled over the "no-man's land" that lay between us and the Atshuaras, and visited an influential Jivaro leader named Taisha who lived on the very edge of Atshuara territory.

When I heard this I eagerly asked him to tell me more about Taisha. Did he know any friendly Atshuaras? And would Taisha consider taking me to visit them?

To my delight, Pitur stated that since Chief Taisha jealously maintained his neutrality in order to carry on his somewhat shaky trade relations with the Atshuaras, he might consent to take us to some of their homes.

This was our first indication of a possible contact with the Atshuaras and we were quick to take advantage of it.

CHAPTER 7

Where Christ Has Not Been Named

Yea, so have I strived to preach the gospel, not where Christ was named. ROMANS 15:20

KEITH AND I HAD BEEN WAITING FOR A LULL IN THE DE-manding routine of Macuma station's growing activities. As soon as we found one we prepared to leave to carry the Gospel to the Atshuaras on our long-planned trip. I could not have asked for a better comrade. Keith was quiet, studious, and uncomplaining about the rigors of jungle life. We laughed together to think how it would have sounded, back when we were students in Minneapolis, if someone had told us that one day we would be fellow voyagers in a dugout canoe headed down the Macuma River.

Having already bid our families good-bye, we stood watching on the riverbank that steaming morning while the five Jivaros that were to go with us lowered our craft into the water. These consisted of a cargo raft with an elevated platform on which would go our food, bedding, clothes, phonograph, records, and goods for trading; and a dugout canoe in which Keith and I would follow with two of the Indians.

We couldn't help admiring the workmanship of the sturdy raft which the Indians had put together with only a machete, stones, and the strength and skill of their hands. It consisted of five twenty-foot balsa logs lashed together with tough vines and strips of inner tree bark wound around hardwood pegs. They hadn't used a nail or a screw anywhere.

The Indians managing the raft were Saantu, Naicta, and Tangamash. In the case of Saantu—the Jivaro corruption of the Spanish word *Santo*, meaning saint—the name was ironic; this slender boy with the black unkempt hair and hollow eyes was anything but saintly. We called him Little Saantu, so as not to confuse him with Big Saantu the witch doctor. We had heard that Little Saantu, too, was studying to be a witch.

We stepped gingerly into the canoe and shoved off behind the raft. What lay in store for us? We did not know.

In the canoe with us were Pitur who knew Chief Taisha, and Jeencham. Pitur stood in the stern, paddling and watching for rocks and rapids ahead. Jeencham poled the canoe along from the prow. A son of old Washicta, he was a very good hunter. He often came to the mission, bringing wild tapir, deer, or monkey meat to sell to us. None of these men were Christians at the time and it had taken some persuasion to get them to go along.

We started out peacefully enough. Both raft and dugout slid smoothly and quickly over the deep quiet pools of the Macuma. But the pools were deceptive. Every few minutes they dissolved into the white water of angry rapids swirling over the sharp-toothed rocks. Whenever we could we kept our seats and shot the rapids as we came to them. But there were times when we had to jump overboard and guide the canoe through from alongside.

We had not gone very far when at the end of a long narrow gorge we came to a falls four feet high. The Jivaros took the raft over first. They lashed tough vines to the sides, maneuvering the raft from either bank, and began to inch it slowly over the falls. Their grip could not falter an instant, for the pounding water would beat the raft into matchsticks against the rocks. All was going well, when suddenly the raft caught. One side reared upward and the other began to slide until our cargo was nearly under water. At this point Naicta gave an almost superhuman tug. The raft righted itself once more and our cargo was saved from a soaking. The job of getting the canoe over was much easier by comparison.

As nightfall approached, our muscles were quite sore and we were glad to stop and make camp.

We built a fire and put some rice and beans on to cook for supper. The Indians went off into the brush to try to find the right kind of leaves and poles to build a proper shelter. We tried to impress on them that they must bring enough leaves to build a big one with a thick roof to keep us dry in case it rained.

I had too many memories of wet and miserable nights spent under poorly-made shelters. At first the musical and rhythmical sounds of raindrops falling on the leaves have a soothing effect. You welcome them, thinking they're going to help you fall asleep. But as soon as the leaves are soaked, the drips start coming through; and the cold water splashing on your face isn't exactly conducive to sweet dreaming.

This time the Indians brought plenty of leaves; we built a rainproof shelter and settled down for the night.

On the next day's travel we left the hills behind. The river widened. There were fewer rapids and longer quiet pools through which our canoe and raft sped swiftly. In the course of the afternoon I shot a wild turkey and Keith caught a fish; we had meat for supper that night.

Afterward we sat by the campfire along the riverbank and pored over a map given us by the Shell Oil Company. We were trying to see where we were. The Indians were uneasy, as they knew we were close to Atshuara country. Naicta, the most talkative of the five, insisted that he knew our position better than our foreign-made map. "We're not in white man's country now and only we Shuaras can tell exactly where we are," he said. "Didn't I go through this very spot years ago on my way to Atshuara Chiriapa's house?"

"Oh," Keith said, "were you not perhaps with that group of Jivaros that went with Catani and Big Saantu to avenge the deaths of Catani's father and brothers? Tell us about it."

Though Naicta at first was reticent about revealing this dark episode from his past, he gradually opened up to us and told the story:

Just upstream from this spot where we are sitting, Catani took us to the house where his father and brothers had been killed. The house had been abandoned; it was now a resting place of the dead. We were almost sixty men who entered that ghostly room. We stood staring in silence at the four mounds in the center of the dirt floor. Here were buried Catani's relatives who had been killed by enemy Atshuaras.

The sight of those graves made everyone so wild all they

could think of was killing. We hurried on to Catani's house. Our leaders repeated the war challenge many times in neighboring houses until nearly a hundred men were ready to go. Three of the witch doctors in the group passed the night drinking *natema*. Under its influence, evil spirits appeared to them, making it plain that an Atshuara named Chiriapa was the one they should kill.

As the roosters crowed the next morning, we started down the trail. After walking two days without coming to any houses, we knew we were getting close to our enemy. Being hungry by this time, we shot and roasted wild turkeys that were easy to find around there.

The next morning, we couldn't go on without making sure that the spirit beings wanted each of us to take part in this war. Fearfully we asked each other, "Have you seen anything in your dreams that assured you that you can go on safely?"

One said, "I saw the *pangi* (water boa) come up out of the river. He appeared to me, promising that in his might I would win."

Another said, "I saw the Devil himself, looking like a mighty Shuara warrior. 'It is I, the leader of the spirit world,' he said. 'I will help you. With my power you will be victorious.'"

Others said they had seen spirits in the form of the ocelot, the jaguar, and different kinds of birds, which told them that they would be the victors.

But there were also those whose dreams revealed danger and defeat. One such said, "I dreamed maggots were eating a hole in the calf of my leg. Therefore I must get back to my own home."

Another said, "In my dream a dog ran at me and bit me. So I'm going back, too."

Another, "I saw myself rolling into the fire and burning my side. I cannot go on."

Many left the party then. Only half of us were left to carry on the war. We could not disobey the commands of the spirits. If those with bad dreams had gone on they would surely have been killed.

We found the *sua* tree. From its small fruit we made a black dye in which we dipped balls of cotton and painted wide stripes and designs on our faces and bodies so it would be harder for our enemies to see us against the shadows of the jungle. We chanted back and forth to each other:

"Now we've become black, black with the *sua*;
It won't be long now, we're getting close.
Tomorrow we'll arrive
Because we're black."

One of our men, named Anang, did not blacken himself as much as the rest. Foolishly thinking he did not need it, he used only a little.

Walking down the trail we came to a stream that flowed by Chiriapa's house. The seasoned leaders said, "We're on the Wild Pig's trail now. It won't be long."

We snickered at this insult to our enemy.

When we came to three trails, all of which led to Chiriapa's house, we hid ourselves and crouched in the brush the rest of the day. Even though our food supply was gone and we were very hungry, the hope that Chiriapa would come walking down one of those trails and into our ambush kept us from turning back. As the sun dropped below the trees we closed in around the clearing. Silently and with trembling knees we approached the house only to discover no one was at home.

As it began to get dark, we felt like giving up the hunt. Someone said, "Let's go back. Let's go home." But Catani shamed us into staying as he snarled, "Why did you think I called you here? Are you women? No one is going back until our brothers' deaths are avenged!" Even though I wanted to go home, I couldn't.

Anang did not have any shirt and he felt chilled in the cool early evening. He put on someone else's shirt but soon took it off again, saying, "I don't feel right. This shirt makes me weak and short of breath." Everyone wondered why he should talk like that.

By the light of palm-wood torches we searched the surrounding jungle until someone found footprints leading away from the house. Assured that Chiriapa and his family had made them, we followed slowly and silently, stopping often throughout the night to rest. But since we couldn't see well we kept stepping on thorns and tripping over vines. Our feet were badly cut and bleeding before the night was over. Just before dawn we came to a banana and cassava patch and, knowing the house was nearby, we snuffed out our torches.

A lone cock's crow startled us all. "We're here now," Catani whispered. "Let's rush them. If you see a woman, catch her. If you see a man, shoot him. But don't shoot his head. We want that whole. All right, you men from the hills, don't lose your nerve, give it to 'em."

We surrounded the clearing and waited, shaking not only from the cold but also from fear. Through the brush and banana leaves we could see the stockade wall. In the morning stillness we could hear the slight creaking of a bamboo bed-rack. Someone was beginning to stir.

Suddenly the dogs started to bark. Then a man's voice gruffly shouted, "Woman! Get up! Don't you hear the dogs? Our enemies must be outside. The Hill People are after us. The Mura Shuaras have come. They have come to avenge the death of their brothers. Get up! Do you not hear their footsteps?"

We looked at each other as we thought to ourselves, "Chiriapa's home all right."

Then we heard a woman's voice saying, "Why do you always talk like that? There are no enemies outside. The noise you heard was only a possum knocking a papaya from a tree. Even the dogs have stopped barking."

Feeling relieved at her words, we looked at each other hopeful of not being discovered.

But again Chiriapa shouted as though he knew we were just outside. Ever since the killing he had been fearful we would retaliate.

"Listen, you head-shrinkers, I hear you! Come on, if you want to fight. You'll find out who is the strongest. Have I not killed many of your men? I will overcome the rest of you!"

"Oh hush!" snapped another of his women. "You are always saying that the Mura Shuaras are after you. Wasn't it just a short time ago that you killed some of them? They are too cowardly to come again so soon. No one is outside now!"

"Well, if you're not afraid, step outside and see if anyone is there," retorted Chiriapa. Then he must have changed his mind for we heard him say, "No, you better not go. You'll surely get it if you do!"

The women laughed as they chorused sarcastically, "You mean you love us and don't want us to get killed, ha?"

Chiriapa's only answer was the chilling sound of bullets clicking into place in his Winchester .44.

"What kind of gun does he have?" whispered one of our men.

Tucupe (holding a bowl of fermented *chicha*) tells Frank Drown of his exploits. As one of Tsantiacu's warriors, he had killed more than twenty men. Later, he became one of the first Atshuaras to embrace Christianity, and gave up killing.

Frank gives a Jivaro baby an injection for yaws, a disease widespread among the Indians. Medical successes gave the Indians confidence in the missionaries.

Tsantiacu's son Yu sits with his arm around Frank. Adults as well as children may show affection as well as curiosity toward the missionaries. But not invariably.

Atshuara gallery: *above, left:* old Aiju, the trader; *above, right:* Shuunta, a witch doctor; *below, left:* Uwitai, a warrior; *below, right:* Chief Tsantiacu, in ceremonial headdress and war paint.

Indians listen with fascination in the big smoke-filled Atshuara house (for exterior view, see front endpaper) as they hear from Frank for the first time the story of eternal life. *Right:* "The paper talks to me!" exults Mayapruwa as he discovers that he can read the Gospel in his own tongue.

Above: The first stage of clearing jungle land for additions to Macuma mission farm. *Below:* The Macuma airstrip, wrested from the jungle, is now kept trim with a tractor-mower.

The Macuma mission today—with station and airstrip hacked out of the wilderness. *Below:* Indian boys pet one of six Brahma calves which had been given tranquilizers and then flown in one by one. Cattle help Jivaros raise living standards.

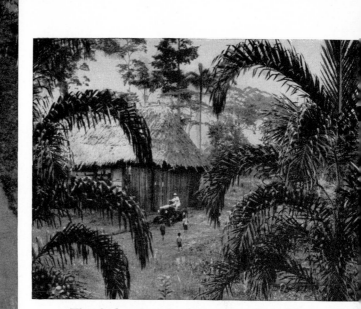

Thatched palm-pole hut was early style at Macuma. *Below:* An Indian couple tell Frank their problems as Christians facing the evil influence of Jivaro witch doctors.

Marie Drown (foreground) and Barbara Youderian check a Gospel lesson hand-lettered in Jivaro. Before the missionaries came, the Jivaro language was entirely oral, had never been written.

Marie (left) and fellow missionary Gladis Gibson examine Chumpi, a young Christian Jivaro, for symptoms of leishmaniasis, the dreaded nose disease. Successful medical treatment was often the missionaries' first step in leading Indians to become Christians.

Indian youngsters come to school naked or in rags. Girls (right) are out-
fitted with white blouses and blue jumpers; boys (below) with T-shirts
and trousers. They learn to use plates, spoons, and forks.

Sunrise prayer meeting on the bank of the Pastaza, opening the annual Bible Conference, or—as the Indians call it—"A Great Feast of the Lord." Former head-hunters come from afar to pray in fellowship with missionaries and with Indians who were once their enemies in endless family feuds.

Left: Ramon, an elder in the Macuma church, preaches in Jivaro as Frank listens.

Above: The struggle to grasp new thoughts, new words, shows on faces of former killers.

Right: A son of Big Saantu bows his head in prayer. Indians are seldom without guns, even during services.

"A carbine," answered Catani, "but that doesn't matter. Don't men die from shotguns, too?"

Then we heard the Atshuara call again to his women, "Is it not broad daylight already? The cowardly Shuaras will not attack us now. Let's go to the river where the *chonta* fruit is ripening. Bring your baskets and we'll fill them full."

We could hear someone push open the heavy door and move toward the stockade gate. Others followed. We watched women and children file out the gate. Then came Chiriapa.

Unpainted Anang fired the first shot. He boldly stepped into the clearing and lifted his gun to fire again when Chiriapa dropped him with his big Winchester.

Then the Shuaras shot from all directions. Chiriapa, realizing he was outnumbered, fled toward the house screaming, "Mura Shuaras! Mura Shuaras! They have come to kill me! They have come to k—"

He fell in the doorway as a bullet tore into his back. Shuara warriors swarmed into the yard and filled the Atshuara's body full of gunshot and spears. I heard the women and children shriek as we burst into the *ekenta*.

"Take the pig's head!" shouted an old witch doctor from the Chiwasa hills. But no one stooped to touch the body. The hesitant younger men began to offer lame excuses.

"I can't cut off the head because my wife is too young. She isn't able to cook the victory feast for such a big crowd."

"My wife has just given birth to a baby. If I touched this dead body my newborn one would die!"

None of us wanted to do it. But the old Mura Shuara from Chiwasa who was wearing a white man's black suit coat knelt beside the dead man. With a machete he slashed the neck first on one side and then on the other. It was so hard it would not cut easily. He wrenched the head back and forth with his hands, then finished cutting it off. Taking hold of the long hair, he slung the head over his shoulder and started out the door. Everyone gasped as he turned his back. The warm red blood was running down his new coat.

The veteran witch doctor commanded us all to follow him.

LEFT: "Heavenly Father, take Daddy to the Atshuaras and help him to teach them of Thy Love." Timothy Frank, four, and Laura Mary, three, join with Marie and Frank in thanking God for the blessings of food and shelter, and in praying for Frank's safety as he prepares to leave home on another flight to take the Gospel to the Atshuaras.

The enemy was dead now and we had to leave quickly. The body on the ground still seemed to breathe but no one paid any attention to it. Before following the bloodstained one, the Shuaras hurriedly ransacked the house of everything valuable—bead necklaces, blowguns and quivers, ammunition, dogs, children, and women. When one of Big Saantu's sons picked up a young girl, no one had to force her mother to go, too. "Don't take my little girl alone!" she cried. "Her father was killed by his enemies and now you killed my third husband. Don't take away my only child. Take me also."

We let her go with us. Then someone noticed one of the women was missing. We knew she had gone for help and that we could not stay there any longer.

I ran outside the house, wrapped Anang in a length of cloth, lifted him to my back and fled as quickly as I could from the Atshuara clearing. Moans from the suffering one and wails from the old mother filled our ears as we hurried over the trail. Before noon the moans ceased and some of us stopped long enough to bury Anang along the road. Fear that pursuing enemies would overtake us conquered our hunger and weariness and forced us to leave Atshuara country faster than we had entered it. By noon we caught up with the rest alongside the river.

There knelt the old man with the head. He was cutting at the neck in an effort to separate the skin from the skull. Turning the soft fresh skin inside out as he cut, he pulled it over the jawbones, chin, nose, and eyes, being careful not to cut the nose cartilage from the skin. Quickly he threw the skull into the river and filled the head-skin with sand and small stones. Although he would have preferred to build a fire to cook it then, we dared not delay that long in enemy territory. Wrapping the skin in leaves, he placed it in a basket on his back and ran with us through the forest.

The next day when we arrived at Catani's house, the old man placed the head-skin in a cooking pot filled with water and brought it to a boil, holding it by the hair all the while. Allowing it to simmer only briefly, he pulled it out and laid it on a leaf to cool. Then with a sharp thorn he pierced two small holes on top of the scalp through which he securely fastened a long piece of jungle fiber. Carefully searing the lips with a heated machete, he pinned them shut with slivers of black palmwood and used more of the twisted fiber to tie them in place. With an air of pleased triumph the old man stood to his feet and carried his trophy to a stream to wash and scrape off any loose flesh. Then he handed it to one of the younger men who took it up the bank to the clearing. There the younger Shuara filled the head-skin with hot sand and stones and closed the neck opening with a tough vine. Then grasping the end of the vine, he swung the head in circles. After he repeated this process several times with changes of hot sand and stones, he rubbed charcoal into the face and neck and ears.

As we began the trip back to Saantu's house, all the women except the one little girl were left with Catani. Big Saantu insisted he have this one as his fourth wife and also insisted the head be taken to his house for the first feast.

Along the journey the head was carefully wrapped in rags and carried in a waterproof basket. At night the men unwrapped it to see if the spirit of the dead man had eaten part of it. Each day the hot sand and charcoal treatment was repeated and each day the head grew smaller, drier, and blacker. The eye and ear openings, now less than a third their original size, were nearly closed and the neck hole would barely admit a man's thumb. With each passing day our pride in the shrunken trophy increased. The *tsantsa* was a symbol of our triumph and victory instead of a loathsome, terrifying head of our Atshuara enemy. No one was afraid to touch it now.

We sent runners to Big Saantu's to tell his wives that we were on our way home with the *tsantsa*.

Shuaras from all over the valley and hills arrived to help prepare the feast and share in it. The day we victors returned to Big Saantu's house the women, having heard us call from a long way off, stood in the doorway eagerly awaiting the first glimpse of the *tsantsa* and of the men who were bringing it. One of the men from the house hurried to the edge of the clearing and placed a stool on the ground and a large wooden shield on top of that. As the men began to appear from the forest trail, the women sang:

> "The victors have arrived:
> The victors have arrived.
> The *tsantsa* they have brought
> The black trophy is ours.
> Now our hearts will be happy and at rest
> Because our enemy is no more.
> He is dead and we have won the victory.

Great is the one who took his life.
Is he not a Shuara?
He is the victor."

When we all gathered in the clearing, the oldest warrior took the *tsantsa*, still wrapped in rags, from the basket and placed it on the shield in the center of the group. The wives in the door-way continued to chant as four of the victorious warriors took their places beside the shield.

The old man solemnly chewed some *tsaangu* and spit a little into the nostrils of each of the four men.

"These are the ones who overcome the enemy!
These are the strong, victorious Mura Shuaras!"

sang the wives of the ones who had killed Chiriapa.

The old one took the hand of Big Saantu, and touched the *tsantsa*. Big Saantu then loosed the trophy from its rag cover-ing and tied its fiber string around his neck, allowing the small black head with its long hair to rest on his chest. The ritual continued with the women chanting in more excited tones.

"The *tsantsa* is coming, let it come in."

As the men slowly approached the house, the group stopped at intervals while the old one spit more *tsaangu* in the victors' nostrils. Finally inside the house the old witch doctor pushed Big Saantu to the center of the *tangamash*.

The old one from Chiwasa also wanted to take the little captive girl's head, but as he and the others were concentrating their attention on the ceremonies, Big Saantu's brother hid her in the *ekenta* and charged an old haggard grandmother not to let the girl out of her sight.

Meanwhile, in the *tangamash* Big Saantu lifted the *tsantsa* from his neck and raised it high in the air. All the women formed a line behind the killer and his wife in the center of the room. Each of the women wore narrow belts with innumer-able dangling pieces of snail shells and hollow dried seeds tied in rows around their waists. Placing their hands on the belt of the one in front of them, they began to jump and dance a few steps forward, then backward, in time with the chanting. The shells and seeds on the forty jiggling belts clinked and rattled with the accented rhythm. The rest of the men sat and watched while the dance continued with each of the four victors and their wives taking turns holding the *tsantsa* and leading the dancers.

After the dancing, the feasting began and continued with much drinking and sexual revelry for three days. The *tsantsa* was fastened to a stick and placed beside the narrow doorway to the *tangamash* where all who entered or left the room brushed by its long hair.

Only the main killers could not take part in the riotous celebrating. Since the spirit of the dead enemy would be especially angry with those who had led in the murder, they needed to stay alert and in their right senses lest an evil curse befall them. Such a curse would rob them of victory in succeeding wars and make them easy victims of some disaster. A tree might fall on them, or a snake bite them, or lightning strike them.

After the days of riotous feasting, visiting Shuaras kept coming to the house to see the *tsantsa* and the captive Atshuara girl. Although accounts of revenge killing were common talk among Shuaras, few of them had the courage and the time during a killing raid to take their victim's head. And none had kept a captive Atshuara girl as his wife. They pointed and laughed at the frightened child as she blew the fire for Big Saantu's women, who were bitter with jealousy and hate. Hunching her shoulders in imitation of the enemy captive, one of them sneered, "Doesn't she look like a turtle?"

"She is afraid and draws her head into her shell!" jeered another amid uproarious laughter.

Hearing angry voices from the *tangamash*, the women stopped to listen. The old black-coated man who had cut off the head was determined to take the trophy to his house in the hill country.

"If you do not give me the *tsantsa* then I will make another from the head of the captive girl," he threatened.

After much arguing Big Saantu and his men finally consented to give up the head. "But first we will cut off some of the hair," they said. "Then we can fasten it on a gourd with some tar and make another *tsantsa*. We must have another big feast after a year with the gourd *tsantsa* in order to insure continued help from the spirits and future victories in war!"

Big Saantu and his men prepared a gourd *tsantsa* and planted large gardens in preparation for another big feast. All but the "little Turtle" looked forward to it. She cried continually during the first weeks she was in Big Saantu's house. But gradually as Big Saantu showed her special favors and the other wives begrudgingly accepted her, she became a part of the household. Now she has borne him a little daughter and seems almost contented.

But Keith and I knew Big Saantu's fourth wife still lived in a cloud of fear. She would never walk the trail with anyone but her powerful husband, and rarely came to our side of the river for fear some Indian from the hills might see her and try to kill her. And we also knew that the war between the Macuma Shuaras and the Atshuaras could flare up again at any time.

After hearing these terrible incidents we did not blame our Jivaro companions for being afraid. Did we dare hope that one day so many Jivaros would go into Atshuara territory, not to make war and shrink heads, but in fellowship with their one-time enemies? Knowing that with God all things are possible, we determined to keep on with our efforts.

That night we could not get to sleep without praying both for the Jivaros and the Atshuaras.

The next morning we had gone only a little way when we sighted a canoe with a lone paddler coming upstream. Since setting out on our journey we had not seen an Indian or a house along the banks. Our Indians gave the familiar Jivaro call "tu-u-u-u-u-u-u-u-u." But the paddler did not answer. Instead, he did a quick rightabout-face and sped away out of sight. Perhaps he thought we were enemies on our way to stage a surprise attack. We wondered if this were a sample of the reception we might expect.

A short distance downstream we saw a house. We hoped this was Taisha's place, since, according to our map, we should now be approaching it. Here we planned to make our headquarters.

We moored our canoe, "tu-u-u-u-ting" loudly to announce our arrival. After making our way through gardens of plantain, cassava, and sweet potatoes, we had a chance to study the large house before us. The first thing that attracted our attention was the roof. The leaves were woven much closer together and in a different pattern from the Jivaro roofs around the Upper Macuma. Otherwise it looked just the same. We felt this must be Taisha's house.

Swinging aside the four poles of bamboo hanging in the narrow doorway, we stepped out of the glaring sunlight into a large room so dark it took a while for our eyes to get adjusted. We saw before us a figure seated in the center of the *tangamash* wearing only a knee-length loincloth. Long wavy hair hung loosely over his plump shoulders. This was Taisha. Without a word he motioned us all to be seated on the various stumps and platform beds scattered about the room. Two women entered from the *ekenta* with clay bowls of *chicha*, which they proceeded to serve to everyone but Keith and me.

Continuing to ignore us, the chief turned to Pitur, the only one in our group he knew. Their salutations were long and explosive. Both men talked at once, sometimes repeating the words the other had just uttered, sometimes introducing new phrases. It sounded as though each knew in advance what the other was going to say. But when we heard Pitur giving an account of our trip, we knew that it was not altogether rehearsed.

Taisha then addressed each member of the group by turn, indulging in the same long-drawn salutations with each one. The sing-song pattern was the same for all five, although the details differed.

When he had finished, Taisha turned back to Pitur and asked him to interpret for me, but Pitur told him that Panchu could speak Jivaro for himself. After a couple of false starts, Taisha slowed his pace of speaking to match mine and from then on we had little trouble understanding each other. I told him we had come down the river as friends to bring him a message from God; that it was our aim to take the same message to the Atshuaras. For this, I said, we would need his help to guide us and to introduce us as friends. He seemed agreeable enough to the idea, but hastened to point out that since the Atshuara families he knew had all been warring with each other recently, he couldn't very well take us to visit them at this time. We were dismayed. Had we come all this way for nothing? The chief was silent. Then he seemed to have a happy afterthought. He did know a Jivaro, he said, who had married an Atshuara woman. He suggested that we get that man to take us to his wife's family.

This possibility cheered us considerably. But not our Indian companions. They had talked bravely enough in faraway Macuma, but now with news of war just across the river it was a different story. They flatly refused to leave Taisha's house. After having listened to their stories on the trip down here, even Keith and I began to have our doubts.

Taisha promised to put us up, so our Jivaros went back to the riverbank to bring up our gear, while we settled in. By nightfall some fifteen men had come to have a look at us and at the goods we brought for trading.

When they were all gathered after supper, we got out the portable phonograph and began to play the Gospel records that Ernest Johnson and fellow missionaries Mr. and Mrs. George Moffat had made in Jivaro. Then we began to sing some hymns and choruses we had learned. After we had their attention, I tried to tell them who God was and what He had done for them. Like all Jivaros, they were curious to know what God's Word had to say about how their world began. This was quite different from the amazing stories in their own lore of how the rivers and forests, the sun and the stars, had been formed. They were especially interested in the story of their ancestors, Adam and Eve, and how they had sinned against God.

But I had to explain very slowly. Since they were hearing these Biblical truths for the first time, they could not grasp too many new thoughts at once. Besides, there were not enough words in my limited Jivaro vocabulary, nor, in all their language, to express some of these ideas clearly. The Devil they knew as ruler of the world of evil spirits, and they feared him. Hell, they believed in as a place of punishment and torment for the souls of men after death, and to most of them it was inescapable.

Through all this, Pitur, Naicta, Tangamash, Saantu, and Jeen-cham sat listening with smug piety. By their remarks to the members of Taisha's household we could tell they were giving the impression that they already knew and believed in everything the missionaries were teaching. They had sung loudly with us and pretended to great saintliness, although none of them had ever attended service regularly at Macuma nor professed to be Christians. Nevertheless, when I had finished they were surprisingly helpful in making my message clear to my listeners. How I longed for the day when they would truly be able to preach the Word with real understanding and power!

We spent the next day visiting other houses in the area, preaching the Gospel wherever we went. In every house we asked the men if they would take us to the Atshuaras. But nobody would. Late that afternoon we had just returned to Taisha's house and were making ready for another evening service when a new group of Indians appeared outside in the clearing. They were picturesquely dressed. The men were clothed in new, brightly-striped *itipis*. Their hair at the back was twisted into pony tails, wrapped with hand-woven belting, and decorated with the brilliant red-and-yellow feathers of the toucan bird. They had bound their long sideburns tightly with string so that they stood out stiffly from their faces like front pigtails. In their ear lobes were pieces of reed about ten inches long.

Again we had to wait through the customary salutations which took about an hour before we could learn who they were. Finally I found out that the key man of the group was the very one I was looking for. After visiting with him a while he readily consented to take us to his brother-in-law, an Atshuara named Timas.

The service that evening was a long one. There were more questions to be answered, more truths to be explained. The Indians were impressed by the fact that we had left our homes and families and undertaken a journey of several days, neither to exploit them nor to attack them, but only to bring them God's Word and news of salvation. Although they did not understand all we had to say, they accepted us as friends.

Early next morning we reloaded some of our gear in the canoe and started downstream again with the visiting Jivaro brother-in-law, our new-found guide. I mentioned to Keith that I could feel the opposition of the powers of darkness. Jeencham, unable to overcome his fears, stayed behind in Taisha's house.

We must have traveled about six hours when our guide gave us the signal to beach the canoe by a barely noticeable trail. It took us about an hour of steady walking before we came to the typical Indian clearing which told us we were approaching a house.

Suddenly, out of nowhere, came a high-pitched shout:

"Don't come any farther! Go on back where you came from! We

don't want any strange Jivaros or white men here!"

We stopped in our tracks. Our guide who knew the voice went on ahead to see what was the matter. The rest of us followed. Since we could see trouble ahead, we felt it would be better to gather in the house than to be scattered outside.

The house was on the other side of the clearing. We approached it cautiously and went in. Inside were a lone young man and several women and children. An ominous silence greeted us. There were no singsong salutations. The women made no move to serve any *chicha*. Timas, the head of the house, was not to be seen. Something seemed to have gone wrong. Our guide looked at us nervously and motioned to us to sit down. Then turning to the frightened young man beside him, he began to talk very fast:

"Don't be afraid. These men have not come to kill. They want to make friends with you. They have brought some cloth and knives to sell. But more than that, they have come to tell you what the great Creator-God has written in his Book. . . . Now send for Timas. Let him know what I have told you and ask him to come back into the house. Tell him I have brought friends to visit him."

As soon as he had finished, one of the young women slipped out of the house. She was gone for quite a long time while we all sat around and looked at each other in silence. Presently she returned, went straight up to the young man and whispered something in his ear. The young Indian looked even more terrified than before. Haltingly, he relayed to our guide what the woman had told him.

She had seen Timas who informed her flatly that he would not receive us and ordered us to leave immediately. If we did not, he would come back and kill us all.

That was enough for our Jivaros. They did not need to be told twice. They all tore out of the house and started running back to the river and the canoe. But our guide stood his ground and Keith and I stayed with him. After a time he sent another messenger to Timas, again trying to convince him that we were friends and meant no harm. Again the word came back. He was angry now with his brother-in-law for having brought strangers to his house; and if he did not take us away at once, he would kill him, too.

I was fearful now myself. I had the impulse to run, like our Jivaros. But if I ran, it would indicate to the Atshuaras that we had really come to kill. Only by walking slowly could we show them that we had come on a friendly mission. We did so, all the way to the riverbank, even though it took plenty of will power.

When we reached the river we found that the four men from Macuma already had the dugout pointed upstream. Our guide stood on the bank to bid us good-by.

I took a new knife from my pack and handed it to him. "The next time you see Timas give him this," I said. "I want him to know that I am his friend."

We cast off. Naicta paddled the canoe away from the bank and out into the middle of the stream. "Why give him that good knife?" he muttered in disgust. "Why not give him a few bullets from the end of your gun instead?"

"What he needs is to be shown the love of Christ," I answered. Naicta did not seem to understand. He just shook his head and lapsed into silence.

By nightfall we reached the house of a friendly Jivaro about half-way back to Taisha's. Five men with their wives and children were at home, and we used the opportunity that evening to play our records and preach the Gospel. We doubted that they would ever have the chance to hear the Word again.

Shortly before noon next day we found ourselves back at Taisha's house. That evening we made the most of our last opportunity to preach the Word and sing to Taisha and his friends.

Now we had to prepare for the long trip home. But Pitur, knowing better than we how impossible it would be to paddle upstream, had sold the canoe. We therefore gave the raft away, packed our gear on our backs, and started off on foot. Soon we found ourselves in the jungle "no-man's land."

Three days of steady walking and we were back once more at the mission station. Our wives and children came running out to meet us. In spite of our muddy, bedraggled appearance and our twelve days' growth of beard, they smothered us with happy hugs and kisses. Disappointed though we were, we could only think then how wonderful it was to be home!

It was not until nearly a year later that we learned of the narrow escape we had had on our visit to Timas' house, and of how only God's protection had miraculously intervened to save us from death. Timas had told the story to an Atshuara, who in turn had told it to a Jivaro. It was a long time reaching us, but we listened with amazement as the Jivaro related it:

On that afternoon when we were walking down the trail from Timas' house to the riverbank, Timas himself was crouched in ambush in the underbrush. He had made up his mind to kill the last man in our party to walk by. This was common practice, as it was easier for the killer to get away. First he saw the Jivaros fleeing, then Keith followed by our guide. I came last.

"I waited with my gun cocked," ran Timas' story. "As I saw the forms of the Jivaros and the white men through the bushes, I tensed my muscles. I was ready to pick off my man. I pointed my gun to his head. Then my arm went weak. My finger would not move. I could not shoot even though I wanted to."

He who stopped the mouths of the lions for Daniel had stopped the trigger finger of Timas that day on the Atshuara trail.

CHAPTER 8

New Creatures in Christ

*Therefore if any man be in Christ, he is a new creature: old
things are passed away; behold all things are become new.*

II CORINTHIANS 5:17

THE INDIANS LOOKED AT ME IN WONDER AND DISBELIEF.
Some laughed. One asked,

"Why do you need another house, Panchu? Do you not already
have one for yourself and your family, one for the single lady, one
for the church, one for the boys' school, others for the chickens,
the wood, and the gasoline? Why do you need a new one?"

"This is not a house for me," I replied. "This is to be a schoolhouse for your girls."

"Our girls?"

"We want them to come live here, to learn to read and write
and know God just as your sons are doing. We will give them new
clothes and medicines and good food. They will learn to be happy,
as God wants them to be. That's why I am building this house."

More explosive laughter and rude comments from the Indians.
Clearly, they did not want their girls to go to school.

"Don't you know we give our girls in marriage when they are
very young?" said one. "Why should they learn to read and write?
They only need to know how to work hard in the garden, to cook
and serve their husbands well."

"What good will it do them to learn about God?" put in another.
"Girls are like dogs who have no souls anyway."

"We will build this house," I insisted, "because I know it is what
God wants me to do. I have talked it over with many of your people.
Two have promised to send their girls. Even if no others come we
will build this house."

When the building was finished and ready, seven little girls came on opening day. They slept and ate and attended classes all in the same building. Their teacher, a young Ecuadorian student from the Berean Bible Institute in Guayaquil, had her room at one end of the schoolhouse and cared for the girls day and night. Señor Segundo and Señora Rosa took charge of cooking the meals for both boys and girls, who ate separately.

The girls came to us wearing the only clothes they owned—a single ragged dress apiece. One barely had enough rags to cover herself, so Marie quickly snatched up one of her own dresses and put it on her. We soon gave them bright, ready-made print dresses that we had bought for them.

The girls, unlike the boys, were no disciplinary problem, since they were used to submitting to constant watchfulness over their lives and were not inclined to run away. But because of their backgrounds, they were extremely shy. If a girl in a Jivaro household opens her mouth in the presence of men, she is considered bold. At first it was hard to get them to say so much as *buenos días* to the teacher. They had never had any freedom of choice nor any chance to think for themselves. In the presence of boys in joint chapel sessions they shriveled into silence. Whatever they did learn had to be drummed into them, over and over again. They responded somewhat to the white chalk, blackboards, and colored pictures, and they enjoyed singing hymns. They loved playing with each other. For the first time in their lives they had a chance to laugh and be carefree.

The next year our enrollment of girls increased to ten. But running the schools was not without its handicaps. For one thing, our missionary staff was suddenly reduced to ourselves and Dorothy Walker. The Berean Bible Institute was moving its headquarters from Guayaquil to Shell Mera and was in desperate need of more teachers. Keith and Doris Austin felt called of God to go and help in training Ecuadorian youth to know and preach the Gospel. From among these students would one day come missionaries to the Jivaros. We missed the Austins' help and fellowship greatly.

There were other problems. We could hold sessions for only four months of the year, both because we were not producing enough food from our gardens and because of the restlessness of the Indian boys. Their fathers taught them hunting and fishing, house-building, cloth-weaving and basket-making, fashioning combs and feather decorations for their hair and the strategy of tribal warfare. Otherwise, they did as they pleased. They had never been used to following any set routine or taking any home responsibilities. Most of them had never had a spanking. Selfish, independent, and irresponsible, they came to school when they felt like it and ran away when anything displeased them.

When the weather was dry, the rivers were low and they played hooky to go fishing. When the weather was wet, they stayed home by the fire to keep warm. They would disappear if they didn't like what they had to eat, or if they thought the teacher was too hard on them. The parents didn't think enough of the school to force them to come and we had to keep constant pressure on them.

It was difficult to get either boys or girls to speak up in class. If they weren't completely sure of the answer to a question by the teacher, they'd rather keep still than shame themselves by making a mistake in front of the others.

Then there was the food situation. Half-starved most of the time, their appetites were insatiable. We cleared more land and planted more gardens. But plantain and cassava take a whole year to mature. Any strong wind would blow down the plantain trees and foraging animals would dig up and eat the cassava. Our efforts were continually frustrated. We didn't get much help from the Indians. They were too lazy, for the most part, to grow enough to feed themselves, let alone any extra to sell to us.

Food, clothing, and medicines were persuasive factors in getting the Indians to send their children to school. We gave them meat more often than they had it at home. Rock salt and brown sugar were attractive delicacies. So long as we fed and clothed the youngsters, the parents didn't care what we taught them. None foresaw that in time their children's *shuartica* would give way to Tius *shuartica* (Christian custom).

At the end of the second year of school came a heartening sign of progress—something for which every missionary strives—the first baptismal service. It would be held in the waters of the Macuma River at the close of a three-day Bible conference in June.

This was a real turning point. To us it was a fulfillment of our purpose in coming to Ecuador. For the first time in the history of the Macuma mission there were Jivaro Christians who wanted to be baptized. These jungles had never before witnessed such a ceremony. There had been times when we feared we would never hear a Christian confession of faith from the lips of a Macuma Shuara. But now here in our midst were five young men and women who had renounced the evil ways of their people. They wanted to make plain that their lives had been changed and that from then on they would live for Christ.

From our own point of view, it was the climax of our first five-and-a-half-year missionary term in Ecuador. From the point of view of the Indians, it was a strange white man's ritual that had no meaning, except to those being baptized.

The home life and tribal customs of our converts had been a constant hindrance to their continued practice of Christianity. *Shuartica* was really grained into them.

Wampiu, the oldest convert, was one of the most intelligent Indian boys I have ever met. In both school and church service he would fix his alert eyes on the speaker and never allow anything to distract him. It was a joy to me to watch his face while preaching, and to see mirrored there the light of understanding of Scriptural truths.

The oldest son of a witch doctor who had died when Wampiu was very young, he had moved to Macuma from the Upano Valley with his mother Chingasu and stepfather Chumpi. When Mistira (as he called Ernest Johnson) first talked about God the Creator, Wampiu was on familiar ground. Most Jivaros believed there was a God, and that He had made the world and all the people in it. But they had never heard that God loved them and wanted them to be with Him through all eternity. When Mistira told that God's Son, Jesus Christ, died on the cross to pay for man's sins, and how He wanted to give men new hearts so they could go to Heaven, Wampiu did not easily understand. These words were new to him and he did not know what they meant. So he came to school daily, learned to read and write in Spanish, but above all he learned more of God's Word and became a Christian.

His faith, however was then severely tried.

Shortly after Wampiu's conversion his younger brother fell ill with chills and fever. He was the disciple of an established witch doctor and for that reason would not yield to Wampiu's pleas to avail himself of God's help and the white man's medicines. He feared losing what power he had already attained as a new witch doctor. An older witch doctor visited him and insisted that he keep using the *natema* drug which would increase his power as a witch. This made him even sicker, so Wampiu's mother, Chingasu, demanded that he take the dying boy to see another witch doctor. She could not understand Wampiu's refusal and kept at him with tongue-lashings until he gave in. Wampiu then set out. He carried his brother on his back over difficult jungle trails, grieving and praying for his brother and mother all the way to the house of the witch.

But the brother died soon afterward. Chingasu, convinced that the first witch must have put a curse on her son, demanded that Wampiu kill him to avenge his brother's death. But this time, in spite of all Chingasu could say, Wampiu steadfastly refused. Tius *shuartica* had taken the place of *shuartica* in Wampiu's life.

The other two boy believers, Tsamaraing and Jimpicti, had also been in every year's session of school. Quick-witted and given to ready laughter, they sang the hymns and choruses with gusto. They were sons of old Chief Washicta. From him they had learned to hunt birds and monkeys with a long blowgun through which they shot poison-tipped darts. They knew the names of all the creatures of the forest, winged and four-footed, and could imitate their calls. They were full of tales of the wars which dominated the conversation at home and gave accounts of the visits of the witch doctor and of how he had called up evil spirits to heal the sick. When their father found he could not keep them from adopting Christian practices, he stubbornly ignored their new-found faith.

The two girls who were to be baptized were Tirisa and Mamaisa. Tirisa had been in school only during the last session and showed a remarkably quick response. But she was the only Christian in her family and life was very hard for her. As a little girl she had already learned to make and serve *chicha*. Now she did not want to do it any more, because it led to drunkenness. Nor did she want to take part in the immoral feasts that followed *chicha* drinking—feasts that seemed to bring such pleasure and excitement to the rest of the family. She preferred to pray and sing and try to win her mother for the Lord. This set her apart from the others and made her life rather lonely.

Mamaisa was having similar trouble with her family. She had wanted to go to school from the time she first heard about it, even though her parents objected.

Puanshira, her father, had come home one day from the mission holding his sides with laughter.

"Guess what!" he said to Mamaisa's mother in the child's presence. "Panchu is paying me to help build a new schoolhouse for Shuara girls. Can you imagine? I told Panchu none of our girls would go. It would only make them lazy to spend their time reading white man's words."

But Mamaisa, who was then twelve years old, listened eagerly to what her father had to say. Her two younger brothers had been going to the boys' school and often talked to her about the things they were learning. And now there was to be a school for girls! As soon as she was alone with her mother, she said,

"My brothers have told me a little about God who loves everyone and about His Son who is much stronger than the spirit beings we know. Isn't that amazing? Oh, how I would like to go there and learn more. And perhaps the white people would give me a new dress the way they gave my brother pants."

Her mother shook her head.

"You know your father won't let you go. Neither will your grandfather, Washicta. And I'm not in favor of it myself. Don't you forget that long ago your father sold you in marriage to Icam from across the river. Three times we have gathered and eaten the fruit of the *chonta* tree since he and Big Saantu settled the bargain. Icam is nearly old enough now to take you as his own. Don't even think about going to school. You must stay home and learn to be a good Shuara wife."

But Mamaisa reasoned to herself:

"My father and mother know only *shuartica*. Yet they are not happy. Doesn't my father mistreat my mother? Long ago he bought a second wife and brought her to live here, then beat my mother when she cried about it. Now he has bought a third wife—one who is smaller than I am. And to pay for her, he has sold me to her brother, Icam. When Big Saantu gave his daughter to my father, he made him promise to give me to his son. But I do not want to marry Icam. I want to go to the missionaries' school."

When the school for Jivaro girls started that year, Mamaisa was there to enter. What had made her parents change? Why had they let her come? It might have been because Icam was going to school and they thought it would be a good idea for her to learn to read and write as well as he. Or it might have been the new dress or the prospect of Mamaisa's eating food which they wouldn't have to pay for.

Whatever their reasons, Mamaisa was in school and very happy to be there. She was having many enjoyments besides learning to read and write: blankets to wrap up in at night when it grew cold, instead of having to shiver by the fire; regular meals three times a day, instead of just whenever there happened to be food on hand; the weekly washing of clothes with soap, instead of letting them get stiff with dirt.

And best of all was the singing about God.

"At the school they sing because they are happy," she told her mother one Saturday on a visit home. "Our people do not have any happy songs, do they? The witch doctor sings while treating the sick. The older men sing about hunting, or killing their enemies in war; and the women wail over the dead or dying. Are not all our songs sad or bad? The missionary songs are so happy it makes me glad to hear them."

One morning in chapel service she knelt in prayer to confess her sins and accept Christ as her Savior. Now she wanted to be baptized.

On the day of the ceremony, everyone was on hand.

Some of our fellow missionaries who had played a part in preparing the young Jivaros for this event traveled from far away to be with us—Ernest and Jean Johnson from their ministry on the coast; Mike and Ella Ficke from Sucúa. The many Indians who had arrived from different parts of the jungle were curious to know what baptism was, although some were doubtful and full of mistrust.

"This is not *shuartica*," one of them remarked disapprovingly as he left the church at the end of the closing conference service and started down the steep trail toward the riverbank.

"What good will it do our children to lie down under water and then come up again?" asked another.

"None at all," retorted a third. "Surely it won't give them any more strength to overcome their enemies. They should do as our old leaders have taught us—go up the mountain and drink the *maicua* and *tsaangu*, so that in their visions they would see the spirits of our ancestors who would make them strong warriors. If they become God's Indians they will never go to war. What a shame!"

"Oh, they're only doing what Panchu tells them," came another voice. "Now that school is over they'll soon forget the white man's words and be like the rest of us again."

"But what are the girls being baptized for?" inquired another. "It will only make them lazy and disobedient. Look at the trouble Puanshira is already having with his daughter, Mamaisa. All she wants to do is go to school and learn more about the foreigners' ways. Now she's even saying she won't marry Icam, Big Saantu's son, even though she was promised to him years ago. That shows how foolish a girl who goes to school can become."

"We'd better be there at the ceremony," put in a more practical-minded one. "If we don't do what Panchu says, he might move away. Then, I ask you, where would we get our medicines and clothing and our machetes?"

So the conversation went all the way to the riverbank. Then, with an audience of about a hundred Jivaros lined up watching, I stood beside the three boys and two girls on a sandbar along the cool waters of the Macuma, and instructed the crowd as to the meaning of bapitism. Each believer took his turn speaking to the Indians in clear voices, to tell of the experiences that led him to Christ. Although few of the older Jivaros hearing their testimonies understood the power of the Gospel, they could not deny that these young people had been freed from the fears of witchcraft and death and were happy in the Lord.

One by one I immersed the radiant young believers and lifted each again to a standing position, repeating five times as I did so the phrases I had memorized in Jivaro for the occasion: "On confession of your faith in Jesus Christ, God's Son, and on your promise to walk in God's road, I baptize you in the name of the Father, the Son, and the Holy Spirit."

When Mamaisa's turn came, she was watched from the bank by her father and mother, her grandfather, Washicta, and Icam. They heard her say that Christ had died for her and that she wanted to live in obedience to Him. They could not have anticipated how much her testimony was to change the plans they had for her life.

Just as Mamaisa was about to be immersed, her father, Puanshira, stepped into the water at her side, evidently to satisfy his curiosity about this strange ceremony. There were a few whispers and suppressed giggles from the crowd on the bank. But mostly they were quiet with awe. They had never heard such words before.

Ernest Johnson closed the service with a prayer that God would manifest His love and power to the rest of the Jivaros through these first Macuma Christians. We climbed back up the hill, confident that the One who had begun His good work in Wampiu, Jimpicti, Tsamaraing, Tirisa, and Mamaisa would go on developing it until the day of Jesus Christ.

The baptism of the first converts in Macuma did not mark the end of their struggles; rather, it was the beginning of even harder battles against the customs that surrounded them.

One who adhered stubbornly to her new faith through many trials was Mamaisa. A few days after the baptismal service, Big Saantu and his son Icam visited her parents. This could only mean that the time had come to complete the bargain made so long ago. Tonight she would be expected to prepare the cassava root with her own hands and enter the *tangamash* to serve Icam his portion, thus initiating the marriage ceremony. She detested the thought of approaching this young man and especially one who was learning to be a witch doctor like his father.

When she brought the steaming bowl into the *tangamash* she handed it to her father and refused to serve the visitors. Her father, with just one more exchange of command and refusal, picked up a stick and beat her until she managed to squirm from his grasp and run sobbing outside. She hid for a few days only a short distance from the house, but one night, fearing her father's continued anger, she ran through the forest to find refuge in the house of the missionaries. Mamaisa knew that Dorothy Walker loved her and would try to help in any way possible. When she reached the house she called softly through the bamboo wall until Dorothy let her in.

The next morning the girl's father, who had been searching for her since she left, arrived at the mission. He suspected she was there and demanded his daughter. "Send her out so I can teach her how a Shuara woman should act!" he shouted.

Dorothy noticed his third wife, who had accompanied him, sitting smugly under a grapefruit tree. Her heart ached for both girls, who were the pawns in a bridal arrangement. She refused to turn Mamaisa over to her father. Later in the lay when Mamaisa's mother appeared along with her father and asked for the girl, Mamaisa agreed to go with her.

Instead of turning to the right from the road by the school, Mamaisa's mother grasped her daughter's arm and started down the trail toward the river. With her father pushing her, they entered the canoe and crossed the river to Icam's house. But rather than become Icam's wife, Mamaisa ran away again. This time she hid for nearly three weeks until her parents and even the missionaries believed she had died. Icam declared that since she had twice run away he now despised her and would not marry her even if she were still alive.

But to everyone's surprise she appeared one Sunday morning at the missionaries' door, ragged and thin but still confident that God would keep her from becoming a witch doctor's wife. Since Icam had lost face and refused to have anything to do with her anymore, Puanshira could let the matter drop and still keep his little wife. Her father allowed her to live quietly once again at home and even to return to the next session of school. Our hearts were full when we heard the story—full of praise to God, who had helped this Jivaro girl.

Not long after the baptismal service we left for the United States on furlough. Dorothy Walker, with the help of another young lady missionary, courageously carried forward the work in our absence. Dorothy started a weekly Bible class especially for the women and also a weekly prayer meeting to encourage the young believers. But because it was not *shuartica* for a woman to preach to the men she did not lead the services herself. Nor did she always give the Bible messages, as she wanted the new Christians to learn to shoulder responsibilities. Upon our return we were thrilled to see the growth in zeal and understanding on the part of our believers.

We felt the need of a separate building for church services rather than holding them in the boys' school as we had been doing. The Christian Jivaros were enthusiastic about the plan and gave freely of their time to put up the simple bamboo-walled structure which they promptly named "God's House." With great pride they spread the news of this first church to be built among the Jivaros in the Macuma area.

The Indians would say with wonder: "No one eats or sleeps here. When we gather together do we talk of war and witch doctors' curses as we used to? No. We pray to God and listen to more of His Word. No one need be afraid to enter "God's House." We want everyone to come and learn with us."

We prayed and began to hope that more would come and that other churches could soon be initiated throughout the jungle.

And come they did. At times the attendance reached nearly one hundred. It was almost becoming *shuartica* to attend church on Sundays.

Although we sang God's praises and preached His Word, these services were never formal and were seldom carried through to the end without noisy disturbances or interruptions.

It was not unusual for Washicta or other respected chiefs to come stomping into Macuma Church in the middle of a prayer or a hymn. He would proceed to extend greetings to everyone present in a loud, deep voice; at the same time he would expect everyone to take notice of him and respond in kind.

Quite often a small bird would unwittingly fly in under the leaf roof and be unable to find its way out again. Thereupon it would dart and swoop back and forth while all eyes followed its flight, with rows of heads moving back and forth in hypnotized rhythm. Often an Indian boy, forgetting he was in church and not out in the jungle, would take after the bird. Then all praying would stop until it was either caught or made its escape.

Vampire bats were also frequent disturbers of the peace. One never could tell when a bat would decide to leave its hiding place in the thatch of the roof and swoop down among the heads of the congregation. A hubbub would ensue as the boys assailed the ugly creature with sticks. When it had made its retreat everyone would settle down again to listen to the Word.

Every service was conducted under the constant threat of dog fights. Most Jivaro families brought their mangy half-starved mongrels to church, sometimes tying them outside, sometimes allowing them to lie under the benches. All dogs were highly suspicious of one another. A sniff, a growl, an answering snarl would be the signal for general bedlam as a whole church full of dogs howled their defiance of one another.

The Jivaro women preferred to sit at their husbands' feet, rather than on the bench beside them. Shielded in their bosoms were pet pigs, monkeys, chickens, or parrots which they fed and cared for as the sermon progressed. They would further divert themselves by picking gnats from their husbands' legs and exterminating them between their teeth.

We learned to take these distractions with patience and good humor, knowing they did not seriously interfere with the growth of the true Church of Christ among the Jivaros.

CHAPTER 9

Medical Missionaries

*I am the resurrection, and the life: he that believeth in me,
though he were dead, yet shall he live.*   JOHN 11:25

WHENEVER A PLANE TOOK OFF FROM OUR AIRSTRIP BEARING
a sick or wounded Indian to the hospital at Shell Mera; whenever
we went on early morning radio contact to describe symptoms or to
ask for a diagnosis, we gave thanks that we were part of a fast-
growing team dedicated to bringing the miracles of modern medicine
to people who formerly had known no succor but the witch doctor's
chants.

We were indebted to a host of others—hard-working pilots, doctors, radio operators, and fellow missionaries—who were prompt
and faithful in their support.

But in the beginning we had to learn by doing. We had no
radio and no planes. Our first dispensary, set up by Ernest and Jean
Johnson, was in the same small room as our store. Our meager
supply of medicines shared shelf space with trade goods. There was
no running water. We boiled our water on the kitchen stove and
carried it in buckets. Most of our patients came in the daytime, so
it did not matter much that there was no light. Since there was
no examining table, patients lay on blankets on the floor. The waiting room was the porch.

The dispensary was improved over the years until it had its own
space in part of a five-room building which we called the "pentagon." The walls were painted; there was running water, and an
examining table with a pad on it. By comparison with earlier arrangements, this was the acme of modern efficiency.

Jean Johnson, when she was with us, then Dorothy Walker,
Marie, and others took turns running the dispensary. The Indians

were suspicious at first and not many came for treatment. But as some were cured and told others, more and more came.

In our innocence, we thought that once they had been healed by our medicines they would turn their backs on their witch doctors. We soon found it was not that simple. With our days so taken up with the routine work of dispensing shots, worm medicine, and aspirin, so trivial and so demanding, there were moments when we wondered whether this medical side of our work was worthwhile. But just as often, God strengthened our hands and hearts to continue.

Our medical successes slowly brought us a good name throughout the jungle. Through this work we came to understand the Indians and their ways. Eventually, many whom we first reached through caring for their diseased bodies, came to know Christ. And we were heartened to see evidence of His power at work in the lives of our patients.

Since Marie, in recent years, has done more of the medical work than I, she tells here some of her own experiences:

One morning as I opened the dispensary door, I saw an Indian, Mr. Hummingbird, and his wife, Tsetsempu, waiting outside. They were bringing their ten-year-old boy for treatment. Tsetsempu had carried the boy on her back over a five-hour trail, bearing also a machete and a basket of cassava roots. Breathing hard and moving slowly, Tsetsempu stepped to the center of the room, got down on her knees, untied the cloth that bound the boy to her back, and gently eased him onto her lap.

Two things were striking about the boy: the extreme emaciation of his wasted body; and the expressiveness of his enormous black eyes, framed by long, beautiful, curling eyelashes. At once I named him "Big Eyes." He could not walk or even stand erect. His hands, hanging limply at his sides, were nothing but bony structures with transparent skin stretched over them. His neck could hardly support the weight of his head. Although his face at first glance looked full-fleshed, it was only so because it was swollen.

Weeks earlier, Mr. Hummingbird had come to our mission from his home along the Cusutca River, seeking medicine for the boy whom he had at that time left at home. He told me the child had suffered from diarrhea for many months. After guessing his weight and height from the father's description, I counted out some sulfa pills and told him he must let the boy come to our school as soon as he was better. Mr. Hummingbird looked slightly shocked at the idea, shook his head vehemently until his pony tail waved back and forth, and said it would be impossible.

Now I understood why and was filled with remorse that I had not taken the boy's condition more seriously. I began to question the mother.

"He vomits," she answered. "All the time he vomits. No food stays in his stomach. He doesn't want to eat and when I do feed him a little, he vomits. I chew his food myself and give it to him from my own mouth just as I did when he was a baby. But it doesn't do any good. And he has diarrhea. Terrible diarrhea. And he says his head always hurts. Don't we Shuaras know that when anyone can't eat he won't live? Give him some medicine for the sickness that has made him so weak and so thin."

I kept asking questions while bringing an aspirin and a little Kaopectate in water. "Big Eyes" just turned away and said, "I don't want it." The low hoarseness of his voice, as he spoke for the first time, startled me. This, too, must be the result of his disease. With gentle coaxing from his mother, he finally swallowed the medicine —only to bring it up a few minutes later.

Tsetsempu fixed me with accusing eyes.

"You see. I told you so. That's why he couldn't take those other pills you sent. Now what are you going to do?"

There was no hope either in the tone of her voice or in the hardness of her gaze.

I was trembling inside, but I tried hard not to show it. At that moment I had no confidence in myself whatsoever. Here was another case I was probably powerless to help. These not-too-friendly Indians had no doubt tried every witch doctor in the neighborhood; then only as a last resort, when the child was nearly dead, had they brought him to the missionary. Yet I took some comfort in the fact they had come at all.

"What are you going to do?" the mother asked again.

"Before I do anything else, I'm going to talk to God in prayer and to the doctor by radio."

Mr. Hummingbird and Tsetsempu looked at each other uneasily while I prayed: "May this experience bring mother and father and child to understand how much they need Thee—not only for physical healing, but for forgiveness of their sins, too."

Then I went to the radio and called the missionary doctor in Shell Mera. He prescribed the shots for "Big Eyes," antibiotics in the morning and vitamins in the afternoon. I could hardly find enough flesh on his shrunken buttocks to accommodate the hypodermic needle. After several injections I was fooled into believing I had found a little patch of flesh on one hipbone. But when I expressed hope to his mother, she pointed out to me that it was swollen only because I had tried to stick him with the needle so often.

For two days a Jivaro woman named Ana and I took turns feeding "Big Eyes" a formula of salt, sugar, paregoric, and water. We began with a half teaspoon every half hour and increased the dose according to what the child could keep on his stomach. We dared not depend on the mother because she refused to give the solution. "He doesn't like it, so I won't make him drink it," she would declare. "He says it stinks." Then an expression of undiluted disgust would pass over her face. Yet, sometimes under my supervision she would encourage him to open his mouth and accept the mixture from the spoon in my hand.

Every morning when I'd ask how much liquid he'd kept down during the night, she'd show me the partially filled quart jar by the bed. This always made me wonder how much she'd poured on the ground. Although I insisted that she give the child nothing to eat in my absence, I knew her fear of his starving to death would drive her to feed him whatever he asked for. She did not trust me or my methods. I did not trust her or her methods. A silent war went on between us.

But in spite of her lack of co-operation, the diarrhea and vomiting gradually subsided. When "Big Eyes" was able to eat a little bit of banana, I would carefully peel one and mash it with a fork before giving it to him. This involved the use of three utensils, the fork, a spoon, and a small plate, all of which had to be sterilized. The mother's method was much simpler. She merely kneeded the banana between her fingers before peeling it, opened it at one end, and allowed him to suck between his lips as much as he wanted. I had to admit that her way was not only much simpler than mine, but more sanitary.

I had a hard time getting him to take other foods I knew his body needed. Milk he refused altogether, protesting that since it came from a cow it must be fit only for dogs. I prepared a chicken broth, but he found it too salty. Then I prepared it unsalted, and put a few crumbs of rock salt alongside. He would smack his lips over the latter with as much relish as any American child for a lollipop.

One day, in desperation, I named every single item of food I had in the house. He refused each one of them in turn until I mentioned bread. This he seemed willing to consider.

"I have heard that white people eat bread and that it is very good," he said solemnly. "I would like to try some."

Highly pleased, I went to the house, cut a slice of homemade bread, wrapped it in a piece of waxed paper, and took it to him. His eyes shone with pleasure as he fingered the package before opening it. The smooth soft paper seemed to fascinate him. Finally he opened one end, broke off a corner of the slice of bread, and put it experimentally into his mouth. He chewed it thoughtfully for a moment. Then he exploded with as much force as his limited strength would allow. Spitting it out as he spoke, he unwittingly taught me two new expressions in Jivaro: "*Yajesmaiti! Yuchatainti!*" ("It is abhorrent! It is inedible!") His mother, thinking this a great joke, laughed and laughed. Then taking the slice of bread from him, she ate it herself. But "Big Eyes" still clung to the piece of waxed paper. He folded it carefully and put it away in his shirt pocket.

For ten days "Big Eyes" remained at the mission, living in a small building only two minutes' walk from our house with his father and mother. Mr. Hummingbird worked faithfully in the mission gardens to help pay for the child's mounting medical bills. Tsetsempu kept the fires smouldering, prepared their food, and cut down weeds around the house. "Big Eyes" himself sat or lay on the bed wearing a shirt I had given him that belonged to our son Ross and using an old dress of his mother's for a blanket.

Soon they began to be visited by many of their neighbors from around Cusutca, who brought "Big Eyes" news of his sisters and neighbors.

And strange were the things I heard them say, as I listened to them belittling me and my foreign ways of treating their illnesses. I knew enough Jivaro now to understand them. But they seemed purposely to ignore the fact that they knew very well my ears were taking in most of what they said. I could have been hurt by them if I had been willing to let myself.

I heard them make many remarks such as these:

"What's that she gives him from the bottle? . . . Just water with salt and sugar in it? How can that help? It's not *shuartica* for a person with diarrhea to drink so much water . . . Doesn't she know that the more water he drinks, the worse his diarrhea will become?"

"Oh, my heart hurts to see how sick he is . . . Tsetsempu, take him home . . . You can't let him die here. See how thin and weak he is. He's dying for sure."

"Don't we Shuaras love our children! Won't we cry and suffer when he dies! Oh, take him back home! Don't let him die here with the white people!"

Every setback the child suffered was always blamed on me and my treatment. His lips and the inside of his mouth and tongue broke out with sores which the mother attributed to the paregoric. When he couldn't urinate for a couple of days she told me it was the fault of the shots. But when he did succeed, she took pride in showing me the exact spot on the ground at the foot of the bed.

In spite of everything, we were becoming friends. The mother's hostility and distrust lessened each day. She tolerated me; then I felt she almost began to like me. "Big Eyes" grew to look forward to our visits together. He would ask me to come back soon and not stay away so long. At my first visit in the morning and the last in the evening I included hymn-singing, a Bible story, and prayer along with the doses of medicine and the shots. "Big Eyes" always listened attentively, repeating and even singing some of the words after me. At first his mother paid little or no attention. She busied herself blowing and arranging the fire, washing and peeling food to cook, and even talking with other Indians.

I had a little wordless booklet with green, black, red, white, and gold pages which represent created life, the sinful heart, Christ's blood, the redeemed heart, and heaven. It was used to explain God's love and plan of salvation for mankind. "Big Eyes" loved it and asked immediately if he could keep it. He had reacted the same way to the colored plastic cup and spoon and the empty injection bottles he was given. I gladly added the booklet to his collection, instructing him that he was not to tear it up or throw it away but rather to read its message to himself and any other Indians that would listen. Each time he came he would take it from his pocket and ask to hear the wonderful story again.

These were busy days in our dispensary, for "Big Eyes" was far from being the only patient. One afternoon a young Jivaro named Tsungi had brought in his fourteen-year-old wife, Juani, in labor with her first child. She had been in labor for two days and was still unable to deliver. I gave her castor oil in lemonade, but it did no good. The next night, feeling sure the baby was about to be born, I sat up with her, her husband, and her grandmother, who had also come along, to time the contractions. Although they were coming now with three- or four-minute regularity, the distraught child-wife suffered in vain. Tsungi kept bringing her food and drink (including beaten egg white with a peppery jungle spice) that, according to *shuartica,* would hasten birth.

The wrinkled grandmother told me over and over again throughout the night hours that Shuara women never deliver while lying on their backs on a table and that Juani would certainly die in that position. Once, to humor the old lady, I helped Juani down from the table to the newspaper-covered floor where she tried to give birth to the baby in a squatting position. The grandmother sat behind, holding her tightly around the waist as she pushed and squeezed with her hands and arms, but it was no use. Finally, at 2:00 A.M. I settled the group with blankets and told them to try to sleep for a few hours. I did the same, resolving to call for a missionary doctor to be flown from the Shell Mera hospital as soon as the 6:30 radio contact should begin.

At 3:00 A.M. the father called, saying that his wife was surely ready to have the baby. I cleaned up the delivery room and table again and lay the suffering girl in place. So far as I could tell, the baby was no closer to being born than it had been the day before.

Suddenly my attention was arrested by the alarmed voices of Indians running up the dispensary steps. It was still too dark to identify the panting, perspiring runners, but their words presented a frighteningly clear picture to my mind.

"He's been bitten by a snake! He's been bitten by a snake! Get the medicine ready quick!"

Before I could ask who, when, where, or by what kind of snake, a Jivaro dashed wildly into the lighted area of the dispensary. Collapsing on the floor, he managed to gasp hoarsely, "I'm dying." It was our convert Tsamaraing, who had become one of the church preachers.

I fully believed him; but fortunately I had enough presence of mind, in spite of my panic, to give him shots of antivenin and morphine. Shortly, he sat up and began vomiting blood-streaked bile into a pail. His lips were swollen double size, his eyes bleary and bloodshot, his hair disheveled. The dreamy young fellow who had stood in front of the church and preached a good sermon just three days before was beyond recognition.

He blurted that a bushmaster, one of the deadliest of snakes, had bitten him on the top of the foot. He groaned that he had been running for two hours through the black jungle night to the mission station.

So here I was with three patients on my hands—"Big Eyes," an expectant mother, and Tsamaraing. All of them desperately needed a doctor's care; with or without it they might be dead by nightfall.

I looked at my watch. It still lacked a few minutes of the regularly scheduled time for radio contact with Shell Mera. I could not wait; I decided to take a chance on getting through. I ran to the house a short distance away and turned on the set:

"Macuma calling Shell Mera . . . Macuma calling Shell Mera . . . We have emergency traffic . . . We have emergency traffic . . ."

The hum of voices told me that the round of contact between Shell Mera and other stations had begun. But at the words "emergency traffic" all other voices died away. I heard Marj Saint answer me. I was getting through.

"Send a doctor and a pilot as quickly as you can."

Then Marj's voice:

"Right away. We have a doctor here from the States."

I hurried back to my patients. Since Tsamaraing had been running for some time, the snake poison would already be circulating through his system. He kept sitting up to vomit and I must try to keep him as quiet as possible.

This past hour had been one of the longest I'd ever lived through. Other missionaries of whom I had read went into a room by themselves at such dark times, and got down on their knees. But there was no chance of solacing solitude for me; I had to do my praying on the run.

And the Lord answered wonderfully.

By 8:30 A.M. the plane came, bringing Dr. Murray Weaver, a distinguished surgeon from California. He just "happened" to be visiting the missionary hospital in Shell Mera. From there he brought truly marvelous equipment: an intravenous set for "Big Eyes," an obstetrical kit for the mother-to-be; more antivenin for Tsamaraing; and his own great kindness, understanding, and skill. To me, this was all the answer to my prayer.

Dr. Weaver knelt down beside Tsamaraing on the floor, gave him morphine to quiet him, administered the antivenin, and a shot of vitamin K. He joined me then in praying for our young preacher. We could see Tsamaraing's muscles relax. He stopped vomiting; and presently, he slept.

The doctor turned now to his patient on the delivery table. He comforted her with soothing sounds to the point where he could persuade her to stay on the table in spite of the grandmother's lamentations. But the worried old woman insisted on climbing up on the table and sitting with her granddaughter's head in her lap. In less than half an hour, Dr. Weaver brought into the world a beautiful four-pound baby boy.

At her great-grandson's first cry, I laughed to see the old grandmother reach into her bosom, produce a piece of freshly cut and peeled sugar cane, and push it into the younger woman's mouth. Judging by the ensuing chewing and sucking noises, the sweet juicy cane exactly satisfied a need at that precise moment.

After cleaning up, we checked the snake-bite patient still on the floor in the adjoining room. Then we went to the little house where our third patient, "Big Eyes," was staying with his family. Throughout that day and the next Dr. Weaver administered two bottles of saline solution slowly into "Big Eyes"' blood stream. Then he diagnosed the child's main affliction as the last stages of tuberculosis. He predicted that even with the best of medical care he had not long to live.

Although it took a good deal of effort, I told his parents exactly what the doctor had said. I assured them that we would do all in our power to help prolong his life. I knew God was giving the child and his hardened parents an opportunity to know Him.

By the next afternoon when the doctor had to return to Shell Mera, all three patients (not to mention the missionary) were feeling much improved and grateful for his help. The proud young par-

ents named their baby Araas after our Ross. The following Sunday
we were thrilled to hear the young father accept Christ as his
Savior. He turned his back on his newly chosen witch-doctor career
to become instead a Tius Shuara. As to Tsamaraing, he improved
so rapidly that two weeks later he could stand again in the church
pulpit and testify how God had saved his life in answer to prayer.

But "Big Eyes" showed no lasting improvement after the doctor's
visit.

Later, as I walked toward the house to care for him, his mother
met me on the path outside their door. She wanted me to listen to
what she had to say before going in.

"I was getting some branches for firewood," she said, "when 'Big
Eyes' called to me to come quickly. I sat down on the bed beside
him and talked to him. But he said that my voice sounded a long
way off. Then he told me that he couldn't see the walls or the roof
of the house any more. He found himself in a place of beautiful
light. I was afraid he must be dying; but in a few moments he
could see and hear me clearly again. I think it must be because he
drank a little of that milk you brought him this morning. I'm
afraid. What can you do?"

Ana, our Jivaro helper, was with me, so I asked her what she
thought. "God is calling him to heaven," she answered unhesitatingly. Although I was quick to express my agreement, the mother
was unable to accept such an explanation. Nevertheless, as I talked
more of God and His ways with men she sat still and quietly listened and she even bowed her head as I finished praying. The next
day both of them prayed and sang with me, asking the Lord for
forgiveness. They thanked Him for the sure hope of a home in
heaven.

The following afternoon was suffocatingly hot. As I approached
the little house, all seemed unusually quiet. The three hollow bamboo poles were placed straight up and down blocking the doorway
instead of slanting toward opposite sides as they usually were during
the day. Although I announced my arrival in the customary Jivaro
manner, I barely heard the response from within giving me permission to enter. Tsetsempu was giving her son a bath. He sat quite
naked on a log next to the fire. He was turned backward and then
forward to receive full benefit from the insect-repelling smoke and

the heat of the glowing coals. A small pot of warm water sat balanced over the embers and from that Tsetsempu filled her bowl made of a half-gourd. For washcloth and soap she used the two halves of a lemon. Squeezing the juice into the warm water, she refilled the lemon halves and gradually poured and rubbed the solution over her son.

No mother anywhere could have been more tender or careful of her invalid son as she wiped the eyes and ears, and dried him fondly with the same dirty dress he used as a blanket. She proudly put his newly acquired shirt I had given him back on, fastening the buttons over his sunken chest and around his thin wrists. Then she gently helped him lie back on his bed, leaving him as refreshed and contented as any patient in the best of hospitals.

That Sunday the little house was filled with visitors as Indians dropped in to and from the church services. Some of them carried leaf-wrapped packages of a real jungle delicacy—large edible ants. September is the time of year when thousands of ants leave their old nests in search of a new environment to start another colony. The Indians knew that on the morning after the first heavy rains that followed several weeks of comparatively dry weather, the ants would swarm. Most of the Jivaros in church that morning had passed the night out in the brush, crouched beside an anthill and waiting for the first sign of dawn and ants. Then, attracting the flying insects with their flaming reed torches, they burned off their gossamer wings. Gleefully they all dropped to their knees and scooped up handfuls of the now-crawling creatures. They then wrapped them in leaves and took them home to be toasted in the open fire.

"Big Eyes" seemed to enjoy having the visitors. The house soon filled with the nutlike smell of toasted ants and the sound of crunching, popping insect posteriors. The ant's pea-sized abdomen is supposed to be the most delicious part. I registered first surprise and then alarm as I saw "Big Eyes'" chin resting on his knees, his mouth and fists full of toasted ants and pieces of cooked cassava root. But he only laughed at my shocked expression. There was nothing I could say. The whole group was in such a party mood that I could only make the best of it and try to join in the fun.

Suddenly "Big Eyes" held out a handful of toasted insects and invited me to have some. Ever since I had come to the jungle I kept telling myself, "*This year* I am going to eat one of those ants and try to find out why the Indians think them so delicious!" But I had never had the courage to put one into my mouth. This was my perfect chance—indeed, one that was unavoidable. I accepted his offer and raised one to my lips. With the round end actually between my teeth, I bit hard and fast. Then I exploded, spitting and sputtering in as noisy an imitation of the Indian fashion as I could manage. "*Yajesmaiti! Yuchatainti!*" I said. "Big Eyes" laughed to hear me use the same words to describe his ants that he had said about my bread. The others joined in, evidently amused just to hear me utter the words. It all came off very well. But on the way home one nagging thought persisted. I still didn't know for sure what those ants really tasted like.

The following morning, Monday, things really began to hum. It was the opening of the fall term of school, and the sudden arrival of more than a hundred Jivaro boys and girls kept us missionaries and two new schoolteachers just arrived from civilization busy. All these children to care for in addition to our medical patients left us very little time for anything else.

In the midst of all the boisterous activity, the greetings and excitement, I suddenly saw a contrasting scene. A family group was making its lonely way down the road from the mission that leads to the river. It was Mr. Hummingbird, his wife, and son. "Big Eyes" was again carried in a sling on his mother's back, his head resting wearily against her shoulder. He looked just as pathetic as when they had brought him here. They were taking him home to die. I ran after them to have a few last words. They told me that "Big Eyes" had had another attack of diarrhea the night before. And now that the school children were coming, they were afraid he might pick up some new disease from them.

I had come to know the boy so well that my heart ached to see him go, especially since I knew I might never see him again on this earth. As I stood looking at him, he took from his pocket his simple treasure, the wordless book, still wrapped in the shiny piece of waxed paper. He smiled wanly. Then as I watched the family continue down the road, I waved sorrowfully at the child.

About two weeks later we heard the news. Death had at last

brought release. Although we had tried to resign ourselves to the inevitable, we felt as though we had lost someone very close to us. But at least there was the consolation that he had lingered with us long enough to come to know Jesus Christ as his Savior through our talks and the wordless book.

CHAPTER 10

The Fateful Trees
of Cangaími

Holding forth the Word of life.   Philippians 2:16

"Panchu, the jivaros around cumai need your help," a young Indian preacher named Tsamaraing said to me. "There are many sick who should have medicines and many children who should be in school. I am the only one among them who knows about God's plan of salvation, but I cannot make them understand. I tell them to come here to Macuma. But they say it is too far and the Pastaza River lies between. They want you to come to them."

Tsamaraing had married a Cumai girl. Obeying *shuartica*, he had to live with his in-laws for a period before he could bring his new wife back to Macuma. As the only Christian in the neighborhood, he was having his troubles.

"Here it is easy to live for God," he said, "but there it is hard. Do I hear the preaching of God's Word every week? Do I sing and pray with other Tius Shuaras? No. I am alone, and I cannot read the Spanish Bible well enough to learn from it."

I asked him what I could do. His eyes lighted up.

"If we had an airstrip, you could fly over often to preach to us. The doctors could come with their medicines. We could have schoolteachers for our children. I have spoken to the other Indians. There is a wide flat place along the river. It would be fine for an airfield and would not take much work. We will build it without pay if you will just tell us how long it should be."

This was an answer to prayer. We were not satisfied to confine our efforts to Macuma and had long looked for a quicker way than itinerating on foot to reach Indians separated from us by miles of jungle trail.

Later I discussed this plan with Marie, Nate, and Dorothy. All agreed that with the help of the MAF plane and our Macuma Jivaro believers, we should take this opportunity to spread the Gospel faster. Macuma would be our main base from which to reach other groups. Cumai would be our first outstation.

We made our initial visits on foot. With us went Chumpi and old Chingasu, the strong-minded Jivaro woman who had once used her biting tongue and strong will to try to keep her son Wambiu from becoming a Christian. The couple had been Christians for over two years. Both now wanted to share in teaching the Gospel to the Cumai Shuaras.

In January, 1954, a new missionary couple, Roger and Barbara Youderian, came to join us. They had helped us the year before while we went to Quito for the birth of Timothy Frank, our fourth baby. Now they were in Macuma to stay and were studying the Jivaro language. These young workers, filled with the love of God, and enthusiastic in all they did, provided the impetus to launch our outstation program in full force.

Just before noon one day shortly after the Youderians arrived, an Indian runner came from Cumai to tell us their airstrip was finished. We contacted Nate at Shell Mera by radio and arranged for him to make a trial landing.

Roj insisted that he walk in first and check on the strip. He would stay to guide Nate in. He would have to leave right away if he was to make it by nightfall, so he started out, not taking time to eat or to let us pack him a lunch.

This tall, ex-paratrooper did everything with a sense that "the King's business required haste." He always worked as if his days were numbered, although he had no way of knowing then that he had only a few years in which to win souls for the Lord.

At Cumai, he inspected the strip, ordered a tree cut down that was standing too close to the airfield, and sent word that all was ready.

With great skill and care, Nate landed the Piper cruiser, and congratulated Roj on his helpful teamwork. We had promised the Indians a visit from the doctor and a hundred-pound sack of salt as a reward for finishing the strip. They were disappointed, therefore, to see the pilot fly in alone. Roj assured them there would be other flights and returned with Nate to Macuma.

The doctor and the salt were soon flown in, along with Dorothy Walker and me. The excited crowd of Jivaros that was gathered in Cumai for the arrival, regarded us as secondary benefits.

Everyone wanted the salt; they smacked their lips over it like children. Everyone's head or body needed the doctor's attention. The day passed rapidly in caring for all these patients. In the evening we held a praise and prayer service. The Cumai outstation was begun.

With Cumai a reality, we laid plans for establishing a second outstation, close to Atshuara territory. There was an airstrip already in existence at Wampimi, about thirty miles southeast of Macuma —one that had been built and abandoned by the Shell Oil Company.

"Maybe a dwelling of sorts could be made from the old company buildings," I suggested one night. "If some of us could stay there from time to time, we could preach to the Wampimi Jivaros; and when the Atshuaras hear we are there, with our medicines and trade goods, they might come to visit us."

Roj was so excited by the idea that he made the first visit on foot, staying just long enough to enlist the Indians to cut down the tall grass on the strip.

Within a few days I flew to Wampimi with Nate to talk over our plans with the Indians. One night there was enough for us. We tried to sleep in an abandoned shack, but chiggers ate us alive. We spent the rest of the night hunched up in the cramped seats of the plane. Before we left we got the Indians started clearing land, planting gardens, and cutting away the thorny vines that had swarmed over the paths and broken-down buildings.

Roj and Barb made ready to move to Wampimi. Before his family arrived Roj patched together several buildings standing in a row, to make a home. One had been a shower room and had a cement floor. He fixed this up as a bedroom. Another building, forty feet away, which also had a cement floor, he changed into the kitchen. He walled in the space between with various boards and odds and ends. He covered the whole structure with a kind of crazy-quilt roof which he made of thatched leaves, tile, tar paper, corrugated iron—anything he could find.

The lower altitude made Wampimi hotter than Macuma, and the place crawled with biting ants and bugs. Their only water had to be carried from a stream half a block away, except for what could be caught in a rain barrel. Roj and Barb did have a hand-crank radio, and the MAF plane made regular landings on that good strip.

They were happy. Their days, filled with language study, treating the sick, and preaching the Gospel, passed all too quickly. When I went to help with a special service a few weeks later, I found forty Indians in attendance—an amazing crowd for this area.

For most of the next six months, the Youderians continued to live at Wampimi. They never gave up hope that one day the Atshuaras would come to visit them.

As the outstations at Cumai and Wampimi were getting under way, a third one was opened up on the banks of the Cangaimi River—one which was to involve us in new crises. The Cangaimi station was about as far to the south of Macuma as Cumai was to the north.

Interest in establishing a missionary station there had been encouraged, as in the case of Cumai, by two Jivaro boys from our school. This was another tribute to Ernest Johnson, who had foreseen that the training of Jivaro boys in a Christian school would one day result in a corps of evangelists to their own people. Now his vision was becoming a reality.

One day the two schoolboys invited me to visit some of their relatives at Cangaimi. They were anxious that I bring a doctor along, as there was considerable disease there. I arranged for Dr. Paul Roberts, one of the HCJB missionaries, and Dr. Ralph Eichenberger of Wycliffe Bible Translators to fly out to Macuma and accompany us.

With the boys as our guides, we all started out on the eight-hour hike. They took us to the home of a Jivaro named Tuitsa, who turned out to be a rough character. Judging by his long gray hair, his straggly whiskers, and his bent-over body, I thought he must be one of the oldest Indians I had ever met. But he was vain about his age. He kept up a running fire of filthy, boisterous talk, obviously trying hard to give the impression that he was still as tough and active as any young warrior.

Tuitsa and his large family group were friendly, perhaps because they were so anxious for the doctor's help. I was amazed that here, on our very first night in the home of a strange Jivaro, we could hold a missionary clinic. We could only surmise that it was because our schoolboys had been such good ambassadors in our behalf.

One small need paved the way for further contact with these people. It was nothing more than a boy with a toothache.

I had learned that a big handicap to the Indians' appreciation of modern medicine was the lapse of time between treatment and cure. The Indian expects his witch doctor to heal him *pronto*. If he doesn't, he is no good. The same demonstration of mystical power is looked for from the missionary doctor. Unfortunately, much of the doctor's routine work, such as dispensing worm oil or cleansing infected wounds, offers little opportunity to demonstrate quick, magical results.

But treating a toothache could be different. Dr. Roberts explained, through interpreters, that he was about to give a general anaesthetic. All twenty-five Indians living in the house gathered to watch.

At first they were merely curious. But as they saw the boy go to sleep, panic seized them. The Jivaros greatly fear the unconscious state. Some began to cry out that the boy was dying and begged us to do something. Dr. Roberts calmly continued with his operation.

When the boy woke up, he did not even know, until Dr. Roberts told him, that his tooth had already been pulled. He couldn't believe it because he had felt no pain. This made the Indians shake their heads in wonder. Afterward they sat quietly while we sang hymns and spoke to them of Jesus and His love, though many of them had not so much as heard of the Gospel before.

That night the doctors, in their turn, had an eerie experience in what it means to live and work among the dark and mysterious forces of the jungle.

The household had settled down. Fires burned lower as the Indians stretched out on their bamboo racks and began to fall asleep. Suddenly and without warning, a strong wind ripped through the forest, tearing leaves from the thatched roof of the house. Outside, giant trees swayed and groaned. Within, Indians jumped from their beds, stirred up their fires to give more light, and ran wildly about the house, all talking at once.

Old Tuitsa, yelling above the storm, dashed to the door. He kept pointing outside to some unseen danger. I ran over to see what was bothering him. He told me that a large tree, quite near the house, was likely to come crashing down on us at any moment. He could have been right; jungle trees do not have to put their roots very deep into the ground to find water; a wind as strong as this could very easily blow them over.

Now the pounding of the rain added to the whining of the wind, and the cries of the Indians created a frightening din.

I sensed in their voices a new note of terror. Tuitsa ran for his gun and returned trembling and shrieking to the door. He stood there shaking, straining his ears.

I understood what it was. The Indians were convinced that the storm had been sent by a witch doctor to give their enemies cover for a surprise attack. Shouting, howling, running about or standing rigid, listening, the Indians were suffering more fear than from an actual attack.

Meanwhile, the doctors were also racing up and down as excitedly as the rest of us. Since I had forgotten to interpret for them, they didn't have the slightest notion of what was taking place. At last when the storm subsided into a steady downpour the Indians grew quieter and I had a chance to explain to the doctors. They were deeply shaken by this contact with the powers of evil. None of us could get back to sleep. We talked long into the night about the destructive practices of paganism and what the power of Christ could accomplish in changing the lives of these people.

A few months later we learned that the Cangaimi Jivaros had picked a site for their airstrip. Our two schoolboys asked Roj and me to come down and have a look at it, inviting us to stay at the house of a pleasant young man named Mayacu, uncle of one of the boys.

We were hopeful that Mayacu might become a Christian like his nephew. He listened eagerly as we told him of God's plan for salvation. He did not say much. But we thought we detected a hunger in the eye he kept fixed on us.

The airstrip site was breathtaking. The Indians had picked a place at the edge of a 350-foot bluff, thus eliminating much of the work of carving one approach out of virgin forest.

Roj and I stood there now, drinking in the view. The terrain at our feet dropped down to the shifting channels and sandy banks of the Cangaimi River. Spread lavishly before us was the dense green jungle, edged on one side by the dragon-tail humps of the Cutucu Range, and cut through the middle by the sweeping curves of the Cangaimi which carried our gaze miles to the southeast.

There was no more time to admire the view. Turning in the other direction, we faced the job ahead: half a mile of tough tangled trees still to be cut down.

With the help of some Indians we began hacking away at the undergrowth. We had made only a small dent in it by sundown. It was now too late to walk back to Mayacu's. An Indian named Jintachi lived not far from the airstrip; we went to his house and asked if he would put us up for the night.

Jintachi was a cocky little man who reminded me of a banty rooster. Grudgingly, he allowed us to stay. But he wanted us to know he was against the airstrip, and would have nothing to do with white men. When suppertime came, he refused to give us— or even sell us—anything to eat. In our exhaustion, however, going to sleep with empty stomachs didn't bother us a bit.

The work got underway. We saw enough indications of enthusiasm among the Indians to make us believe they'd go on with it; so the next day we hit the trail back to Macuma.

Late in November of that year, 1954, an Indian runner reached our mission with the announcement that the airstrip was ready for use. I set out on the trek to Cangaimi with a light heart. I could imagine Nate Saint coming in to make the first successful landing after I had checked out the strip, then flying me back to Macuma.

What a shock it was to find many tall trees still standing at the jungle end of the approach. There was nothing to do but go on with the job. The Indians were even unhappier about this than I, as they thought they had finished it. Silently, they picked up their axes and followed me. All that day and the next, the air rang with the whack of blades and the groan and crash of giant timbers thundering to the ground. We were pushing back the solid wall. Again I imagined myself flying out over the Cangaimi with Nate.

I was lost in such daydreams when the crack of a tree followed by sharp, anguished cries pulled me back to reality.

I ran, picking my way over the criss-crossed logs to the spot where the cries were coming from. The figure of an Indian loomed up before me. It was Jintachi, the banty rooster. I had not expected to find him here at all. He had just reported for work because he didn't dare lose face by refusing to help with a project so widely supported by the other Indians.

Jintachi glared at me defiantly and almost gleefully declared, "A falling tree just killed one of the *Shuaras*. It's Jisma, he's dead."

There was no mistaking his implication: "It's *your* fault—it's all *your* fault."

I ignored Jintachi and turned to the others.

"Where is he?" I called.

"Here—pinned down by the trunk!" someone shouted back.

I vaulted a log and headed in the direction of the voice.

Hurdling one log after another, I reached the scene just as the Indians were dragging a limp, skirted form from the brush into a clearing. I knelt down and examined the injured man. His nose was smashed; some teeth were gone; his head was all bloody. I wondered if he could still be alive. Then he groaned. I gave thanks that there was still breath in his body.

I had no medicines with me and no bandage. Suddenly I remembered that I had brought long strips of torn white sheets to mark out the length of the landing field so it could be seen from the air. I sent one of the Indians to get the bundle.

I needed help badly, but in emergencies, Jivaro Indians are totally helpless. When one of them faces the mere prospect of death, the rest give him up. Even while the afflicted one still lives, they start plotting vengeance against whoever has caused him to die. This was no exception. Superstitious taboos kept anyone from touching the doomed man. No one would give a hand in bandaging Jisma's wounded head. No one would bring water, nor any clean leaves for him to lie on.

An angry muttering arose. I heard one Indian say, "If this, my brother-in-law, dies, the man who cut down that tree will never eat another mouthful of food. I am strong enough to finish off the one responsible for this awful deed. And I will do it."

The threats increased. They all started asking one another who had felled the tree. It never occurred to them that it might have been an accident. Somebody had done it purposely and they were going to find out who it was.

To my consternation, I heard the name of one of our Cangaimi Christian schoolboys being mentioned more and more. Was he not the one who had first urged the idea of the airstrip? Was it not he who had persuaded the Indians to work on it? Then was not he the one who cut down the tree?

This was the moment Jintachi had been waiting for. He was going to prove his point. He began to talk the loudest, his voice coming out above all the others:

"Have I not been saying right from the beginning that to build such an airstrip was all foolishness? Are we Indians being paid for all our sweating? Now look what has happened! See what those who have toiled so hard can expect for their labors!"

He pointed to Jisma lying on the ground.

"Will *he* ever eat again?"

Jintachi's words were having their effect. The muttering became a chorus. If Jisma died, I feared for the life of our Christian boy.

But I had to turn my attention to the victim. His breathing sounded a bit more normal. His wounds were beginning to clot. But he couldn't stay here—he would have to be taken to a house. And how could this be done, with the Indians feeling as they were? Summoning up my will power and drawing strength from the Lord, I literally forced the stubborn Indians to improvise a stretcher from poles and borrowed shirts, which I then covered with leaves. I made them carry him to the nearest Jivaro house, although it was half an hour's walk away.

There I checked his condition and found it fair. But he needed medical care. If I could just get to Macuma in time to catch Nate and his plane, I could tell him to fly over Cangaimi and drop at least sulfa powder and clean bandages, since the airstrip wasn't yet fit for a landing.

I never walked so fast in my life. On the way, I looked at the situation from every angle. Matters at Cangaimi had come to a crisis. If Jisma died, it could set off a new wave of vengeance killings. Our hopes for evangelizing the Cangaimi Jivaros would be blasted.

To make things worse, I could not go back to help Jisma myself. I was already committed to attend the regular meeting of the mission council in Quito. I had also promised to bring Linda and Ross home from school for Christmas and was due to leave Macuma the following morning. I could only cling to my faith and pray that Jisma would not die.

Most important now, beyond seeing that remedies got back to Jisma, was to impress on the young Jivaro walking at my side the immediate need to get the remaining trees chopped down and the airstrip in usable shape, in the event Jisma had to be flown out to the hospital. But could the Indians, gripped by superstition, be persuaded to resume the work after such an unfortunate accident?

When I reached Macuma, I learned that Nate was grounded in Shell Mera by rain. Since there was no way to fly the remedies to Cangaimi, I sent them—with instructions as to their use—back with the Jivaro guide. The next day the skies cleared and Nate flew to Macuma to take Dorothy Walker and me to Shell Mera. Marie would be left alone during our ten-day absence. She promised to inform Nate of Jisma's progress.

I had been in Quito about three days when I was wanted on the radio. It was Nate calling from Shell Mera.

He had just heard from Marie. Jintachi had showed up over at Macuma with the news that Jisma had taken a turn for the worse. He had developed a high fever and was out of his head. Jintachi, knowing the sick man would die unless he got help from the missionaries, had put down his antagonism to come and beg Marie to have Jisma flown out to a doctor at Shell Mera. He kept assuring her that the rest of the trees were now down and the strip safe for a landing.

Nate was willing. But could I let him go ahead? Was the strip actually ready? While I was trying to decide what to do, Roj called from Wampimi. He volunteered to go to Cangaimi and check the airstrip himself.

It was then ten o'clock in the morning. Roj arranged to meet Nate at Cangaimi at four o'clock that afternoon. Roj was to start some small brush fires to indicate the wind.

Roj's hike was something of a feat. He made it over eighteen miles of that tough jungle trail in slightly less than six hours.

No one could appreciate what Roj had done better than Nate who later wrote of it:

"At 3:55 P.M. I was approaching the new strip, a mere cut in the matted grass and almost invisible until you got right over it. My heart rejoiced as my eyes spotted smoke drifting skyward from the cliff end of the clearing. There was Roj running from one smudge to another, stirring them up so they'd throw more smoke. He signaled 'Okay' on the condition of the strip. The wind was almost calm, slightly favorable. No downdrafts. I went in, committing the operation to the Lord.

"The landing surface was the roughest I've been on for a long time, but firm and perfectly safe. Roj was the ghost of his usual self. He was haggard and pale and sweating profusely. His shirt was in shreds. His heart pounded visibly and he panted for breath as he shouted to the Jivaros, instructing them to bring the wounded man as quickly as possible. I had some food for Roj in the plane . . . but he had no appetite for anything but a ripe pineapple which he promptly finished off. He hadn't had anything to eat since we had talked on the radio in the morning. Why? Why, because he could not stop even a minute . . . could not spare himself and still arrive in time.

"Off through the jungles I could hear the excited calls of the men who were bringing the victim. They carried him on a bamboo pallet slung between shoulder poles. His face was horribly mutilated . . . bones broken . . . one eye was opaque, probably blind before the accident . . . the other was blood red. He looked so dead I was shocked to see him move."

Nate reflected:

"Here was one of the hopelessly lost ones that the Lord Jesus had come to seek and save . . . a poor old one-eyed killer who rarely had seen or shown any expression of pity. He probably trusted me only because his own people had given him up. Death to him was the horror of the unknown; the anguish of a starless night forever. He knew nothing of God and less of Calvary. If only I could make it to Shell Mera maybe Doc Fuller could pull him through the night. The Lord willing, he might still be snatched from the brink."*

The Lord was willing; Jisma lived. A few months later he was back at Cangaimi strong and well. I gave praise that impending tragedy had paved the way to victory for the Gospel.

If one were to attend church in Cangaimi today, there, listening attentively to the service from the front bench, would be seen the cocky Jintachi himself!

* Russell T. Hitt, *Jungle Pilot: The Life and Witness of Nate Saint*, pp. 246-48.

CHAPTER 11

Crack in the Wall

Be ready always to give an answer to every man that asketh
you a reason of the hope that is in you. I PETER 3:15

WHEN I LEFT QUITO TO TAKE THE CHILDREN BACK HOME
for that Christmas of 1954, I had no inkling of what was in store
for me.

We stopped to spend the night in Shell Mera with Marj and
Nate. Marj was on regular radio contact next morning when she
suddenly summoned me to the set.

Roj was calling from Wampimi.

"I have traffic for Frank. Is he there? Over."

"He's right here, Roj. Over."

"Tell him to stand by. I have a visitor—a very important visitor
—who wants a word with him. Over."

Bursting with curiosity, I asked Marj to find out who it was.
Roj wouldn't tell her. He would only say, with an air of great
mystery, that this was a friend very dear to me, but someone I
hadn't yet met.

"Ready. I'll put him on. Over."

It was against the general rule for anyone but missionaries to
use the jungle network. With some misgivings, Marj handed me the
microphone. I called Roj and waited. It was not Roj's voice that
I heard, but the resonant tones of a stranger, speaking in Jivaro.

"Panchu!" said the voice, "I am Tsantiacu, Atshuara chief."

I could hardly believe my ears—a leader of the tribe I had been
trying to reach was calling me on the radio!

"We have heard much about you," he continued. "We want
to be your friends. My people hope you will come to our country.
They are waiting to see you. I invite you to stay at my house."

The chief and I talked back and forth for a few minutes; he was perfectly at ease with the microphone. My heart was full of thanksgiving for this unexpected opening to the Atshuaras.

His voice faded. Roj told me later that Tsantiacu had kept on talking even though he stopped transmitting because his arm got tired cranking the generator. Marie, listening in from Macuma, was overjoyed to hear the Atshuara's message.

This opportunity had come about only because Roj and his family were willing to endure the discomforts of living in that hot primitive outpost.

A few days later, when Roj brought Barb and the children to spend Christmas with us at Macuma, he told us how God worked to bring this contact about.

Tsantiacu lived three days by trail to the northeast of Wampimi. He hadn't been this deep in Jivaro territory for years.

The Atshuaras, however, carried on trade relations with some Wampimi Jivaros who lived not far from the mission station. These Jivaros had plenty of wild pigskins. The Atshuaras were more skilled than any other tribe at making blowguns and poisoned arrows. The Jivaros traded their pigskins for blowguns, and the Atshuaras in turn traded the skins for cloth, machetes, guns, and ammunition.

Word went through the jungle that there were missionaries at Wampimi who had medicines. Hoping to find a cure for his illness, Tsantiacu had come as far as the home of a neutral Jivaro from where he sent word to Roj that he would like to see him.

Roj found the chief both impressive and friendly. Tsantiacu consented to come to the mission house. There Roj gave the chief and his party medicines and presents of foods, played Jivaro Gospel records, and arranged for him to talk to me on the short-wave radio. Then he discussed plans for us to visit Atshuara country.

At the right moment, Roj spoke of the trip Keith and I had made several years before. He told the chief how Timas had threatened us and wanted to know if he were likely to make trouble again. Tsantiacu then revealed for the first time why Timas had tried to kill me.

"Did not Timas fear both white men and Jivaros from Macuma?" the chief said. "Did he not think Panchu had come to spy, so that the Jivaros could come back later to kill him? But since that time he had learned more about missionaries. He knows you are his friends and only want to help us." He grunted. "Anyway, he lives now in another part of the country, so he will not make trouble for you."

Roj tried not to let his eagerness to take advantage of this opportunity blind him to the dangers involved. He put another question to Tsantiacu:

"If Panchu and I travel to your house soon, will you come back to Wampimi and go with us over the trail to make certain no other Atshuaras try to hinder us?"

Without hesitating, Tsantiacu said he would. He was a man of quick, sure decisions. Having given his word, he would keep it. The two men set a date for the trip.

"By the time two moons have passed I will be back," promised Tsantiacu, "unless the rains swell the river so we cannot cross—or you send me word you cannot come."

The two moons had nearly passed when Roj returned to Wampimi after having stayed to help us for a while in Macuma. There the Indians brought him discouraging tidings. They were all saying war would break out at any moment between Tsantiacu and Timas. The latter's little son had died. Timas claimed the baby had been cursed by Shuunta, a young witch doctor who was Tsantiacu's nephew and who had accompanied the chief on his recent visit to Wampimi.

Roj had every reason to fear that the looming war would make our going impossible. But he did not change his plans. "By faith" he sent Indians to Tsantiacu to let the chief know he was back in Wampimi and ready.

After two days the Indians returned. They had not been able to reach Tsantiacu's house, as the lower Macuma was too swollen to cross. Roj didn't believe the Lord had brought Tsantiacu to Wampimi in vain; the baby's death, the flooded river, were only the Devil's work to keep us from taking the Gospel to the Atshuaras. He instructed the Indians to try again later.

Roj said nothing of this to us in Macuma, but only reminded us that by the middle of February the "two moons would have passed."

And sure enough, on February 16, Tsantiacu, with one of his wives, appeared at Wampimi. War had not broken out; the river had receded; the Indians, on their second trip, had reached Tsantiacu's house and found the chief ready to return with them.

Roj sent word to us in Macuma and to Nate in Shell Mera that everything was going according to plan. He also asked that Marie go with us as far as Wampimi in order to stay with Barb and her children. Dorothy offered to care for Timmy, who was then twenty months old, and also our new baby, Laura, so that Marie could go. Nate flew to Macuma to take Marie, myself, our six-year-old Irene, and a visiting friend, Dr. William Reyburn, to Wampimi. Dr. Reyburn, an anthropologist working with the American Bible Society, was eager to go with us to the Atshuaras.

At Wampimi we packed our loads to go on the backs of Jivaro carriers. These included a phonograph, records, blankets, medicines, food, one change of clothing each, and a compact shortwave hand-crank transceiver. The Wampimi Jivaros would never have ventured through "no man's land" by themselves. They went with us reluctantly for pay.

I saw Tsantiacu for the first time at Roj's. The chief was a man to command respect. His piercing eyes could be steely cold with hate or warm with friendliness. The Winchester .44 which never left his hand was as much a part of him as the geometric designs painted across his high cheekbones. He wore no shirt, but a new striped *itipi* reached from his waist to his ankles. His black hair was cut in even bangs across his forehead and hung down his back in a long ponytail adorned with toucan feathers. His sideburns were twisted into forward pigtails, bound with string and also decorated with bright feathers. Ten-inch hollow reed plugs stuck through the lobes of his ears.

Just before our party left the clearing, Chief Tsantiacu, deftly and without embarrassment, changed his costume. First he took off all his brilliant feather ornaments and tucked them into his shoulder bag. Then he fastened an old dirty *itipi* around his waist, at the same time dropping the new bright one to his feet. As he fell into line behind his pudgy little wife, he no longer looked the chief, but like any other Indian on the trail.

Late in the afternoon we came to the last house on the Jivaro side of "no-man's land." We unlimbered the hand-crank radio and watched the Indians fasten the antenna up in the trees. In a few minutes, from that remote spot we were talking to Marie and

Barb in Wampimi, to Marj in Shell Mera, and to Dorothy in
Macuma. We took the radio contacts by now as an everyday
affair; even the Indians no longer marveled at them.

But it brought joy at the other end to hear our voices. Marie
wrote in her diary:

"February 20. Praise the Lord for radio contacts. Barb and I
take turns on the hand crank. It is so hard I cannot turn it sitting
down. By leaning my left leg on the seat, standing on my right
leg and turning the crank with all my strength, I can barely produce
enough power to transmit for a minute or two at a time. But it is
well worth the effort to know how the fellows are."

And Dorothy wrote to friends,

"One of the Indians came to chat before the Sunday service. He
asked me, 'Do you suppose the Atshuaras have killed Frank and
Roj?'

" 'No, they have not,' I said, 'because I talked to them by radio
this very day. They are well and will soon be at Tsantiacu's house.'

"What a joy to be able to reassure them—and myself."

We had two more days of hard travel through virgin jungle,
jumping over logs, fighting thorns, often crossing flooded rivers.
We slept on the hard ground which was cold and damp, with no
mattress but a thin layer of tropical leaves. Then, unexpectedly,
we came out into a clearing and saw before us Tsantiacu's huge
oval house.

In all my travels I had never seen a larger Indian dwelling. It
was about forty feet wide and must have been ninety feet long. It
was arranged like a Jivaro house: The *tangamash* had six bamboo
sleeping racks; the *ekenta* had eight or ten, with bamboo partitions
between. Smouldering fires at the foot of every rack in both sec-
tions filled the house with a thick blue haze. The roof, about forty
feet up at the highest ridge, was beautifully woven in an intricate
pattern of folded palm leaves, and was sooty black from the smoke
of many fires. The longer we stayed the more our eyes smarted
and our throats burned.

We sat down and changed our water-soaked socks and shoes.
Tsantiacu showed us our bamboo racks. Then he called to the
women to bring us some food. They filed in from the *ekenta*, bearing pineapple, papaya, bananas, plantains, boiled eggs, cooked

meats, and sweet potatoes, more than I had ever been served in any Jivaro home.

Looking around us, we could see how the Atshauras lived. Large bundles of unhusked corn, along with rolls of dried pigskins, hung from the rafters. A signal drum made from a hollow log stood against the wall. Above the men's racks were blowguns and quivers, small snare drums, a violin and flute, monkey-skin bags, and many baskets of brilliant feather ornaments.

The *ekenta* crawled with assorted children, dogs, parrots, and monkeys. A pet pig squealed and skittered behind one woman's skirt as she worked. The floor was littered with pots, vegetables, and fruit. The women were not nearly so strikingly dressed or lavishly adorned as the men. They all wore simple outfits of the same dark, coarse cloth, in the same two-piece style. Their skirts were gathered in a big roll around their hips, resting on their protruding abdomens. Their loose blouses were purposely cut short the better to nurse their babies.

More women than men made up this jungle family. As visitors came throughout the day, there must have been at least twenty adults, almost that many children, and fully as many dogs.

The Atshuaras appeared more industrious than the Jivaros. Their gardens were larger and better kept. They were always on the lookout for chances to trade.

They appeared healthier too, although there were plenty of signs of the usual diseases—tropical ulcers, skin trouble, and the distended bellies among the children that indicated worms. We looked forward to the day when we would come back with a missionary doctor. There was so much we could accomplish with proper hygiene and medical care.

For two days and two nights we lived in close quarters with the Atshuaras, amid the smoke, heat, bugs, and strange smells, sleeping on their racks and eating what they ate.

They were almost embarrassingly friendly and inquisitive. They could hardly keep their hands off us or our belongings, apparently they were more curious about us than we were about them. We had long prayed for the opportunity to get to know these people and understand them. It had come; we made the most of it.

The conversation was especially satisfying. They never seemed to tire either of talking about themselves or of listening to us. The differences in pronunciation from Jivaro weren't hard for us to grasp, although every once in a while they lost us altogether in the intricacies of their grammatical constructions.

We did better than we had hoped on a first visit in getting through to them. Every morning, afternoon, and evening we called them together to listen to the Gospel on the phonograph, to hymn singing and preaching. They had never heard the story of God's Son or of the salvation offered to all men.

Alternately standing or sitting on the hard stool, I would begin with the story of creation, go on through the fall of man, and the redemption bought on Calvary's cross for our sins. Each time I finished, Chief Tsantiacu would look at me with emotion and say, "Never have I heard such beautiful words. Tell them again." The other Atshuaras would nod their shiny black heads in agreement with their chief.

My voice grew hoarse. My bones ached from my cramped position. But we were so delighted at their interest that I told the story again and again. They never seemed to get enough.

Once, when I had finished, Roj whispered to me, "Just to see the expression on their faces is reward enough for plowing through all those mudholes. Praise the Lord for bringing us here!"

We made a point of getting acquainted with the members of Tsantiacu's household. We learned their names, tried to keep straight in our minds their relationships to one another, and listened to the stories they had to tell.

Tsantiacu had three wives, one daughter, and one young son. I asked him which of his wives was the mother of his children.

"None," he answered. "Their mother is dead."

"What caused her death?" I asked, thinking perhaps it must have been some illness.

"Oh, she was bewitched. But the witch that killed her isn't alive any more."

"What happened to him?"

Without the slightest trace of embarrassment or guilt, Tsantiacu said,

"I killed him."

This was a healthy reminder that, in spite of their fascination with my Bible stories, conversion of the Atshuaras would not be a quick or easy task.

Their own talk, like that of the Jivaros, was filled with tales of wars, of violent death, and of curses inflicted by the witch doctors. At no time were their guns far from their hands. This feeling of fear was especially noticeable at night. I have always been a light sleeper, even at home on a comfortable bed. Here, tired though I was, I had trouble dozing off on the hard bamboo rack. Through all the hours until dawn I was conscious of the noiseless step of one Indian or another, prowling about, gun in hand, his eyes and ears alert for sight or sound that would betray the surprise attack of some unseen enemy.

We had a reminder again in the morning of the unpleasant primitiveness of the Atshuaras' way of life. Before the first rays of daylight sifted through the cracks in the walls, we were startled by awful sounds of retching, vomiting, and belching. Then there would be light bantering conversation and even laughter interspersed between repulsive gargling and the sound of splashing on the hard dirt floor. We realized that this must be the voluntary "stomach washing" which we had heard they practiced. It signified nothing more than the start of a normal day in this household.

During the last afternoon of our visit, old Tsantiacu invited Roj and me to go with him over the land he called his own. As we walked we came to a stretch of road, about half a mile in length, which was remarkable for its width and straightness.

How had it ever come to be here, right in the heart of the jungle? Why had it been made so straight? We asked Tsantiacu.

"It is just a trail we used while bringing leaves for our new house," he replied.

Roj and I looked at each other. We both had the same idea. This would make a perfect site for an airstrip!

We sounded out Tsantiacu. The instantaneous smile that brightened his rugged face told us that the same idea had already occurred to him. He started talking.

"Do you mean that if we made an airstrip here you would come to visit us often and tell us more about God's Word?"

"Yes."

"Then that is what we want to do. If you will tell us how to build an airstrip, we will make one."

Roj didn't lose a moment. He started right out, pacing off the desired length and breadth. Then he stripped branches and stuck them in the ground to indicate the boundaries. We promised that as soon as we got back to Wampimi we would send in shovels and axes to help speed the work. As inducement to push ahead, we assured him that we would fly in a missionary doctor as soon as there was an airfield fit to land on.

We left with the old chief's declaration of friendship and warm invitation to come again ringing in our ears. I couldn't help contrasting this experience with my last visit to another Atshuara chief five years before. That one had ended with our being ordered to get out or be killed. There had seemed to be no hope of ever making contact with these strange people. But now, in His mysterious ways, God had opened the door to make it possible for us to bring them the Gospel.

CHAPTER *12*

A Voice from the Sky

All things to all men that I might by all means save some.
I CORINTHIANS 9:22

THE WITCH DOCTOR WENT INTO HIS TRANCE. THE DEMONS in the form of anaconda, fer-de-lance, and jaguar writhed and danced toward him. He gave up his will to theirs. In return, they disclosed to him the name he was seeking.

"Catani!" he moaned. "It was Catani who put the curse on your nephew and caused his death!"

That was all Tsantiacu needed. He organized a war party, descended on Catani's house, and killed one of his relatives for revenge.

Catani then secretly summoned a large group of Jivaros to his home. There they drank the *chicha,* whipped themselves to a frenzy by their hypnotic war dance, and departed en masse for Atshuara country.

Wampiu brought us this news with a stricken look on his face. Full-scale warfare was breaking out again. We should not have been so optimistic about establishing good relations with the Atshuaras.

Everything had been proceeding according to plan in building the airstrip to reach Tsantiacu's people. The axes and shovels had been sent on as promised. The clearing of the strip was well along; Roj and I were planning another trip soon to check on progress.

Now we faced a setback.

"Catani and his men mean to get Tsantiacu's head and bring it back for a *tsantsa,*" Wampiu whispered. "And if they can't get the chief's head, they are bent on making a *tsantsa* of the head of some other Atshuara."

155

His report filled us with consternation. Tsantiacu and his people would blame us for Catani's attack. They would look on us as spies who pretended friendship only in order to help our Jivaro neighbors destroy them.

It was clearly our Christian duty to stop this attack. But how? We did not have much time. It would take Catani and his party, at the most, three days more to reach Tsantiacu's house; and according to Wampiu, they had already set out on the trail.

I racked my brain but nothing came. At the next contact I turned on the jungle network radio and put in a call for Nate Saint at Shell Mera.

Nate I knew to be a fellow of great mechanical ingenuity. He did not fail me this time. His first notion was to fly over Tsantiacu's house, lower an aerial telephone in a bucket at the end of a long cord, and warn Tsantiacu of the coming attack. But Nate quickly discarded that one, pointing out that Tsantiacu, never having seen a telephone, wouldn't know what to do with it.

Then he hit it. Why not rig up a loud speaker in the plane and warn Tsantiacu from the skies? I agreed. Nate signed off, saying he would get right to work on it.

The weather turned against us. All that day it remained too thick for flying. The second day, the same. The third day dawned murky and threatening. Along toward afternoon I advised Nate that it was wide open at Macuma. He said it was still heavy at Shell Mera, but he'd take off anyway.

Nate brought another missionary, Bill Gibson, with him. The three of us took the cabin door off the plane and set up the loud speaker in its place. Then we left for Tsantiacu's house.

We found it without much trouble and began circling overhead. Now my efforts at learning the names of Tsantiacu's family paid off. I could see the Indians running about down below. When I took the microphone and called them by name, they knew it was Panchu speaking. One woman dropped her basket and streaked for the brush. Several men remained, jumping up and down and waving their arms like college cheer leaders. I warned them that Catani and his men were on their way to take them by surprise. Nate cut the motor and we glided over, so they could hear my voice free from the engine noise.

Now we had to let Catani know that Tsantiacu had been warned.

We flew back to Jivaro country until we saw the house where Catani lived on the edge of "no man's land." Again we circled. There was no one in the clearing, no smoke coming up from the house, no sign of life anywhere. But we knew that even if Catani and his men were there they would not show themselves. Again we broadcast our message from the plane that Tsantiacu had been alerted and was ready for them. We had no way of knowing whether Catani heard us. But we had done our best. We put back to Macuma, and just in time, for dark was coming in.

Through succeeding days we waited apprehensively for news of the attack. But we heard none. Later, we learned that the Lord had worked through us. Catani had been along the trail that day within earshot of my voice. He had heard our message, and as a result had given up the attack and sent his war party back home.

But the respite in the bloody warfare was not to last very long. About six months later, another relative of Tsantiacu's died from illness. Again the witch doctor named Catani as responsible for the death. This time it was the Atshuaras who organized a raiding party and set out to avenge themselves on the Jivaros.

For several days Tsantiacu and his men law in ambush along the trail leading to Catani's house. They grew jumpy with waiting. At last they heard footsteps on the path. Tsantiacu's Winchester split the air as the first shadowy figure appeared. An Indian crumpled to the ground. The Atshuaras, thinking they had got their enemy, fled.

The man they shot, however, was not Catani, but his brother-in-law Mangash, who had attended our school in Macuma and become a Christian. Miraculously, he had not been killed. Tsantiacu's bullet had cut through the flesh of both arms and grazed his chest, just missing his heart. Mangash had fallen to the ground more from fright than from injury. A week later he came to us for treatment. His wounds were almost healed by then and he praised the Lord for saving his life.

Mangash had had enough of feuds. He moved from his old home near Catani's house to Macuma to be close to the church. But the attack set off a new series of killings. The Jivaros knew it was Tsantiacu who had shot Mangash—how, it was hard for us to say; perhaps by the sound of his gun; perhaps by his footprints, for the Jivaros can read footprints as they can faces. They even knew how many Indians Tsantiacu had brought with him. The war was no private affair between the two chiefs. All their followers were involved; and even we Christian missionaries had difficulty staying neutral.

This time it was Catani's turn to set out with a raiding party, bent on killing Tsantiacu. Then a strange thing happened, unknown to us until some time later.

One afternoon we flew over Tsantiacu's house to show the new airstrip to a distinguished Ecuadorian army officer. We found, as we expected, that the airstrip was not yet in shape. So we circled the house several times, dropped some clothing to encourage the Indians to continue working, and turned back. As we dipped for the drop, we noticed a newly-built high stockade which Tsantiacu had put up around his house as further protection against his enemies.

While we were flying back over "no-man's land," Catani spotted us from the ground—so the Jivaros told us later.

"It's Panchu! He's gone to warn my enemies again!"

When Catani and his party sighted the plane they were going to turn back. But they were now so near to Tsantiacu's house, and so worked up with rage, that they decided to press on.

They crept up as far as a little stream that flowed just outside the stockade. There Catani hid in the bushes, waiting for the moment when an Atshuara would come for water. Soon a woman appeared, carrying two large water gourds. She stooped, filled them, and was starting back to the house when Catani fired, killing her instantly. Although they heard the shot, the Atshuaras did not dare leave their stockade to see what had happened. Guns in hand, they waited until dark. When they found the woman's body, they needed no witch doctor to tell them who had done the killing.

A month later, Tsantiacu set out to get his revenge on Catani. Once more he lay in ambush along the trail that led to the witch doctor's house. After a while, Catani and his family came up the path. This time Tsantiacu did not miss. He took aim carefully and fired many times. One bullet passed through the body of Catani's favorite wife and through a young child she carried on her back. The baby died instantly; the wife, before daylight next morning. Four of Tsantiacu's bullets entered Catani's body. He fell to the ground. His friends found him there some time later. Amazingly, he was still alive.

Word of the shooting spread like wildfire from house to house. Catani lay dying from his wounds. Jivaros from around Macuma went to see him, and urged that he let himself be brought to us for treatment, saying,

"Panchu and his woman have powerful medicines that will make you well."

But the stubborn old warrior shook his head.

"Was it not Panchu who warned Tsantiacu? Is it not Panchu on the side of the Atshuaras? Then why should he want to help me?" he asked.

The believers from the Macuma church tried to tell him that the love of Christ was a free gift to all men—that it applied equally to Atshuara and Jivaro. But their words fell on deaf ears.

Catani held out for five days. Then, failing fast and with no other hope, he consented to come. Indian runners hurried ahead to tell us he was on his way. As we questioned them about his condition so that we would be better prepared to treat him, it appeared that his case was too grave for us to handle by ourselves. We put in an emergency call for Dr. Fuller at Shell Mera.

Our yard filled with Indians who had come from miles around. They stood there recounting Catani's feats as a warrior and a witch doctor.

The slow jungle ambulance moved through the clearing, up to our porch. Lying there, wrapped in a blanket, Catani looked at us with his pleading, suffering eyes. Here was no longer the arrogant chief, the witch doctor with magic powers. He was another helpless soul, lost without Christ, terrified by the thought of death.

I knelt beside him, explaining that God had not spared him for nothing, that he had been given another chance for salvation and must make the most of it. He listened without reaction as I prayed that God would save him—both his body and his soul.

The plane came and bore him off to Shell Mera. As its motor faded into silence above the trees, the air was rent with the piteous wailing of the women who believed they would never again see the sick one alive. To die away from home, especially among white men, is greatly dreaded by all Jivaros.

Catani was on the operating table for eight hours while the doctors probed for bullets and cleaned the neglected infections. He did not quickly respond to the anesthesia, as his system was too saturated by Jivaro narcotics. Doctors and nurses said he made that hospital room a fearsome place as he fought and struggled and moaned the weird chants which he was accustomed to singing as a witch doctor in treating sick Indians.

A week later, he was back home almost as strong as ever. Our church members came to us and offered to pay what they could toward the expense of Catani's hospital care as a gesture of love for this wicked man. Then they visited him. They hoped they would find him chastened and grateful, and interested in the Lord who had saved his life. Not at all. Catani's heart remained unchanged. He shunned the church members and avoided me. He had no intention of giving up his witch doctoring, his warfare, or his hatred of Tsantiacu.

Tsantiacu was sure to find out that we had saved Catani's life, and we wondered how he would react. Would he think we were now enemies of the Atshuaras? Would our efforts to reach them with the Gospel come to an end? I prayed,

"May the Lord help Tsantiacu to understand that God's ways are higher than men's ways, and that we, as God's people, could not possibly take sides in jungle warfare."

With Catani well again, fear reigned once more in the stockade of the Atshuaras. They kept watch through many long nights, determined not to be taken by surprise again.

Word reached me that Tsantiacu had said to his Indians,

"Have you heard what Panchu has done? After I shot Catani and left him to die, Panchu gave him medicine and sent him to the big doctor in Shell Mera who made him well. If Panchu hadn't helped him, Catani would be dead. Besides, the Wampimi Jivaros are now saying that Panchu plans to bring soldiers here to catch us. He is Catani's friend—not ours."

This was discouraging. The outlook for establishing a church among the Atshuaras looked darker than ever.

But I was not ready to abandon hope. Somehow—in God's good time—our chance would come.

CHAPTER *13*

The Open Door

For a great door and effectual is opened unto me, and there are many adversaries. I Corinthians 16:9

THERE WAS NOT MUCH THAT WENT ON IN ECUADOR'S Oriente which we didn't know about. But now I was hearing only hints and indications of a bold, imaginative operation being initiated in the northern jungles. My comrades Nate and Roj were busy with mysterious activities. When I asked Nate directly what was going on, he answered me just as directly that he could not tell me. He was engaged in a project that called for the utmost secrecy.

I was occupied in trying to follow up our first contact with the Atshuaras. In the fall of 1955, the job in hand was to finish the airstrip so that we could more easily visit Tsantiacu.

Roj was working in Shell Mera, helping to build the hospital. When he returned to Macuma, Nate flew us over Tsantiacu's house to check on how the airfield was coming along. We saw the Indians working down below. But we were unhappy to observe that they were extending the strip in the wrong direction so that it pointed toward the house.

Roj insisted on going in and directing them. We landed at Wampimi and had one of the Indians walk in with him. Others were to follow with his bedroll, food, and radio. Several days went by without any word from Roj; although we called him on schedule, he never answered. I thought something must have gone wrong. Nate came to Macuma with his plane; we rigged up the aerial telephone and flew the half-hour to Tsantiacu's place.

There were a few low clouds, but through them we glimpsed Roj working with the Indians. That made us feel better. We let the phone over the side and began to fly in a tight circle. Half the

161

time we were in the clouds and half the time in the clear.

"It's like fly casting," Nate said. We had to make several tries before we landed the phone.

Roj came on and explained that the other Indians hadn't followed him, so he had no radio. He faced a bad situation: influenza had broken out and the Indians were in need of medicines. He asked us to come back three days later, assuring us the strip would be ready then for the first landing.

Nate went back as agreed. Although he found the strip still quite rough, it was good enough to land on. He flew Roj out and brought me back the following week to take some more medicines and to hold services. Nate seemed to enjoy the challenge of landing on the short rough strip. When he remarked that this was good practice for him, I knew he must be thinking of landing somewhere on an even rougher, shorter strip.

I had heard that three missionaries up in the north jungles had been doing some flying that wasn't talked about. Putting two and two together, I figured they might be trying to make contact with the Aucas as I had been with the Atshuaras. The Aucas were one of the fiercest and most dreaded of savage tribes; they lived cut off not only from white men but from other Indians. They carried long spears with which they attacked anyone who tried to come near them. They had even been known to throw their spears at planes flying overhead.

Other hints were dropped. During one of Nate's regular visits to Macuma, an Indian returned a borrowed trap of mine. When Nate saw it, he asked if he could have it, saying cryptically, "It's just what I'll be needing one of these days."

I asked him how the project was coming.

"I'm sorry, I can't tell you a thing about it," he said. "All I can say right now is that it looks encouraging. Pray for us."

Roj brought his family to Macuma to spend Christmas. He informed us that after the holidays they were going to stay a while with the Ed McCulleys, who had charge of an outstation far to the north. This was close to Auca country. I knew then that Roj was in on the operation, too.

Just before they left, Roj, with Nate's approval, told me about the project and why it had to be kept so secret. It was such an adventurous undertaking that if word leaked out in advance, it might be misunderstood or exploited by the outside world, which would ruin their carefully-thought-out preparations.

When Nate came to get Roj he asked if he could borrow the transceiver we had used on our trip to the Atshuaras. He said they were going to establish themselves on a beach in Auca territory and needed the radio to maintain contacts with Shell Mera. But he didn't tell me what day they would be there or any other details.

I shall never forget our farewells. We all went out to the strip to say good-by. When they were strapped in and ready to go, I said to them, "May the Lord bless you. Come back soon." Nate looked at me and said, "Yah."

All through the next week I tried to get news of their activities. But nothing was said on the regular contacts. I had no success. Then one day a message was sent out for Jim Elliot to get on over to the "conference." That must mean they were ready to start their plans a day or two early. After that, no one said anything.

A couple of days went by, then curiosity got the better of me. I wanted to know what was happening. They were using the plane; therefore I surmised, they must be using the radio. They must be having secret contacts on another frequency. Then I remembered something: Nate had a crystal which he once used to call the Shell Oil Company tower. I tried listening in next morning on that wave length; Roj was talking from some unknown point in Auca territory with Nate at Arajuno and Marj at Shell Mera.

They were using a kind of code language. Roj was telling Nate, "We took on a little water on the football field last night. If the sun comes out in an hour or so, everything will be okay." To me this meant that the sandstrip along the edge of the Curaray River, where Roj had told me they were going to land the plane to make contact with the Aucas, was usable. Roj told Marj that they had a good "conference" the day before, and that "three had come." To me this meant that three Aucas had appeared in friendship.

On Sunday I was busy getting ready for the services and did not have time to listen. Monday morning nothing was yet revealed. When I turned on the radio at contact time Tuesday, I heard Marj's voice calling me. It was steady as usual, but strained. By this time Operation Auca was being made known to everyone. But I had not yet heard the news she was about to give me. She said, "The fellows are missing. The last contact we had with them was Sunday noon. Johnny flew yesterday morning over Palm Beach, the landing place in Auca territory. He saw the plane. It has been stripped of all its fabric. None of the fellows are there. We don't know what has happened to them. Would you come and lead a rescue party to the site?"

My quick reaction was that of course I would. Roj would have gone anywhere to help me.

"I'll ask Marie if it's all right with her. If she says 'yes' I'll be right back with the answer."

I ran across the yard to the house and told Marie the sad news. "They must all be dead. If the plane's gone, they're gone," I said.

"Of course you must go," she replied. "That's the only thing for you to do."

I ran back to the radio.

"Macuma calling. Yes, Marj, I'll come."

Pilot Johnny Keenan, who had joined Nate in Shell Mera eight months before, came for me in the one remaining MAF plane and took me to Shell Mera. People were coming from everywhere— from Quito, by bus and car; from Panama, by plane.

On Wednesday we started for Arajuno, which had been headquarters for Operation Auca. There our ground party made its final plans. We had a good group, among them seven missionaries. Any one of them could have directed the search as well as I.

We went on foot straight across country to the Curaray River. From the few Quichua Indians living there on the edge of Aucaland, we obtained some dugout canoes and started down the river.

My heart was sad. I had never expected to find myself in a situation like this.

We were paddling along when we saw overhead the helicopter that had been sent from Panama. It landed on a nearby beach, kicking up a great storm of sand. The occupants stepped out. They had worse news for us. They had just returned from a trip over Palm Beach. The bodies of three men were lying there in the water, with spears in them. One of them was wearing bluejeans.

I didn't say anything. Who, of that group, always wore bluejeans but Roj? I couldn't bear the thought of Roj being dead. We had

walked hundreds and hundreds of miles through the jungle together; we had built houses at Macuma together; we had opened
outstations, built airstrips together. In my mind I could see him
lying there in the water, a little way ahead of us downstream.
Would I be equal to picking him up out of the water and giving
him a burial?

And there was Nate. He had become as dear to me as my own
brother. He had always been there to pull us out when we were in
a tight hole. He had been unfailing in his faithfulness, ingenuity,
and good nature. There would be other pilots, but there was only
one Nate Saint. The other three missing men I didn't know so
well as they had been working in the northern jungle. But Roj and
Nate had been my pals.

As our canoe slid over the rapids following the helicopter I
prayed, "Lord give me strength."

We were approaching Palm Beach. I was weak with a double
fear—the fear of seeing the bodies of the ones I had loved, and
the fear of being killed by the Aucas. But the experiences of the
next few minutes—looking at the skeleton of the plane on the
beach; climbing the ladder to the tree house where my friends had
slept; bringing the bodies of my dead companions up from the
river—were good for me. I felt the Lord calming my heart and
giving me a new determination to serve Him, regardless of what
might happen to this body of mine.

We laid the men on that sandy shore. The fact of death could
not have been more real; but so was the truth of "absent from the
body and present with the Lord."

We said to one another, "They are not here. This is only the
house they left behind."

Their burial ground was under the tree house. How close were the
forces of evil in that dark and dismal hour! Black clouds cut off
the sun and a fierce wind and rain beat upon us.

I had a Bible with me in my rubber pack. But neither time nor
weather allowed me to get it out. I conducted the service from
memory, while the rain poured down and mingled with my tears.
I bowed my head in prayer, commending the bodies of our loved
ones to God's care until they should rise again on the Day of
Resurrection.

The aftermath of that killing—the Christian forgiveness shown by the widows and relatives—is one of the most inspiring chapters in Christian missionary history.

Barb soon returned to Macuma with her children Bethy and Jerry. As they climbed out of the plane, four-year-old Bethy looked expectantly toward us.

Barb greeted us with a smile and explained, "Bethy thought her daddy would be here to meet her. Although I've told her many times all that has happened, she was sure she would find Roj in Macuma."

During the several weeks the three of them stayed in our house, we never heard a word of complaint or self-pity, although we knew Barb felt her loss greatly. We praised the Lord for the wonderful privilege of having her back with us and the Jivaros.

She was truly happy to continue in the work that she and Roj had begun and soon moved with Dorothy to spend several months at the outstation of Cangaimi.*

At Macuma, the outlook for continuing contact with the Atshuaras was disheartening. Almost every day, visiting Indians brought fresh reports that Tsantiacu and his people had turned against us. Every Jivaro had a different story: Tsantiacu had rolled logs onto the airstrip; his women had planted the field to cassava bushes; the chief said I was coming back with soldiers to take him away. Worst of all was the rumor that since the Aucas had killed Roj and Nate and suffered no consequences, Tsantiacu now felt no compunctions about killing me. The trouble was, we had no way of knowing how many of these tales were true, and how many merely the product of the fevered Jivaro imagination.

There were physical difficulties, too. The only plane we could count on to make a safe landing on that tricky Atshuara airfield —Nate Saint's—was lying on Palm Beach, stripped by the Aucas. Johnny Keenan was still on the job with the other MAF plane

---

* The story of the martyrdom of Nate Saint, Jim Elliot, Pete Fleming, Roger Youderian, and Ed McCully is told in detail in *Through Gates of Splendor* by Elisabeth Elliot (Harper, 1957). See also *Shadow of the Almighty* by Elisabeth Elliot (Harper, 1958), *Jungle Pilot: The Life and Witness of Nate Saint* by Russell T. Hitt (Harper, 1959), *The Dayuma Story* by Ethel Emily Wallis (Harper, 1960), and *The Savage My Kinsman* by Elisabeth Elliot (Harper, 1961).

and was always eager to lend us a hand. But his little Pacer was much too fast to land on Tsantiacu's small clearing. With the big house at one end of the strip and the tall trees at the other, there was no margin for tail winds or any slight miscalculation.

Another thought lay heavy on my conscience. I could see, after having helped to pull the bodies of Nate Saint and Roj Youderian from the cold waters of the Curaray, that my life might go in the same way. Besides my own life, the reputation of those five martyrs who had died for Christ at Palm Beach was at stake. I reasoned this way: Their sacrifice had electrified the entire Christian world. From all continents had gone up the spontaneous cry: "Wonderful! Great courage!" But if, within a few months, there were to be another violent death in that same part of the world, the cry could very easily change to "Those fool missionaries have done it again. Why do they take such risks?"

Yet I could not put from me the need to bring more of the Word to the Atshuaras. When I thought of how much preaching and teaching people in my homeland receive and how long it takes them to understand the necessity of salvation, I realized how much greater was the need of the Atshuaras. I felt the urgency of the situation. The wars were still going on. Besides the Atshuaras, the Jivaros, too, would soon be wiped out. Only knowledge of Christ could redeem them from their senseless slaughter.

I made up my mind to go. It was God's will. But I would take every precaution to make sure that I wasn't killed.

A few months later, my chance came unexpectedly. The Wycliffe Bible Translators had brought a new plane into the country, a slow-landing, fast-lifting Helio Courier plane ideal for a cramped airstrip. With it had come a new pilot, Bob Griffin.

In March I had to go to Shell Mera, then on to Quito. This gave me the opportunity to get the expedition organized. Johnny Keenan introduced me to Bob. When I asked Bob if he thought he could fly us in, he replied promptly, "Sure thing! When do we start?"

Mindful of my promise to Tsantiacu to bring a missionary doctor, I put it up to Dr. Ev Fuller in Shell Mera, who readily accepted. Faithful Mike Ficke also consented to go along.

I had one other thought. I recalled that on that sad day at Palm Beach, as I walked away from the newly-dug grave, Major Malcolm Nurnberg of the United States Air Force had asked if he could go with us whenever we went to visit another tribe of Indians. A warm friendship had grown between us. I wrote to him now, inviting him to come. To my pleasure and surprise, he replied promptly, saying he had just returned from a trip to the States and would soon be able to join us.

Since we had learned that it is never wise to venture into the jungle without an Indian companion, we decided to take one who was also a believer. He could then help with the preaching.

Icam, son of Big Saantu, offered to go. Icam had grown up in our school and had become a Christian. He would be able to make Tsantiacu understand why we wished to be friends. Also, I wanted the chief to hear of the love of Christ from the lips of a jungle Indian like himself.

On April 16, 1956, we all gathered at Macuma, ready to start. First, Bob and I made a reconnaissance flight with Johnny Keenan in his little Pacer. We wanted to see if the airstrip had really been planted with cassava and strewn with logs.

As we drew near the clearing, Johnny kept a fair altitude. We could not be sure that rumors that the Atshuaras would shoot at us were untrue. We were pleased to see that, contrary to what we had been told, the airstrip was bare both of vegetation and of logs. A minute later, Tsantiacu himself came running out of the house, followed by a swarm of men, women, and children. They waved to us in a friendly way. Johnny banked, circled the field, and cut the throttle so that I could make myself heard. I called out to the Indians below: "We'll be back later!" They waved and nodded as though they understood me. We dropped a length of cloth before Johnny turned the plane and headed back to Macuma.

That night we talked over our plans. The Atshuaras had convinced me by their actions that they would welcome us as before. Bob Griffin thought the Helio plane could get in and out of there. My doubts looked foolish to me now. After all, what was there to fear?

We flew both planes next morning to Wampimi, about halfway from Macuma to Tsantiacu's airstrip. There we repacked our cargo, and planned to make the final lap in four shuttle flights.

This was my first visit to Wampimi, where Roj and Barbara had once been stationed, since Roj was killed. The sight of it made me sad. No Indians came running to greet us. There was no sound,

save the screech of the katydids and the humming of myriad insects in the trees. The trail so grass-grown, and the crazy-quilt house
that Roj had so energetically pounded together, were sorrowful
reminders of happy times gone by. Wampimi had served its purpose as a steppingstone to the Atshuaras, but for lack of personnel
it would soon be abandoned.

I put aside these mournful thoughts and we set about repacking
our gear. Johnny Keenan and Mike Ficke would go ahead in the
Pacer; Major Nurnberg and I would follow in the Helio plane.
Icam would remain behind at Wampimi, and go in on a later trip
with the doctor and the rest of the cargo.

The plan was that Johnny and Mike would keep circling the
sky in the Pacer above us, while the Major and I landed in the
Helio plane. They would be in constant radio contact with Shell
Mera, reporting on all our movements, in case the Atshuaras turned
tricky. Also, we reasoned that the presence of the second plane overhead would discourage them from attacking us, since they wouldn't
know the Pacer could not land there.

We watched Johnny and Mike step into the Pacer and take off.
We shoved the Helio plane back onto the strip; the Major and I
took our places beside Bob Griffin. As we fastened our seat belts
I had a last twinge of misgiving. I looked at the major.

"Remember, Major," I said, "the same thing could happen to us
that happened to the five. Do you still want to go?"

"I wouldn't miss this for anything," he replied. Bob revved up the
motor and we were off. As we climbed into the sky, we waved back
to the tiny figures of Dr. Fuller and Icam, who were bidding us
Godspeed from the ground.

Everything seemed to be made to order for this day and hour.
The sky above was blue; the jungle below a gentle, friendly carpet
of green. From time to time we were reassured by the sight of
Johnny and Mike in the Pacer alongside, not far off our wingtip.

Looking down on the familiar terrain brought memories of hard
experiences hiking over those jungle trails. Now we passed the
place where Taisha's house once stood. It called to mind that first
attempt to reach the Atshuaras Keith Austin and I had made long
ago, and of how we had been threatened and driven off.

A scattering of cumulus clouds began to veil our vision of the
jungle floor. But now, drifting lazily upward in the cool morning

air, was a thin column of smoke, pinpointing what looked to be a tiny clearing. We were coming over Tsantiacu's house.

I fixed my eyes on the yard within the stockade, watching for any sign that might give a clue to the Indians' reaction. Ant-sized figures began to pour out of the *tangamash*. But I saw no cause for alarm.

Bob circled the clearing three times. The only way to land was over the house.

He lowered the flaps and throttled back for a landing. The Helio plane backfired as usual. We banked steeply and skimmed over the housetop. Coming down smoothly, we rolled to the trees at the far end of the strip and stopped with the plane's tail toward the house.

I jumped out and looked around. Then I stopped in my tracks. A cold sweat broke out all over me. I could feel the prickles go up my spine. There was not an Indian in sight.

I turned back to the plane.

"Something's wrong," I called.

Then I shouted.

"Stay in the plane. Be ready to leave any second."

The major was already on the ground. He was pulling his army rifle from the luggage compartment.

"Put that back," I yelled. "The sight of it will only make them more suspicious. You stay right here. But don't use that gun unless they start to shoot. Then don't shoot to kill—only to scare."

I faced about and started toward the house. There was no sound. I had not taken twenty steps when three Indians moved out silently from the garden in front of the house.

In the middle was Tsantiacu, flanked on either side by a warrior. The chief was waving a gun at me with one hand, and with the other, motioning me to go away. As he did so, he would take a few steps forward, then a few steps back, then a few steps forward again. His warriors weaved back and forth in unison with their chief. The way they brandished their guns and the meanness of their looks left me no doubt as to their message. They were telling me to get out of there quickly. Nevertheless, I faced those Indians and kept on walking toward them. They still motioned me back.

Then I remembered I was wearing a hat they had never seen before, a big white one with a wide brim. Perhaps they did not recognize me as Panchu. I took the hat off and threw it on the ground. It didn't change things a bit. They still brandished their guns and danced and threatened. I kept on walking slowly.

From the corner of each eye, I checked the sides of the strip for the stirring of a leaf that would betray an ambush. I saw none.

By now I was fearful. But I had worked and waited and hoped and planned for this moment. If I were to turn and run, the door to the Atshuaras would be closed to me forever.

The nearer I crept, the more Tsantiacu and his men danced and shouted. My thoughts flashed back to the Curaray River. The picture of those bodies of my friends lying there in the sand came again into my mind. But this time it gave me courage. Those men faced death and had not drawn back. They had not counted their lives dear unto themselves. Was I any different from them? Did I have any more right to live than they? I thought: "Our lives belong to God. May He be glorified in me—whether 'by life or by death!' "

As I continued to inch forward, Tsantiacu and his men kept edging toward me uncertainly. Then I remembered the gun in my own hand. I always carried it when visiting Indians, not that I ever intended to kill one, but an ounce of prevention is worth a pound of cure. It occurred to me that the sight of it might be one cause of their fear and suspicion. I laid my gun down on the ground, hoping they would take this as a sign of friendly intent. But it brought no change in their attitude. They kept on shouting and threatening as before.

Cold sweat poured from my body. I was right on the point of turning back. Instead I prayed, "Lord, give me strength to take a few more steps. Then, if they don't change, I'll have to get back in the plane."

I took those steps. I called out as I did so, "I am Panchu. You know I am your friend. You do not have to be afraid of me. I have come to tell you more about God. I am bringing you the doctor I promised you long ago."

At the sound of the word "doctor" Tsantiacu changed in one instant the motion of his hand from "go" to "come." Thus encouraged, I moved closer to him. The hand went up again, this time with wide palm out. His meaning was clear, in universal sign language: "STOP! Right where you are."

Now we were less than twenty paces apart. I was conscious of three pairs of sharp black eyes fastened intently on mine. Then I saw that they were less concerned with my words than with trying to read my expression. Indians can always tell more by the look on one's face than by the word spoken. I, in turn, tried to read their faces. I thought I saw expressions that were less distrustful, more puzzled, if not friendly. I stepped forward as I repeated my plea. Finally I went all the way and stretched out my hand to Tsantiacu. He reached his hand out to me. He gripped me in a bear hug and we danced around, patting each other on the back. Suddenly he held me off and fixed me with a piercing gaze.

"Why did you shoot at us from the plane?" he demanded.

Now I understood. When the plane backfired he thought I was shooting at them.

The tension eased. I looked up at the sky and signaled to Johnny in the Pacer that all was well. He waggled his wings, then streaked off for Wampimi.

But Tsantiacu's suspicions were not entirely dispelled.

"Why do you come this time in a different plane?" he demanded. I explained that the one he knew had been destroyed by Auca spears and that the Helio was the only missionary plane left which could land on such a short strip as his.

The major had made his way up to us by then. As he and Tsantiacu shook hands rather stiffly I explained that the major was the one who had gone with me in search of Roj.

Linking my arm to the chief's, I said,

"Come with me and have a look at the new plane." He shook his head and refused to move.

"No," he said suspiciously. "It's a trap. You have soldiers in there."

Rumors spread by the Macuma Jivaros had definitely reached him. He had believed the story that I would come one day with soldiers to take him away. Another good reason for his hostility . . .

Tsantiacu thawed a little when I asked his permission to send the plane back to Wampimi for Dr. Fuller. But he grew wary again when I told him the pilot would also bring a young Christian Jivaro from Macuma.

"Is this young man a witch doctor like Catani?" he asked. I assured him that Icam was no witch doctor, but a true Tius Shuara. I hoped I was making the distinction clear to him, because his knowledge of God's power was still very limited.

A little later, when Icam arrived, a situation arose which I had not anticipated. As the two men were greeting each other in the formal Indian fashion, Tsantiacu stopped in mid-sentence.

"Are you not the son of Big Saantu, the old witch doctor who killed my cousin Chiriapa?"

"Yes," replied Icam without hesitation.

"And was it not Big Saantu who at the same time captured and married my niece?"

"Yes, you say the truth," Icam answered calmly.

"And where is the girl, now that the Big One is dead?" Tsantiacu wanted to know. "Tell me, does she still live?"

"She lives," nodded Icam. "She has since married my uncle. She now has children by him."

Tsantiacu's troubled gaze wandered out over the jungle. In his eyes I could see two forces striving for mastery—the memory of tribal injury calling for personal revenge, and Christian forgiveness with which he had so little experience. If the former were to win out, our work among the Atshuaras would again be threatened.

The chief turned back to Icam.

"But you are different," he said very slowly. "You are not like your father, Big Saantu. You are a Tius Shuara. And Tius Shuaras do not send curses, or carry on wars."

His next statement was conclusive:

"You are welcome here."

The warrior's face broke into smiles. The two members of enemy tribes put their arms around each other's shoulders in token of fellowship. I praised the Lord that the few lessons in the love of Christ we had been able to give the Atshuaras had found their mark far beyond anything hoped for at the time. This gave me fresh courage.

We spent four days with Tsantiacu and his people. Three times daily we held singing and preaching services, and as before, the Atshuaras could never get enough. They loved to sing, and we were pleased to find that they had learned several of the hymns from the phonograph records Roj and I left behind on our previous trip. Indians awakened us in the night, or interrupted our meals, to ask us to sing a song about Jesus just once more.

On this trip, we found we had a new and powerful spiritual weapon. That was Icam's moving personal witness as to how the Lord had saved him from a life of cruelty and terror, of witchcraft and warfare. This held the Atshuaras spellbound.

They wanted to know in great detail everything that had happened since our last visit. When I told of the tragedy at Palm Beach on the banks of the Curaray, the chief's eyes flashed with anger. He interrupted me.

"When I first heard that the Tawi Shuaras [Aucas] had killed Uruchu [his name for Roj Youderian]," he said, "I was so angry I wanted to call all my men together and go kill them. Wasn't Uruchu like a brother to me? I still have in my house the box of things he left for me to take care of. Didn't Uruchu suffer in the hot sun to help us build this airstrip? I tell you, if I knew the way to Tawi Shuara country I would go there with my men and kill them with guns. They with only spears wouldn't have a chance. They should suffer and die for what they did to Uruchu and the *pirutu* [pilot]."

I was both moved by this demonstration of loyalty and affection for Roj and disappointed that he should still believe so firmly in "an eye for an eye."

Meanwhile, Dr. Fuller had arrived and gone right to work. Some of his first cases were minor: he extracted a thorn from the foot of a man named Tucupe and an infected tooth from the jaw of one of Tsantiacu's women. He dispensed worm medicine wholesale, giving it to all the children and many adults. He also gave shots of penicillin to many who suffered from tropical ulcers. Upon examining the men, he found there was hardly an Atshuara in that household who did not have a scar from a bullet or lead lodged in his flesh. As he won their confidence, the married adults began coming to him and complaining that they were unable to have babies. Dr. Fuller quickly diagnosed their trouble as gonorrhea and administered the proper treatment. This was to earn their lasting gratitude. Many of them later were able to have children; and for years afterward they still remembered affectionately the kind doctor who had made this possible.

In our few minutes of free time when we weren't conducting services or assisting Dr. Fuller, we went hunting or fishing. One afternoon while Tsantiacu, the major, and I were out together, a rain squall caught us by surprise. Tsantiacu began gathering a few leaves to make a shelter for us. The wind was blowing hard. Suddenly Tsantiacu straightened up, faced the wind, and gave a strange whistle. This aroused Major Nurnberg's curiosity. He asked me to find out from Tsantiacu why he did this.

"I am communicating with the spirit of my dead father," the old chief replied. "When the wind blows, my father's spirit might come very near me."

As I interpreted these words for the major, I noticed him shudder a little.

"What a creepy feeling that gives me!" he said.

I understood that the chief's contact with spirits was a real part of his daily life. We began to speak about it.

"You pray to God whom you can't see, don't you?" he said. "We talk to the spirits of our ancestors whom we can't see. Tell me, is there any difference?"

I tried to make clear to him what the difference was. But he seemed unimpressed.

"When we drink *tasaangu* and *natema* we can see the spirits of our ancestors, and hear what they have to say to us. Do you have any such medicine that will help you see God?"

I answered him emphatically that we did not. Then I explained, "God has revealed Himself to us in the person of His Son. He has written in His Book all he wants us to know of Him. But we will see Him someday in Heaven. And there we will be like Him forever. He has done much more for us than the spirits of dead men can do."

I could see that in spite of the hunger with which they received the Gospel and the gusto with which they sang hymns, there would have to be many, many more such conversations before Tsantiacu and the other Atshuaras really grasped what we were trying to tell them.

Throughout the visit, and underlying the spirit of friendship and good feeling, I was burdened with a growing uneasiness. I could not dismiss it. Tsantiacu and I had never discussed Catani, so I did not know if he still held a grudge against me for having helped save the life of his bitter enemy. The answer came on the last day of our visit.

The chief and I were talking. Suddenly and without warning, he said to me bluntly,

"This Catani. Does he still live?"

I nodded. Tsantiacu scowled.

"I thought I had finished him for good."

"You killed his favorite wife and child," I told him. "As for Catani, you wounded him in the hand, leg, and chest. His Indians brought him to me. I sent him on to the hospital at Shell Mera where the doctor took out all those bullets you put into him. Yes, Catani still lives. He is back home once more and getting well."

Tsantiacu gave an outcry as of one betrayed.

"What did you do that for? Why did you not let him die? Are you not my friend?"

I decided we might as well have it out.

"What's more," I told him, "the doctor who is here now, helping free your family from sickness and pain, is the very same doctor who took the bullets from Catani and saved his life."

Again the question, "Why? Why?"

I faced Tsantiacu.

"We wanted Catani to live. Only if he lived could he hear God's Word and become God's child."

The old chief appeared to be struggling to understand this new thought.

"Do you mean that if he becomes God's child, then he will have a new heart and will not want to kill any more?"

"Yes, you say the truth."

"Then preach to him plenty!" he said as he walked away.

Had I made an impression on this tough old warrior? Could he see that God's bounty was great enough to give me love for both him and Catani? Had the strain between us been resolved? I could not tell.

The plane came. I was to fly out on the last shuttle to Wampimi.

As Tsantiacu walked with me to the plane, he put his arm around my shoulders and said,

"Panchu—I will never threaten you again so long as I live. Come back and tell us more about the Bible as soon as you can."

I praised the Lord. After all our struggles, setbacks, and disap-

pointments, the door to the hearts of the Atshuaras was open.
There was every reason, too, to hope that it would stay open so that
Christ's church could someday be established here. This experience
was a lesson in God's power to us missionaries—as well as to these
Indians.

CHAPTER 14

Shuartica Begins to Shake

For the weapons of our warfare are not carnal, but mighty through God to the pulling down of strongholds.

II CORINTHIANS 10:4

ROJ WAS GONE, BUT THE IMPACT OF HIS TESTIMONY WAS strongly felt in Macuma. When I had first returned from Palm Beach I told the Jivaro believers the story of Operation Auca. Their hearts, too, were touched.

"He was our brother," said one, "and now he is dead."

"Oh, but we will see him again," said another. "He has gone to Heaven just a little while ahead of the rest of us. We will soon catch up to him."

And they all agreed that because he had died for the sake of reaching wild men for Christ, they would be willing to do the same. Their zeal to preach the Gospel increased. Attendance in the church services rose. Back-slidden members returned to the Lord, seeking forgiveness and promising to live righteously.

I encouraged the leading believers to take more responsibility in conducting the services and business meetings. Within a few weeks during one of the monthly business sessions, the baptized believers, who by this time numbered twenty, elected six of their number as elders. These became the main preachers, manual work directors, treasurers, and evangelists. They also enlisted other members to help them. There was no paid pastor. But the organization of the church was no longer only my responsibility. We worked together. Although I continued teaching the Wednesday Bible studies, I would not preach on Sundays unless they asked me. When the church needed repairing, or land had to be cleared for new school gardens, they accepted these duties as a part of their job.

In January, 1958, a group of the elders came to me with a new proposition. "Panchu," they said, "we think you are right when you tell us we should hold school for nine months of the year. With only short sessions, such as you have held up till now, the children forget what they have learned from one term to the next. How can we help?"

"You will have to help a great deal," I told them. "This is not my school; it is yours—for your boys and girls. You will have to take much of the responsibility. You will have to see that the children come and that they stay in school. I will find the teachers. We are in need of a new dining hall and kitchen. These you must build. Someone must be found to cook for the children. Above all, you will have to plant bigger gardens if we are to have enough food throughout the whole nine months."

After further discussion, they were satisfied and I was satisfied.

Shuartica was loosening its hold. By this time many parents wanted to send their children to school, and were persuading some unbelievers to do the same. I was no longer alone in my battle. When problems came up about the cooks, food supply, new buildings, teachers, clothing, medicines, or runaway boys, I took them to the Jivaro church leaders and together we prayed and worked out solutions. The Indians began to respect these joint decisions—changes that were being made, not by a white man alone, but by their own people as well.

The following October we launched our first nine-month term. The Indians had built a big new dining hall; Chingasu and Chumpi did the cooking, with half their salaries paid by church offerings, half by us. The school enrollment had reached nearly a hundred, so we employed two Christian Ecuadorians as teachers.

But now that we had to feed all these children for a full nine months, the gardens weren't nearly big enough. The Indians themselves helped by bringing basketloads of cassava, plantain, and smoked tapir, mostly to sell, and occasionally to support the Lord's work. This supply at best, however, was spasmodic.

I gave much thought to this problem and kept encouraging the Indians to plant bigger gardens. By improving my own jungle farming methods I could show the Indians how to get more out of the poor clay-type soil. As I studied the way the Jivaros farmed, I knew that here, too, *shuartica* would have to change.

Since the planting as well as the cultivating and harvesting is done by the women, I would have to talk with one of them about it. Who was better than wise old Chingasu? She was always at hand, cooking for the school children.

One afternoon, as she stood in the kitchen watching a huge kettle of soup bubbling over an open fire, she seemed in a talkative mood. I asked her a few questions to draw her out, then sat on a stump stool and listened as she related the Jivaro women's age-old way of insuring a good crop.

This is Chingasu's story:

"I think of a time when we had just finished planting a new, big garden. Our whole family had suffered much trying to get established in a new place. I was only a little girl then, but I remember it well. We had made a big clearing and built part of our house. We had to carry our food from so far away, that even while we worked we were weak with hunger all the time. None of us wanted to go through this again. We wanted to make sure we had plenty to eat in the future.

"At last our garden was all planted. True to *shuartica*, we had to perform a secret ceremony. My mother got me up early one morning. We left the house quietly.

"Mother carried in her hands a small clay bowl. Within it was a little stone with mysterious powers—a little stone we called *nantar*. We had painted our faces and our arms bright red with a dye from the *annotto* tree; without this protection, my mother told me, the spirit in the stone would draw the blood from our bodies. Mother looked to the right and to the left to make sure no one was watching. I carried some more of the *annotto* dye to paint the *nantar* when we reached the garden.

"My great-grandmother had used this very stone in her gardens; and so had my grandmother; and so had my mother after her. Only now I was learning its true meaning. The *nantar* is always passed from the mother to oldest daughter in the family. Being the oldest girl, the *nantar* was to come to me as soon as I married. When I was younger, I knew my mother had often gone out to see the *nantar*. But we children were never allowed to go near the spot where it was hidden. Mother told us that if we touched it we would become sick and might even die. I don't think this was really so. I think she was afraid we might show other people where it was, because there were lots of women who did not have any *nantar* to hide in their gardens. They wanted one, because it would make their food grow well and they would even steal a *nantar* so they could have a good crop.

"Now, out in the far end of the garden, just as the sun was coming up, my mother made a pile of sticks. She set the bowl down on them and took the clear flintlike stone gently in her hands. I handed her the dye, and as she applied the fresh covering of pretty red, she sang a strange song.

"She told me that in this stone was the spirit of her great-grandmother. Her own grandmother, whom she remembered, had been a great woman, too. She never lacked for food. Everything she planted grew wonderfully well; her cassavas were of tremendous size, her sweet potatoes the largest and sweetest anywhere around. She was a hard worker and had lots of children.

" 'So now, dear child,' my mother told me, 'we must treat this stone with much care and secrecy. If we do, our gardens will grow and grow and we shall not know hunger. I am the best-loved of my husband's wives because I feed him the most. Learn, my child, and you, too, will be loved by your husband and your name will be well-known throughout the jungle. Just look at our neighbor's family. Are they fat? If their mother had a *nantar*, maybe she would have a bit more energy and would work a little and more of her children would live. As it is, her husband looks like a snake and a hungry one at that. No wonder they are always coming here to beg food. What a shame to be so lazy! My dear daughter, don't you ever be like that!'

"Placing the *nantar* back in the bowl, my mother covered it with some wide leaves so that the rain would not wet it. 'The spirit must not suffer,' she said. 'If it does, you will be awakened in the night by its cries: "I am suffering, oh, I am suffering so. Come see me, come see me. I need you." When you hear the voice of the spirit you must obey, and the next morning before it gets light you must come and see the *nantar*. You'll find that it has become moldy or wet. Then it must be repainted with the *annotto* dye. But before you touch it, be sure you have plenty of the red dye on your face and hands. I don't want you to lose all your blood.'

"Having finished her instructions, my mother stretched her hands out over the garden. Then she sang a song to Nungui, the earth goddess. She sang as feelingly as you do when you pray. The sacred stone was well-covered and hidden, and we returned home.

"So the *nantar* is handed down from mother to daughter and moved from garden to garden to make things grow. We thought it would help; we knew no better. If I had known the true God before, I would have prayed to Him. But how were we to find out about Him if you missionaries hadn't come?"

I agreed with her. She turned to her soup. I thanked her and went about my chores.

We needed to clear more jungle to plant more gardens, so I bought a section of land from the Ecuadorian government. This made us the owners on paper; but the real owner was the stubborn, tangled, snake-infested ancient growth. We now began our attack.

Cutting down trees anywhere calls for skill; but the Jivaros are the best axmen I have ever seen. Since the vines are so thick, there is no room for the horizontal swing we use. Instead, they bring the ax up after the stroke and around their heads in a smooth continuous motion, flashing it down to the cut again.

First the smaller trees in the area to be cleared are cut about halfway through the trunk. Then the middle-sized trees are hacked until they begin to weave. Finally the axman singles out a big tree in a key position that can be made to fall on the smaller ones. He chops away until a creaking sound warns him to run clear. As the giant falls it starts a chain reaction like a tenpin in a bowling alley. With leaves and branches flying, it carries all the smaller, weakened trees in its path, laying the whole space open to the light and warmth of the sun.

This could be a dangerous moment for the axman. If he had to re-enter the area now, he might run afoul of poisonous snakes angered by having their hiding place in the branches disturbed. But long before the trees are cut down, the underbrush has been cleared away and the corn sowed broadcast. No one need enter the patch till harvest time. Their method, though shocking to an Iowa farmer, is no doubt best for these sons of the jungle.

Planting cassava requires a different procedure. Every inch of the ground must be grubbed of its vegetation and small bushes which are piled around the field literally by the ton. The trees are then chopped down one at a time, and the leaves and limbs trimmed away before the next is felled.

A man and his wife will work from one to three months to clear a patch 100-yards square. If the weather is bad it may take much longer. When the space is what the Indians call cleared— although it may be littered with hundreds of trees large and small— the women loosen the ground with a pointed stick and put in place the six-inch cuttings of the cassava bush. Within two months the weeds start to grow and the women must spend more hours slashing away with machetes to keep them down. Since it takes a year for this crop to mature, the long tuber becomes expensive in terms of labor. For lack of food the Indians are likely to start eating the cassava tubers before they are full-sized, thus reducing the harvest further.

Hunger, an ever-present phantom, stalks the Jivaro. He looks upon it as an inevitable fact of life. Nor does a good harvest insure the Indian of having enough for his household, for visiting relatives may descend upon him at any time like locusts.

I learned more of this from Wampiu, when he complained that so many relatives had been staying with him for so long that he was about to run out of food. I asked if *shuartica* demanded he carry hospitality to such extremes. He replied that it did, explaining that if a Jivaro didn't feed his relatives when he had enough himself, he was considered selfish. For this reason, many Jivaros planted their small gardens close to the house, and had big ones off in the bush where they could not be seen.

The Indians would farm their hard-cleared patches for a couple of years; then, upon finding the weeds too thick to fight, they would move away and start the process all over again elsewhere. To have an Indian here today and gone tomorrow was not very healthy for the church. He might have become a Christian while with us; but for him to move too far to come to services or send his children to school was not good. He would have no Bible instruction and no fellowship with other Christians. His children, finding no other believers with whom to marry, could not found Christian homes. No indigenous church could well develop among a roving population.

More food for our school children, a different way of life for our church members—these were some of the goals before us. To achieve them, we would have to make basic changes in our mission-ary methods for these primitive people. The Gospel was saving their souls. But if the church did not have a better climate in which to grow, it would never be able to stand on its own feet without missionaries. More food, and a more stable way of life, could result only from better ways of farming. But we could not learn, nor could the Indians learn, overnight. We would have to proceed by trial and error. It would be a long undertaking.

Perhaps one of the most significant things we had already ac-complished was to help the Indians get cattle. When their gardens reached the point of no return, we encouraged them not to abandon the land but to plant it to pasture grass. For several years we had had our own small herd of cattle to supply milk for our children. We had obtained some calves over in the Upano Valley and while they were still young, Nate and Hobey had flown them to Macuma.

We worked out a program whereby we gave heifer calves from our herd to the Indians. Since they had so little money, and we did not believe in outright gifts, we kept a half-interest. When the animals were sold, our half went toward educating their chil-dren. In this way they got a start for nothing and helped them-selves at the same time.

Ramon, the chief Jivaro elder in the church, was our first cus-tomer. He bought his heifer outright with money he had earned sawing boards for the missionary dwellings. Ramon treated his heifer like a pet and did such a good job of raising it that he set an example for the others.

This encouraged us. We saw that the cattle program could be a stabilizing influence. As Marie pointed out, "It would be hard for an Indian with a cow and a pasture to put his possessions in a basket and move away."

Our mission farm was becoming an agricultural experiment sta-tion as well as a source of food. Rice was introduced and proved very successful. Lima beans did remarkably well. A new strain of corn produced three times as much as the scraggly Indian maize. But for the first five or six years we had done all our farming with no other tools than machetes, shovels, and axes.

Then new help came to us in the form of a small tractor, a gift from a friend, Mr. Leonard Reimer, a Canadian Christian businessman. With this equipment we could expand our program. One of our time-consuming chores was to keep the airstrip clear. Where ten Indians were needed for a week every two months to cut the grass with machetes, now with the tractor and sickle bar we could do it in a matter of hours.

The Indians were greatly impressed with the new machine. On one occasion I heard a Jivaro say to a visitor,

"Does not that beast do much work? Does it ever get tired? Does it ever feel the heat of the sun?"

But the Indian babies cried at the sight of it whenever their mothers took them past the place where we were working.

I began to experiment with methods of planting cassava. Having read in a magazine that cassava cuttings in the Far East were planted in the ground vertically, rather than horizontally, I decided to try it. Opposition arose immediately.

I plowed a piece of land near the house and asked the school-boys to bring me some cassava sticks. They protested: only women planted cassava. I told them we were going to try a new way.

A serious old Jivaro mother watched me, and shaking her head, assured me that cassava planted in that way would produce nothing.

Contrary to all expectations, the cassava grew very well. Then everyone said, "But will it yield any fruit?" When the cassava matured, the Indians were surprised and I very pleased. The tuber was almost half again as large as their former ones. No doubt plowing the land had as much to do with it as anything. But I had a lot of fun letting them think my new way of planting might have helped.

Now that we had food in plenty, we could watch the growing number of children coming to school with happiness and confidence. We were especially pleased that more than a third were girls.

We hoped their lives would be better from now on, for we were making progress in teaching the Indians many new customs, all of which would affect the future of these children. Among these customs were: postponing marriage until the girls had at least reached their teens; replacing polygamy with marriage between one man and one woman; learning to call on God for help, instead of on the witch doctor; learning to accept death as from God, rather than as a curse from an enemy.

At this time help came to us from an unexpected source. Representatives of the Ecuadorian government in Macas co-operated with us in helping to stop tribal wars and polygamy.

But *shuartica*, so long entrenched, was not to be quickly or easily routed. Heartbreaking situations arose to plague this generation in the years of changing from the old to the new. There was ten-year-old Tsapacu, for example. Although her father, Jeencham, had heard the Gospel since Ernest Johnson first came to Macuma in 1945, he still adhered to all the old customs of *shuartica*. He let his daughter come to school only because her mother had died and there was no one to care for her. But to obtain a new wife for himself, he planned to sell Tsapacu. She was just the age of our own Irene, which impressed on us how unready the child was for marriage. But not so Jeencham. He was going to take her out of school and give her to a young man named Jua, the son of an old Cangaimi witch doctor. In return, Jeencham would receive the witch doctor's desirably fat teen-age daughter as his own wife.

I heard about this and, knowing that Tsapacu didn't want to be married, sent word to Jeencham that either the child would come to school or I'd call the government soldiers. Tsapacu came—but so did Jua.

Although they lived in separate dormitories, the others looked on them as man and wife. Jua kept track of everything Tsapacu did and sent her little presents of soap and bobby pins. As she soared on the swing, or played tag, she looked like any other care-free child. But when we asked her if Jua was really her husband, she ducked her head in shy assent. In spite of the fact that the bargain had been struck and the old custom not completely changed, the young couple *was* attending school. This showed that *shuartica* was giving way, even among the unbelievers.

Besides helping with the outstations, school, and farm, the believers in the church often worked together with us on the language. Although it was not *shuartica*, they wanted to learn to read the Bible for themselves and were vitally interested in translation and literacy problems.

Even some of the women could give Bible lessons and help Marie translate. Old Chingasu, though she could not read, often taught the weekly women's Bible class. Her first attempt years before was one that Marie would never forget. A group of nearly forty women had gathered to sing, pray, and learn more of the Word of God. At that time most of them were still unbelievers. Chingasu stood before them, her dark eyes flashing to the challenge. Impatiently, she flung a lock of unruly hair out of her eyes and spread her open hands for all to see.

"I do not hold any paper," she admitted simply. "I am one who cannot read to you from God's Book. Only what I have heard and know in my heart to be true, can I tell to you. Listen well, and you will learn, too."

She then proceeded to tell with amazing accuracy the story of creation and man's fall into sin, and of his redemption through the death and resurrection of Jesus Christ. She spoke with such vividness and eloquence that she held her audience enthralled. No one scratched or turned a head to look outside. She made the way of salvation clearer than we foreigners could do.

As Marie listened to Chingasu's presentation, she was more convinced than ever of the importance of teaching the Indians to read as well as of encouraging them to help us translate.

"If we should have to leave them without the written Word, they could not last long in the battle against their old evil customs," she said. "The Jivaro church needs the Bible in the language of its people."

Marie was not alone in her conviction. She was only one of several missionaries who had labored toward this goal.

While Roger Youderian was still with us he had worked long hours with the Indians to develop reading materials in Jivaro. Just before he went on his mission to the Aucas, he handed Marie a big oatmeal box.

"You probably won't have time to look at this before I get back," he said, "but in case you do, here it is." He smiled and left the room.

When she opened the box she found it filled with hundreds of illustrations of animals, birds, reptiles, insects, plants, trees, and other visual objects of the Jivaro world. Some he had traced; some were original sketches. All were accompanied by the Jivaro names he had learned from the Indians. We were awed to think how many hours he had devoted, without our knowing it, to that monumental work. We hoped to carry on what he had begun.

His was one more contribution to the missionary effort. Mr. and

Mrs. Charles Olson had begun the job of reducing Jivaro to writing. At that time Jivaro had no written alphabet. The Olsons based their proposed grammar on the structure of their own language and Spanish. An Italian priest, Padre Juan Ghinassi, who worked most of his life among the Jivaros in the southern Upano Valley, put together a grammar which he had printed in the early thirties. This was a help to all of us. The priest and the Olsons had also compiled dictionaries. Ernest Johnson added simplified grammatical forms and illustrative sentences. Dorothy Walker further revised the grammar and taught it in lesson form to the Youderians and other new missionaries.

While Dorothy and Barb carried on the work at Cangaimi, we were joined in Macuma by Mr. and Mrs. Glen Turner, of the Wycliffe Bible Translators. Glen, a linguistic scholar, further analyzed the grammar and shortened the alphabet to twenty-three letters, thus making it phonetically scientific. Then we and the Turners incorporated everyone's contributions and produced the first five simple Jivaro reading primers. Marie taught them to the school children and to classes of adults. Believers like Wampiu, Chingasu, and Tsamaraing were delighted to discover that their own language could speak to them from marks on paper. Some of them took copies home to teach other members of their families. They began to hope they could learn to read God's Word.

In all the world there were less than twenty thousand people using the Jivaro language. With its limited alphabet, its nasalized and voiceless vowels which changed the meaning of words, it was one of the most difficult of languages to learn, and particularly to set down in written form. Yet if these Indians were ever to understand the true meaning of the Gospel in the only way it could be brought home to them, namely, in their own tongue, the job had to be done by someone. We and others dedicated ourselves to this task.

Then we enlisted the aid of the Christian Indians in translating passages of Scripture from Spanish to Jivaro. They had already helped us coin words and phrases needed in preaching Scriptural truths—words for God, Jesus Christ, Devil, "prayer," and "peace." Even "Tius Shuara" had been their own choice for "Christian." We knew we could not produce accurate translations without their co-operation.

When the leading believers, who by now were growing rapidly in knowledge of the Word and Christian responsibility, first sat down with us to write God's Word, they thought it would be a simple task. Some of the very ones who years before had ridiculed our preoccupation with paper and pencil, began to understand that this was hard work. A new door of intellectual accomplishments was opening up before them. Day after day we improved translations of already familiar verses and worked on new ones.

When we dealt with John 1:11, 12—"He came into His own creation, and His own people would not accept Him. Yet where-ever men did accept Him He gave them the power to become sons of God. These were the men who truly believed in Him"—I was puzzled by the word "accept." Although I considered using the Jivaro words for "buy" and "take," neither of these fitted this situation. I explained to the Indians that we needed a word that meant "to receive into one's heart" as they would a visitor in their homes.

"I know a word," said Wampiu. "Once when Tsantiacu came to visit an Indian in Wampimi they wouldn't open the door to let him in. The door was barred. Tsantiacu called 'I am Tsantiacu, Tsantiacu, Tsantiacu,' but they would not '*itaacharmiayi*,' accept him."

"That is the word I want," I said immediately.

Our finished translation read thus: "He came to the things that He had made but His own people did not bring Him in. But to any person who does bring Him in, God makes to become *His* people—to all those who say 'yes' to His Son."

When through our joint efforts such verses as these became clearly understandable to them, they gained a new appreciation of the missionaries' task and of the important contribution they themselves had to make.

But greater victories over *shuartica* were still ahead.

Shuartica refuses to accept death as a natural end of life—but attributes it to an enemy's curse. Our Macuma Indians had to learn from experience how faith in Christ could triumph over their most dreaded enemy, death.

It was a quiet morning, something unusual at the mission station. The silence was broken by the shrill voices of our little school girls calling, "*Shuar winawai! Shuar winawai!*" This warned us we were about to have Indian visitors.

Marie and I stepped out to greet Uyungara, a powerfully-built warrior from the headwaters of the Macuma who had an evil reputation as a killer. His skin was hideously mottled from the ravages of *pinta*, a blue skin disease.

But he appeared gentle and soft-spoken. By his side stood a tiny Jivaro woman, who was plainly very ill. Uyungara's small restless eyes shifted from the woman to us and back again before he could find words to speak. Then they poured out, the gaps filled in by the other Indians who had come with them. The woman was Masuinga, Uyungara's favorite wife. Sick as she was, she had walked the long trail from her home on the other side of the Cutucu Mountains in the hope that we could help her.

As Marie and I looked at her, our first impression was that she must be not only pregnant, but past due by at least a month. Her relatives, however, hastened to assure us to the contrary. Just three months ago, they said, she had been normal and it was only since that time that her abdomen had swollen to its present enormous size. Here was something baffling. She did not seem to be suffering a great deal of pain, but she was very tired and had difficulty breathing.

We took Masuinga to the dispensary for an examination, and Marie wrote down her symptoms on one of our cards:

"Huge swollen abdomen. No fever. Bowel movements normal. Urination normal. No swelling of feet, hands, or face. No engorgement of breasts. Respiration, 36; heartbeat, 105. Abdominal cavity appears to be filled with liquid."

We lost no time in communicating these symptoms by radio to Dr. Fuller at Shell Mera. He offered to come, and arrived next day by MAF plane, bringing with him the instruments necessary to perform a minor operation. He went directly to our dispensary where Marie was waiting with Masuinga.

Marie now continues with the story, since she was the one most closely concerned:

Masuinga sat on the edge of the operating table, her feet swinging freely. Uyungara stood behind her, holding her little hands in his rough, mottled paws. He showed as much concern for her as Frank would have for me in a similar situation. Watch-

ing the tenderness with which he comforted his wife, it was hard
for me to think of him as having taken part in many murders
and head-shrinkings.

Dr. Fuller gave Masuinga a local anesthetic. Then he skillfully
made a small incision and inserted the trocar. With this instrument he passed through the abdominal wall, allowing the liquid
to flow out slowly into a pail. We measured six gallons before
the liquid stopped running. When Dr. Fuller had finished stitch-
ing the incision, Uyungara turned to me with tears in his eyes
and said pleadingly, "Now give her one of your injections so her
stomach won't fill up again."

I interpreted for him. Dr. Fuller solemnly shook his head.
"There isn't any cure. Tell him there isn't any hope of her ever
getting completely well. She appears to have either cirrhosis of the
liver or cancer. All that can be done is to remove the fluid again
when it fills up, which we'll be glad to do."

I repeated to Uyungara in Jivaro what the doctor had said. He
was heartbroken at the news. He begged us to fly Masuinga to
the hospital for treatment. "If only you will make my wife well,"
he said, "I will work for you for the rest of my life."

I talked to him all that afternoon. Knowing how hopeless it
was, I could only comfort him by telling him of the beautiful
heavenly home that waited for Masuinga if she would become a
Christian. Once he interrupted:

"Oh, as for me, yes, I'm a wicked Jivaro, I know. I have killed
many Shuaras. But my wife is not bad. She does not kill. She only
prepares good food and serves it to me. Why should she have to
suffer and die?"

This I was unable to explain to him; he was not yet ready to
understand.

For several days they stayed with us near the mission station.
Our Jivaro believers did their best to give her an understanding
of eternal life as they visited with her. After gaining strength she
walked to her relatives' home. Christians from our church took
her a portable phonograph and the Gospel records she had first
heard and enjoyed in Macuma.

Six weeks later Uyungara brought Masuinga back again in the
same unwieldy condition as before. This time we did not have
to send for Dr. Fuller. Fellow missionaries Bill and Gladis Gibson

had just come back from furlough. Gladis, who had had medical training, was able to drain off the liquid with a borrowed trocar. Once more Masuinga thanked us; but it made us sad to know we could offer only temporary relief. We wondered how much longer she would live.

She heartened us one day by saying in a firm, confident voice that she was no longer afraid to die. She now had sure hope of everlasting life with the Lord; therefore it no longer mattered to her what happened to her earthly body.

Uyungara worked faithfully every day to help pay for Masuinga's medical care. Once he disappeared and we learned he had gone fishing in a nearby stream. In the Jivaro way, he built a dam, then rinsed a basket of pulverized rotenone roots in the water just above it.

The milklike fluid, mixed with water, suffocated any fish unlucky enough to be there. Uyungara could then wade in and pick them up with his hands.

Late in the afternoon he appeared at our door, offering his basket of fish. The largest were not so big as his fist, the smallest not so large as his little finger. There was hardly a meal there for Masuinga and him, let alone for us. Yet to have refused would have hurt Uyungara, so I gladly accepted the tidbits which we found were delicious.

The next day I returned the favor by taking Masuinga some ripe plantains as a gift from us. This led to a long talk with Masuinga, which brought us much closer together.

It was late in the afternoon, a beautiful hour. We sat together in her doorway, watching the sun go down behind the Cutucus. The familiar saddle hump and the lower ridges stood out black against the brilliant pink and orange of the sunset sky. Masuinga looked at me inquiringly.

"Is the country where you used to live anything like this one?" she asked. Then, before I had a chance to answer her first question, she went on, "Do you have a living mother and father? Or any brothers and sisters?"

As I groped for words in Jivaro to picture sights she had never seen, I described our large cities, farms, the highways, and the factory where my parents worked in the United States. I told her about my only sister and her family.

She seemed surprised that I had living parents and a sister. She couldn't understand why I had left them, why I had chosen to live so far away.

"Don't you love them?" she asked.

This viewpoint was not unfamiliar to me. I had found that most of the Indians—not unlike many people in the States—thought we could only have come here for reasons of personal gain; or because we lacked the intelligence to make a living at home.

I told Masuinga why we were here. I explained to her in terms she could grasp that the Creator-God who had made the sunset and the mountains had called us to come and give His Word to her Shuaras.

"We have found so much joy and so much satisfaction in serving Him," I said, "that we would not change places with anyone in the world." A warm smile of understanding lit up her face.

She wondered why, since my parents were still living, I had no other sisters or brothers. She wanted to know if people in my country killed one another like the Jivaros. This led her to tell me a moving account of her life as a Jivaro.

"Long ago when my dear mother was very young and I was just a child," she began, "my father was killed. We lived then, far away, on the other side of the hills near the big volcano, Sangay.

"One night the rain was beating hard on our roof. The wind was blowing—'Ooo-ooo-ajawai.' Suddenly many enemy Shuaras rushed upon our house. We could not see them until they were among us, shouting and shooting. They killed all the men, among them my father. Mother tied my baby sister to her back and we ran out into the rainy night. Never did we go back to live in that country. Never have I had any more brothers or sisters."

The sun had gone down behind the Cutucus. As I looked out over the beautiful landscape and thought of what Masuinga had just told me, I recalled the words of the old hymn: "Where every prospect pleases and only man is vile."

We sat for a few minutes longer and prayed together. Several days later, Masuinga went back to her relatives' house with her husband.

A month passed. Then we received word on the radio that Uyungara and Masuinga had appeared at the hospital in Shell Mera. That tireless strong-willed Indian had carried his wife on his back over the two-day trail from his home to Macas. With money earned by working for white colonists, he had paid for their passage on a small commercial airline to Shell Mera. Uyungara stubbornly refused to give up hope that his wife would yet improve, if only she could get better treatment.

At the hospital, he encountered Dr. Fuller again. But Masuinga now had malaria as well.

Throughout the night she lay unconscious while Uyungara watched at her side and the missionary nurse despaired of her life.

At this time I left Frank in Macuma in order to visit our children in school at Quito. I went by way of Shell Mera. But since my schedule was tight, I hadn't thought of stopping in to see the Indian couple. Masuinga was in good hands and there was nothing, really, that I could do for her.

When I reached Shell Mera, the pilots told me to eat a quick lunch as they would be ready to take off for Quito by 1:00 P.M. Our flight, however, was postponed again and again owing to heavy clouds over the mountains. After the first delay, I lay down to rest and fell fast asleep.

I was awakened with a message from Uyungara who had heard I was in Shell Mera. Masuinga had regained consciousness and wanted me to go to her. I felt rebuked. How could I have gone to sleep after lunch when these people were so in need of my encouragement and fellowship?

It was distressing to see Masuinga lying there, her face drawn with pain, her eyeballs yellowed with the disease, her lips and eyelids puffy from the high fever.

All afternoon we talked and sang hymns, repeated Scripture, and prayed in Jivaro. Again Masuinga gave sweet testimony of her trust in the Lord. Again she declared she was not afraid to die, now that she was God's child. The radiant smile on her face, the light in her eyes, the sound of her high thin voice as she joyously sang the new and wonderful words of the hymns, made me feel she was already closer to Heaven than to earth.

Now that I was assured Masuinga knew the Lord, I wanted Uyungara to know Him too. Turning to the Indian, I asked, "When do you expect to become a Tius Shuara? What are you waiting for?"

His face broke into the most beautiful smile—yes, in spite

of his blackened teeth and his mottled skin, his expression made it beautiful—and said, "I am already God's child."

I could hardly wait to tell this to Frank and the Jivaro believers back in Macuma.

When I asked Uyungara to pray, he addressed the Lord God in Heaven who had given him a new heart and began describing his present situation.

Halfway through, he started talking to me instead of to the Lord. I opened my eyes and looked at him. His eyes were still closed and his black brows knit in the conscious effort of pretending to talk to someone he could not see. He seemed totally unconscious of the fact that he was using "Señora" where he should have used "God." He had not yet learned to close with "In Jesus' name, let it be so," so when he came to the end he merely declared, "That's all I have to say right now," and opened his eyes.

In spite of these small lapses, I really believed that this sinful old Jivaro had accepted Christ.

I left Shell Mera feeling very humble. I thought to myself, "What reason have I ever to complain? Why should I waste time and effort on nonessentials when there are people so hungry for the knowledge of the Lord?"

After my visit in Quito, I returned to Macuma where Frank told me that Masuinga and Uyungara had come from Shell Mera and were now staying again with their relatives in the neighborhood.

I asked Frank if Uyungara had said anything about having become a Christian. Frank told me that he had asked Uyungara point blank whether he were God's child. The old warrior had turned away his head, muttering only that he was thinking about it.

My high hopes were dashed. Uyungara must have purposely deceived me then, hoping that if he professed Christianity, he would get better care for his wife. Then I thought of his faithfulness to Masuinga. Could I blame him? All I could do was to pray for him.

Another month went by. One night, while I was on my knees in our bedroom, I felt I had an urgent message from the Lord. He was trying to impress on me that I ought to go visit Masuinga. I would not have had such an impulse by myself, because she was already beyond my help.

Before I could get ready to go, word came to us by way of the jungle grapevine that Masuinga had died. I found this very puzzling. I could not understand why the Lord had asked me to go to her, knowing that she was already dead.

The next day came the explanation; the rumor was false. Masuinga, though still living, was so emaciated and distorted that she could hardly sit up or move. To the Jivaro mind, weakness is the same as death, so the mistake was a natural one. However, it confirmed my faith to know that the still, small voice, which had spoken to my innermost being, had not come from my imagination.

Almost immediately thereafter, Masuinga's brother-in-law came to say that she wanted me. She needed badly to be tapped again. Unhappily, Bill and Gladis Gibson were away. But another friend and I decided that we would go. Chumpi and Chingasu volunteered to come along.

The room in which we found Masuinga seemed cluttered and full. Several dogs were tied to the bed poles. Little children sat or stood about eyeing us shyly. Women were busy nursing babies, tending their fires, and preparing the food for cooking.

On a rack at one side lay Masuinga. The eyes she turned on us were clear and bright as she welcomed us with a smile of recognition. She remained cheerful and talkative for the three hours of our visit.

She told us how much it meant to her to have another Christian in the house. She was referring to the eleven-year-old girl from our school, with whom she prayed and sang hymns.

About twenty-five Indians gathered around as Chingasu and Chumpi each gave testimony of what God had done for them and recited truths they had learned from the Bible. When it came Masuinga's turn and she began to pray in her weak, yet unfaltering voice, no one stirred or whispered. Even the dogs were hushed and still. She prayed for everyone in the room, repeating their names and asking that all would be changed in heart, as she had been, in order that one day they would be unafraid of dying.

Masuinga proudly but sadly showed me a dress she had been making out of some material that Uyungara had bought for her. This was most unusual, for among Jivaros, it is *shuartica* for the men to do the sewing. She was sad because she had almost finished the dress and now she would have nothing to do with her hands, no way to fill the long, empty hours.

This made me think of all the dresses for the schoolgirls that would have to be sewed before the beginning of the next term. I asked Masuinga if she would not like to do some of this sewing. She responded with delight, so I promised to send her material, scissors, and thread. Her face brightened as she said she would make the first one for her little Christian friend who had been such a comfort to her.

I noticed that Uyungara was conspicuous by his absence. Masuinga told me quite frankly that he was searching for another witch doctor, one who would be powerful enough to effect her cure. I reminded her then of the scene at Shell Mera, and of how I had been convinced of Uyungara's conversion. She shook her head slowly.

"He has not really become God's child," she said. "He told you that so you would think well of him and give me more help. But he has not changed his old ways one bit."

She asked me to pray for him. But even more, she wanted me to pray for her one young son, Wachapa, who would soon be left without her care.

"I want Wachapa to learn God's way. He is old enough now to be in your school. But his father will not let him go. He is bent on teaching him *shuartica* in order that he will grow to a strong warrior—one who will kill, and drink, and have many wives. But that is not what I want. I want him to learn God's Word and be a Tius Shuara."

As I sat listening to this Jivaro woman lying on the bamboo rack in the dimness of that smoky room, I realized I had never been in the presence of anyone closer to the Lord. Heaven was real to her—and she was almost there!

But I was sorry I had neither the skill nor the instruments to relieve her of the burden of liquid that had again stretched her abdomen to such unbelievable limits. Before I left, Masuinga made me promise that I would be back in a week—the following Wednesday—to help her. I gave the promise readily. At the moment I could see no reason why I couldn't fulfill it. Gladis and Bill were due back in Macuma in five days. I was certain that Gladis would go with me to perform the simple operation.

A day or so after my return, I was dismayed to hear over the radio that the Gibsons would be detained for several days more. How could I keep my promise now? I pictured Masuinga lying there on her bamboo rack, with her perfect faith in the Lord and in me, waiting in vain—hour after hour—for me to come. She might die before Gladis could get there to help her.

Prayer was all I had left. "O God," I prayed, "send someone before the week is over—someone who will be able to relieve Masuinga before it is too late."

My answer came in an unexpected way.

Two days before the week was over, on the regular morning radio contact Dr. Fuller sent me a message from Quito that he had a good friend from the States to whom he wanted to show some of the medical work being done among the jungle Indians. He asked if it would be convenient for them to come to Macuma at this time, and if there were any Indians particularly in need of a doctor's care. We sent back a quick affirmative to both questions, with a prayer of thanksgiving in our hearts.

We trusted the Lord for good weather. Wednesday dawned clear and cloudless, and we soon saw the yellow MAF plane over the trees, bringing in Dr. Fuller and his friend, Mr. John Copley, from Oley, Pennsylvania. Dr. Fuller had the trocar in his pocket and tennis shoes on his feet ready for the jungle hike. Mr. Copley insisted on going along in spite of his sixty years and lack of experience with jungle mud. His special interest in herbs and running comments on jungle plants enlivened our journey.

We found Masuinga even larger than when I last saw her. As she smiled her welcome and reached for my hand, she seemed to know that God had enabled us to keep our promise.

Dr. Fuller sat cross-legged on the bamboo rack and opened his black bag. The usual audience of naked children and long-haired Indians gathered round to watch. The incision was made and the trocar inserted without difficulty. Mr. Copley held a large clay pot while it was filled three times before the liquid would stop flowing. Then after a short service and visiting a while with Masuinga, we started homeward. Mission accomplished. Hearts contented. Promise fulfilled.

Three weeks later, just after Christmas, Gladis and I were planning to visit Masuinga again.

"We'll go next Tuesday," I said, "as soon as our children have returned to school in Quito."

But on Friday an Indian runner came to Macuma. He brought word that Masuinga had died. This time it was true.

"Did she die like the rest of your people?" Frank asked the young man, who looked frightened at the very mention of the word "death."

"No," the Indian said at last. "It was very strange. Masuinga died differently. She wasn't afraid. When we heard her say 'I'm dying,' we all gathered around her bed to watch. But she did not scream or cry as others have done. She shut her eyes and smiled. She only said, '*Shiir jeajai*' ['I have arrived beautifully'] That was all."

We could not be sorry that Masuinga had been released from her distorted body. To know her had been a blessing and it was a comfort that we would see her again.

It would make Masuinga happy to know that little Wachapa left Uyungara's house with his grandmother soon afterward, and never returned to live with his father. He and his grandmother live now with their relatives near the mission. Wachapa, who became a Christian, has been in our school every term since then.

From Masuinga's testimony on her deathbed, several Jivaro men, women, and children have come to know Christ and have been freed from the fear of death that oppressed them for so long. This was a great triumph over *shuartica*.

CHAPTER 15

Evidence of the Holy Spirit

But now in Christ Jesus ye who sometimes were far off are made nigh by the blood of Christ. EPHESIANS 2:13

THE TIME HAD COME FOR OUR CHRISTIAN JIVARO BELIEVERS at Macuma to take the Gospel to the Atshuaras. But they could not go on foot because Catani was at large again. And we had no plane with which to fly them there.

Early in May, 1956, we received word that the replacement plane had arrived. Johnny Keenan and Hobey Lawrence were both available to us as pilots; both wanted the experience of flying to all the outstations and landing on the short tough strips. Now we could proceed with our mission.

One Sunday morning in Macuma at the close of service I stood before the Indians and asked that everyone interested in teaching God's Word to the Atshuaras remain seated. Most of them stayed.

"Since a new plane and pilot have arrived, I made a trip with them last week to visit the Atshuaras," I began. "Tsantiacu and his people were happy to see us. They told me they would like us to come often so that they, too, may learn the Word of God. But I cannot speak as clearly to them in their language as you can. Therefore it is up to you as Christians to go teach the Atshuaras what you have learned of Christ.

A hush fell over the room. Then came an outburst of excited voices.

"Will you go with us, Panchu, or do we go by ourselves?"

"There are no Tius Shuaras among them. They may kill us."

"Catani lives between us and the Atshuaras. He has said he intends to kill Tsantiacu. If Catani finds we are going to the chief's house, he may attack us, too."

I raised my hand for quiet.

"Listen," I said. "I will tell you what passed between me and Tsantiacu. Perhaps that will quiet your fears. I told him, 'Don't think that only foreigners like me know God. Do you remember Icam, who came to visit you? I want you to hear more of God's Word from other Tius Shuaras like Icam. If I sent some to visit you, you would not feel like killing them, would you, because they were once your enemies?

"Tsantiacu looked at me solemnly and said without hesitating, 'Oh, they aren't our enemies now. They are God's people. We wouldn't kill them.'

"I asked if he would let you stay in his house, if he would feed you and take good care of you. He assured me he would. He only cautioned that you do not go hunting or visiting, as other Atshuaras who do not know you might shoot at you.

"The plane will take you to Tsantiacu's place. I will go with you but I won't stay long. Now—who will say to me 'I will go'?"

There was a buzz of uneasy conversation. Some were afraid of flying, others of what might happen to them. At last Naicta—the one who had accompanied Keith and me on our first trip—and Ramon volunteered to go.

A few days later I flew with them to the Atshuaras and introduced them to their one-time enemies. Both Ramon and Naicta were Mura Shuaras from the Upano Valley, whose people had never been friendly with the Atshuaras. I bluntly told Tsantiacu that Naicta had been one of the war party who, years ago, killed his relative Chiriapa.

The two men and the chief greeted each other with no trace of fear or distrust. The change in Ramon and Naicta was plain to Tsantiacu. Instead of guns they came bringing mimeographed copies of Christian hymns and Scripture. I returned to Macuma, leaving the men happily counting off on their fingers those who had heard of Christ and those who had not.

Five days passed before the plane went back to bring them home. As Johnny flew over the landing strip he told us by radio he could see Ramon, Naicta, and the Atshuaras walking with their arms around one another's shoulders. An hour later the Jivaros stepped from the plane at Macuma loaded with gifts—beautiful feather ornaments, a live parrot, and some roast pig. They smiled at us, exclaiming, "Already many of them want to become Christians."

But we knew with what ease Indians can say "Yes—I want to become God's child," so we were not persuaded. However, we rejoiced with the two faithful witnesses while following in our hearts a policy of "wait and see."

Some days later I went to visit Tsantiacu again. He awkwardly tried to tell me that he was becoming like God's people. But he admitted he had gone with his warriors on a killing raid.

"We did not kill anybody," he told me proudly. "You and the believers from Macuma have taught us that God's Word says 'Do not kill.' So all we did was capture some of their women and bring them back in our canoes and turn them over to our own people."

I felt like crying and laughing at the same time. How absurd that he should think that capturing and selling women would be acceptable Christian practice—even though it was somewhat better than killing. But at least it indicated that he was beginning to feel, in his own strange way, some concept of sin.

On another occasion Tsantiacu, greatly agitated, asked me if I'd help him learn to pray. "I know God is powerful," he said, "and I need His help." I asked why. "I am getting threats from my enemies," he replied. "I hear they are planning a raid to kill us. I have my gun ready. But you tell us that God's Shuaras do not kill. If I am to defend myself, I must have God's help. I want to learn to pray."

I couldn't tell whether Tsantiacu wanted to obey God no matter what happened, or whether he just wanted God's power to help him out of a tight situation. But I prayed with him, asking God to prevent the killers from reaching Tsantiacu's house. I told him to keep on praying, that I would return after two moons, and that in the meantime God would make it unnecessary for him to use that gun.

Two months later, Tsantiacu told me triumphantly that his enemies, the Copatasa River Atshuaras, had never reached his stockade. Word had come that they started out, then suddenly turned back when they were halfway over the four-day trail. This seemed to convince Tsantiacu that God could answer prayer.

I once asked Tsantiacu point blank if he had become a Tius Shuara. This I rarely do with Indians, because they are inclined to answer in the affirmative, just for the sake of pleasing. I have learned that it is better to wait patiently for them to take the initiative in expressing a change of heart. But I put the question to him now because I wanted to know how much understanding of the Gospel he had obtained from the believers. He looked at me a moment, then answered, "Yes, I asked God's Son to come into my heart. But he hasn't done it."

Then I knew that he did not yet understand the way of salvation.

After that first courageous visit of Naicta and Ramon, other Indians from Macuma went to stay with the Atshuaras, to teach them to know Christ. Among them were Chumpi and Chingasu who remained on different occasions for weeks at a time.

It is usual among the Indians for the men to become converted first. But in this instance most of the women became Christians before the men, largely due to the wonderful work of Chingasu.

She would gather a group of the Atshuara women around her and begin her lesson as follows:

"I am a Shuara woman who never heard about God when I was young. I never went to school and I do not know how to read. But I know God loves me—He has saved me from my sin. Because Christ is in my heart I am happy. Even those of you who are old like me and have never been to school can learn about God and find happiness by giving your hearts to Christ."

Chingasu's clear, sympathetic presentation won many converts. Tsantiacu's niece, Mamatu, was the first to be saved. When I visited there later, others in the household told me with awe that Mamatu had become a *Tikishmamtaicawaru* (one who has bowed the knee). "She kneels and prays by herself every day," they told me. "The rest of us would like to do it. But we don't know how."

One by one, through successive visits from the Christians from Macuma, many of them were converted.

I had long tried to persuade Chief Tsantiacu to come to Macuma to see the Christians and their church for himself. We discussed this possibility many times. But there was Catani to be reckoned with. Tsantiacu pointed out that the walk over the five-day trail would give his old enemy too many chances to do away with him.

I promised to send the plane for him, and this seemed to overcome Tsantiacu's objections. Since I could not go myself, I recorded a message which Hobey could play to Tsantiacu upon landing:

"This is Panchu. Don't be afraid. Just sit quietly in the plane, and soon you will be in Macuma listening to God's Word with many Tius Shuaras. They are not your enemies. They love you and want to help you know God. Without fearing, you come."

But Tsantiacu's reaction was unexpected. His old Indian superstition took hold of him. He was mystified by the voice coming from Hobey's little battery-powered tape recorder. He thought this was some piece of deceit on the part of his enemies to lure him away from his home so they could kill him.

There was poor Hobey on the ground with nothing but sign language to encourage the stubborn Tsantiacu who was refusing to come. Hobey called me at Macuma by radio and asked me what to do. I told him to put his earphones on the chief and let me talk to him. Hobey complied. Tsantiacu had worn the phones before and they did not frighten him. After much persuasion, I convinced him that this was really Panchu talking, and that he would be in no danger if he took the trip.

The chief took off the earphones and disappeared into his house. He was gone for forty-five minutes, leaving the pilot fidgeting and wondering what was going on. When at last he came out again, here was a different Tsantiacu. His face was startlingly painted with alternate straight and wiggly lines. His long hair had been done up and decorated with brilliant multi-colored toucan feathers. He had discarded his drab and shapeless garment for a clean, new black-and-white striped *itipi*. Across his chest were rows of small, round, flashing mirrors, held in place by narrow belting. He was an impressive figure.

With Tsantiacu were his favorite wife and his only son, equally decked out in their best ceremonial paint and finery, and obviously expecting to climb into the plane with him. Hobey radioed me for further instructions. I thought a minute and then told him to bring them all, if he could do it within the weight limit.

In the next few minutes, Tsantiacu spanned the centuries. He stepped proudly into the plane and submitted to the safety belt with the self-assurance of a much-traveled diplomat. As the plane soared into the skies he laughed loudly and kept up a constant stream of talk. Then he began to sing one of the hymns he had learned, as though practicing for the meeting with the Tius Shuaras. As he looked out the window, he pointed at every river and ridge they passed, recognizing them all.

When the plane circled Macuma for a landing, he shouted down to the people in the houses below in the expectation of being heard as he had heard my voice at times from the plane.

The first few hours of his weekend in Macuma were happy ones for the chief. He listened to testimonies, and prayed and sang with Jivaros who, but for the teachings of Christ, would have still been his enemies. I was reminded of this when I saw him sitting side by side with Mangash, whose chest still bore the scars of bullets from Tsantiacu's gun.

Then, some time on Saturday, came a disturbing rumor that Catani had entered the jungle across the river from our settlement and was threatening to kill the Atshuara chief.

When this word reached Tsantiacu he went wild. He shouted and stamped and waved his gun. He recited instances where members of his household had either been shot by Catani, or died from the curse he had put upon them. The chief upbraided us for bringing him here and exposing him to danger.

We had scheduled a baptismal service at the river for that afternoon and looked forward to showing Tsantiacu how Christians were baptized. But to reach the spot he would have to walk down a short jungle trail. If there were any truth in the rumor, this would provide too good an opportunity for Catani or his men. So, regretfully, we left the chief at home, while the rest of us went to the river.

By the next morning the rumors of Catani's presence had been proven false. Tsantiacu relaxed and began to enjoy himself once more.

He was especially impressed by the Shuara church. He had heard, he told us, of this building used solely for thinking about God and learning more of His Word—a house where no one slept or ate. But he had not believed there could be such a place until he now saw it with his own eyes.

Just before stepping aboard the plane to take the Atshuara family home, Tsantiacu said earnestly,

"Some day we will build a church among our own people."

We saw more fruits of the missionary work of our Indians among the Atshuaras the following fall when seven of their boys, including Tsantiacu's own son, appeared to attend our school at Macuma.

At first we were worried. Would our Jivaro boys accept the newcomers? Or would they make fun of their long hair, naked bodies, and queer-sounding dialect?

Our fears were foolish. Most of the boys treated the Atshuaras as their special friends. They helped them learn the rules of school life, taught them to play their games, and were quick to take their part against any who mistreated them. Only one Mura Shuara, who reflected the attitude of his father, persisted in bullying the new boys until I had to send him home. The Atshuara boys proved apt at learning. By the time their year was out, most of them had become Christians and learned many hymns and passages of Scripture. They went home again well-equipped to help their people to know the Lord.

Some months later—in February, 1957—when Ernest Johnson was visiting the Atshuaras with me, came a moment I had long prayed for. We had just finished conducting a service at Tscantiacu's house. As we were getting ready to lie down for the night, I felt a touch on my arm. Turning, I saw the chief standing beside me.

"Panchu," he said softly, "I need to bow the knee. I want God to forgive me the many evil things I have done. I want Him to give me power to overcome the Devil."

Then and there, we knelt togetner. He talked directly to God as he had talked to me, asking His forgiveness and help. While I prayed I heard two other male voices raised to God in the native tongue. I knew that two more Atshuaras had become Christians that evening.

When we arose, we found ourselves surrounded by women of the household. "Now Tsantiacu has become a *Tikishmamtaicawaru*," they cried happily. "He and his men have bowed the knee."

On one of my trips nearly a year later Marie went with me to the Atshuaras and wrote of her experiences to our four oldest children in school at Quito:

Dearest children,

I am writing to you while sitting on a bamboo rack in Tsantiacu's big house. A little Indian boy wearing a pair of baggy shorts big enough to fit his father is standing beside me, open-mouthed, watching me. My arms are stinging and itching from the bites of tiny gnats. In fact, I itch all over—even inside my clothes—from chigger bites. My eyes burn and feel tired because of the constant smoke in the air.

I just changed my blouse for one with slightly longer sleeves to protect my arms from the gnats. None of the women and children paid any attention while I took my blouse off and revealed my slip. But when I opened a tin can that we brought with a few cookies in it, they all gathered around to see what I was going to eat.

This is the biggest jungle house I have ever seen—almost as big as a circus tent. There must be fifteen beds around the outside wall, and one in the middle full of snarling, mangy dogs, and a big, ugly monkey. About eleven women, a dozen children, and three men are here now.

Daddy and I arrived at noon yesterday. Tsantiacu is not at home. They told us he had gone visiting with his two younger wives and they do not know when he will return. After the plane left, we walked slowly to the house. Daddy visited with two men. Staring, giggling women crowded around me, touching my hair and clothing.

I singled out the oldest woman in the group and learned what her name was from a little one standing beside me. Then I got the oldest one to tell me the names of the others. Indians never like to tell you their names. You must always learn them from someone else. After repeating their odd names until I had learned them thoroughly, I asked about their husbands and children.

Six of them are wives of living husbands; four are widows; and one of them is *ajapamu*. That means "thrown away"—or maybe it is like being divorced. Her husband is still living with his three other wives, but the women gave me the impression that he would probably kill the new husband if she tried to remarry. She looks like a very young girl to have had such troubles. They told me she has lost a baby, too. Her name is Antri.

The widows' husbands have all been killed by their enemies; none died a natural death. They told me these women had come to Tsantiacu's house to hear more of God's Word. But I think they said that just to please me. I believe he brought them here to protect them.

One has a baby boy. She must have shaved her head as a sign of widowhood and grief when her husband was killed, because now it is about an inch long, sticking out in all directions like an overgrown "butch" cut. Another has a baby girl who looks exactly like her—shy eyes above puffy cheeks, framed by ragged, tangled hair. Their faces are even dirty in the same spots.

When I asked a third widow if she had always lived in this house, she laughed and said, "Oh no. I am only the dung of the Atshuaras. They threw me away."

"They? Who are 'they'?" I asked.

"The ones downstream. My husband gave my daughters in marriage to Chiipa. After my husband was killed I thought I would go live with my daughters, but they did not want me. They feared that their husband would love and marry me, too. My husband's friends would not let me stay with them either. They were afraid that if I did those who had killed my husband would kill them, too. Everyone was afraid. I was all alone, I had no place to go, no one wanted me. Then my uncle, Tsantiacu, brought me here." These Indians often use the word "uncle" just as you do for your missionary uncles—to express endearment, rather than exact relationship. 'Come learn a new way of life,' he said to me. 'Take God's way and you will be happy.'"

The fourth widow is a deaf-and-dumb woman whose husband was killed two years ago. It is inspiring to watch her; she takes part in all the household activities just as though she had no handicap. She talks with her hands and seems to understand those who talk to her in sign language. She made friendly signs at me. I tried to guess what she was saying, and when I answered with a smile and some made-up motions, everyone laughed.

The women told me that all the adults in this house have now become Christians. They sing and pray and apparently have quit making war plans and calling on witches.

Two men have just arrived. The little boy who is watching me write tells me they have been hunting for seven days and have brought back two wild pigs to skin and roast. One of them is Shuunta, a relative of Tsantiacu's. Shuunta used to be a witch doctor, but he says he is a Christian now. One of the women told me that when Shuunta was a witch he drank the *natema* and called up evil spirits. But he does not do so any more. He still has the powerful witch's arrows in his body, she said. But the last time her baby was sick he put his hands on the child and prayed to God. He did not drink *tsaangu* or *natema* or call up the evil spirits. And the baby got well.

Daddy and the other men have come into the house and the women are bringing us all some food, so I will put this letter away until later. Wish you could be here with us to know and love these strange people.

Macuma—a week later

I want to tell you about the rest of our visit with the Atshuaras.

When the Indian hunters came into the house, each man sat on his own *cutanga*, making a circle around the food the women served them. They all bowed their heads and, in a loud voice, a man named Tucupe thanked the Lord for His goodness. They didn't so much as look at us before or after praying, so we don't think they were just trying to impress us. When I commented about it to one of the women, she said, "Oh, they always thank the Lord before they eat."

On Friday morning most all of the men and women went to work with Daddy to lengthen the airstrip. I stayed in the house with Tayujinta's attractive bride to watch her dye some shirts and blouses. I knew the Indians dyed their clothes when they got stained but I had never seen them do it. I supposed they boiled them as we do. But she just used cold water, mixed with the leaves of a certain plant which turned it the color of grape juice. After dipping the garments in the dye several times, she squeezed them as much as she could and then spread them on the roofs of chicken houses to dry. From a distance they looked like people lying there.

As we walked out to the airstrip she showed me the plant she used. She crushed some of the leaves between her teeth to make the juice run out. It was green at first, but soon turned dark purple. "We use this as you use soap," she said, "so all the ugly dirt stains won't show." How would you like to change places with her?

The sun was so hot on the airstrip I wished I had some lemonade to give to Daddy. But I thought of something almost as good. Borrowing his jackknife and calling a couple of little boys to help me, I picked several papaya and peeled them. A leaf spread on the log was the table; the juicy fruit was sweet and thirst-quenching. I thought the Indians might enjoy it too and Daddy said I should offer them some. I served the most important men first, just as the Indian women do, and then all the others. They laughed and laughed. Guess they thought it was a big joke that the "white mother," as they called me, should be serving them. The men teased the women, telling them they, too, should learn to feed them while they worked. Some of the women were too embarrassed to eat in front of the men.

Maybe it was while I was picking the papaya that I got more chiggers. Anyway, I still have their bites here in Macuma to keep reminding me that I really visited the Atshuaras.

You, Timmy, would have loved their pets. They had dogs, monkeys, birds, and one little wild pig. He had a longer nose than pigs we know, and longer legs, and stiff, bristly hair. The women fed him from their mouths and he followed them everywhere. The boys had tamed a young tapir and then set him free. Every evening he'd show up in one of the gardens to be fed and petted.

The most exciting thing of all was the amazing evidence of God's power at work in the lives of these people. We held services for them morning, afternoon, and evening, but they couldn't seem to get enough. After dark, when all the beds were full of sleepy Atshuaras, we could hear different ones praying and then Tucupe's voice singing until we fell asleep.

Friday afternoon Chiip came to visit, bringing his two short, fat wives and six dogs. When they came into the house, Shuunta's wife stirred up a choking dust as she tried to sweep the floor clear of its dirt and garbage. I was longing to go outside, but didn't want to miss anything, so I stayed and watched.

Tucupe started preaching to Chiip, who is not a Christian. Tucupe told him that since he had become one, the Lord gave him a heart of love for everyone—even his enemies. "We don't make war any more," he told Chiip, "and you wouldn't either if you had a new heart.

"Would you kill your own brother or sister?" he went on. "Of course you wouldn't, because you love them. Well, that's the way it is when you become a Christian. Every other Christian is your brother and sister and every unbeliever can become your brother and sister too.

"But we ourselves are newborn ones as yet. We have learned just a little about God. Others, like Panchu, know a lot more. He is like our older brother because he was the first one to bring God's Word to us."

Then the women came and sat down on the dirt floor and the men drew up their *cutangas*. Tucupe quit talking and sat down too. Now we could begin the service. I had my flute and so I played some of the hymns before we started to sing. Daddy taught them the one about the thief on the cross who asked Christ to forgive him. They sang it several times, but they were afraid they would forget it, so they wanted to sing it over and over. After a short message, we all bowed our heads and everyone, except the deaf woman and the visitors, prayed aloud.

The women wanted me to play the flute some more so they could sing. When I had first arrived I wore long cotton hose for protection against insects. But after supper I went to the spring and took them off and washed my feet and legs before returning to the house for the service.

Now when someone noticed I did not have any stockings on they became curious. They pinched and felt my legs and one of them said, "Take her shoes off. I want to see what her feet are like." So I took off my tennis shoe and bared one big foot for all to examine. They pinched and rubbed it until I began to think I must be a freak. And what remarks!

"Look how white it is."

"And it is so soft—just like a newborn baby's flesh."

"Poor thing, that's because she always wears shoes. If she stepped on a sharp stone it would cut her foot wide open."

"See how close her toes are. It must hurt to have to have them all squeezed together in shoes like that."

They laughed, and so did I, at my poor, tender, strange feet. But how glad I was that even though there were many differences between me and these ladies, they still accepted me as their friend and sister.

When the women returned to their fires and babies, Daddy suggested that we go for a walk on the airstrip. It was perfectly beautiful and seemed especially so by the light of the full moon, in contrast to the drabness of daytime. Earlier that evening we had watched the flaming and fading of a gorgeous sunset. It thrilled us to think how lavishly the Lord spreads out His beauty, even in this faraway corner of the jungle. There is no place where one is shut off from the presence and power of God. As we lifted our eyes to the beauties around us, we had the warm feeling of being right at home and close to the Lord.

But we were not to enjoy our walk alone. As we started out, Tucupe and several of the young boys came running up. They wanted us to sing some more about the dying thief. So we walked back and forth along the airstrip in the moonlight, lifting our voices in harmony with those who, only a few short years ago, did not know anything about the Lord.

On the way back to the house we came to the garden where cassava bushes stood shoulder high and sweet potato vines covered most of the ground. A little way beyond me, I saw a woman, and walked toward her while Daddy went on with the men. As I drew nearer I saw clearly that she was kneeling in prayer. So I knelt in the dirt beside her and prayed with her. An old woman, she was lifting her heart in praise to the Lord who had saved her and in petition for His help and protection over her son. At this time he had gone on a long trip through the jungle to visit relatives and she was afraid for his safety. "But even if my son should die on the trail from a bite of a snake, which is what I always fear," she said, "I will love and trust Thee, knowing I will see Mayapruwa again in Heaven."

Tears filled my eyes as I listened, and I wondered if I had ever heard a more trustful prayer. As she continued, this primitive jungle garden became to me holy ground—a place where fellowship with God had brought beauty of soul to this Indian woman in her haggard, stooped old body.

When she finished she took my hand and told me that she knelt to talk with the Lord in this place every evening when it wasn't raining. As we walked to the house, I asked her when she had become a Christian. "A long time ago—when Chingasu was here," she answered. "She's old like me but she taught me to kneel and pray to God."

Back in the house with Daddy, I told him I felt these Atshuara Christians, though they knew so little, had helped and encouraged me more than I had them. Our visit with them was a wonderful experience and we were sorry when it ended. They begged us to stay longer and teach them more of the Bible, but we could not. Knowing the Lord cares for the Atshuaras, we pray for them and want you to pray for them, too.

We love you much and pray for you each day.

Mom

CHAPTER 16

The Testing of Tsantiacu

No man can serve two masters.   MATTHEW 6:24

A FEW WEEKS LATER IN APRIL, 1959, I RECEIVED AN urgent message that Tsantiacu wanted to see me. This was good news, for we had been concerned about the Atshuara chief. Some of the women had expressed their anxiety to me on former visits. He was far from being steadfast and growing in his new belief.

"Tsantiacu is not always happy," one of them said. "When there is no Tius Shuara here to remind us of God, it is easy to forget. More of the Devil's Indians come here than Christians from Macuma. Do Indians who do not know God talk beautiful words? No, they talk only of witch doctors and wars. When Tsantiacu goes visiting he tries to tell of God's Word. But nobody listens.

"Lately men have come from down stream to tell Tsantiacu about the wars to the south. His favorite nephew has been killed, they say, and they want Tsantiacu to go and avenge his death. They also try to stir him up to kill his enemies nearby—Timas and his brother, Cashijintu—who have threatened him. When Tsantiacu listens to the Devil's Indians, he goes wild and wants to kill. Then he remembers he is *Tikishmamtaicawaru* and does not want to do wrong."

From what the women told us, the chief might already have gone to war had not the Lord put a series of obstacles in his way. First, his warriors, Shuunta and Tucupe, whose Christian faith was stronger than their chief's, refused to go with him. Then he hurt his leg. By the time it healed, a trader came for pigskins. Tsantiacu went hunting and forgot his plans for war.

Now I hoped I could revive his faith before he reverted to his old ways.

Tsantiacu was waiting for me.

"Panchu," he said, "I am going to visit some of my kinfolk who live far to the south. These people have never heard the wonderful words from God's book. If they die without knowing Jesus Christ, they are sure to go to the big fire that burns and burns. Also, I wish to bring back with me the widows and orphans of my nephew who was murdered. I wish you to go on this journey with me, to preach the Gospel to these, my relatives. Be ready after two moons—at the time the moon is straight up."

His words filled me with joy. I had long wanted to reach those Indians living farther away who had never heard of God. But it would have been too dangerous to go by myself. I needed a Shuara to go with me who was known to them. I had intended to suggest such a trip to Tsantiacu. But this was better; it came as his own idea, in fact, his command.

Upon my return to Macuma, I wrote to Ralph Stuck, a fellow missionary, who had once said he'd like to go with me on a trip like this. He wrote back that he was still interested. Wampiu said he'd go along to help preach and teach.

When the moon was straight up, we flew to Tsantiacu's house.

Before the pilot left us, we had to decide when he would come back to pick us up, as we had no equipment with us for radio communciation. Upon questioning Tsantiacu and his men, we learned that the farthest group of relatives whom they wanted to visit, lived not along the Huasaga River as I had supposed, but two days' walk inland. I had recently injured my foot in Macuma, and I could not possibly walk that far. After much discussion with the Indians, we said we would go with them only as far as the first settlement of Atshuaras, three days downstream. Ralph and I would stay at the house of an old Indian named Aiju, while Tsantiacu and his men walked on inland. We made an appointment to meet the pilot at Tsantiacu's house after eleven days.

We went to work repacking the clothing, thread, knives, and other trade goods into rubber packs for stowing in the canoe. The Atshuara women were busy getting things ready. The men rolled up the pigskins for trading. Tsantiacu still seemed troubled in his mind.

"Many moons have passed since they murdered my nephew," he

said. "Should we forget? Are not his women and children still crying?"

"My gun is clean and ready," put in the warrior, Shuunta. "But can I use it on the dirty killers? Have I not learned that Christians do not kill?"

"Must we not then bring the widows and orphans back with us?" said Tsantiacu, changing his mind again. "Will they not be safe here from their enemies? Will we not teach them God's Word and so save them from burning in hell?"

Both men nodded. They now appeared satisfied that the plan for the expedition was a wise one.

I had brought my outboard motor, which, to the Atshuaras, was a wonderful new toy. Women and children followed us to the river to watch us try it out. We took them on test runs down to the rapids and back. Those aboard clapped their hands and shouted; those ashore clamored for a turn like children at a pony ride. It looked as though our journey would begin in a lighthearted spirit.

Then a remark from Shuunta, who had been looking at the motor, cast a shadow on things.

"It may be that this engine will make too much noise." He frowned. "Can we forget that between here and where we are going, we pass through the country of our enemies? Do not Timas and his brother, who have sworn to kill us, live close to the river? If they hear the big noise going down will they not be waiting in ambush for us when we come back?"

In the silence that followed, Tucupe spoke up.

"God has told us to go; we must obey. With His power, we will return safely."

Wampiu pursued his theme when he preached that evening.

"God does not promise His children any easy road to Heaven," he told the Atshuaras. "But He does give them courage to sing and pray even in the face of danger."

In the morning there was murmuring among the women: "Tsantiacu should not go . . ." "Have you heard that Timas is saying, 'Will not my enemy be an easy shot? Is he not weak as a woman since he has become a Tius Shuara?' No, Tsantiacu should not go."

At the riverbank, the Indians were already waiting with their loads on the ground. They were standing silently, looking at one another. I quickly called them together to pray. After the final "Amen" I gave them no chance to say any more, but stepped into one canoe, while Ralph eased himself into the other. The Indians followed. One of them, Wajari, gave us a push with his pole and we were off.

In the first few hours of travel the stretches of smooth water were too short to use the motor. We had to rely on the pole. But soon we lashed the two canoes together with vines and drove them with the outboard motor.

The Indians forgot their fears. We all had a good time, singing hymns together, talking and laughing.

Later a smaller river emptied into the Huasaga, making it considerably wider and deeper.

"The river will be like this for a long way," Tucupe assured us.

"Yes," agreed Shuunta, "until we get to a certain point near where Timas and Cashijintu live." At the mention of the two names, dark eyes flashed signals of alarm.

If I encouraged them to talk freely about this man Timas, I thought, it might relieve the tension. So I asked the Indians just how far he lived from the river. Unfortunately, Shuaras have no accurate way of measuring distances. Long distances are reckoned by the number of nights spent sleeping on the trail, while short distances are calculated according to opinion or circumstance.

Some of the Atshuaras seemed to think that Timas' house was quite a long way off, while others didn't think it far at all. Some tried to describe, by pointing their fingers to imaginary positions of the sun, how long it would take them to walk it. Since they didn't move their fingers very far, I judged that Timas' house might be a mile or two from the river. This was reassuring; for from that distance Timas' Indians would not be likely to hear the sound of our five-and-a-half horsepower motor—especially since it would be passing in a deep river canyon bordered by heavy vegetation. I said so to the Indians. But their fears were not easily quieted.

"What if they happen to be hunting on a trail near the river?" one of them asked. This idea seemed to frighten them anew.

I tried another approach.

"Are they not also Atshuaras? Why should you fear them? And Timas—did I not meet him a couple of years ago at your own house?"

"Timas has long hated us hard. When you saw him, he had forgotten for a while. Since then, has all not changed?"

"How?" I asked.

"A child in his house died. He thinks Shuunta sent the curse. Oh, would not Timas kill us quickly if he could!

"Don't forget," he went on, "we hate Timas, too. He cursed a child of ours and made him die. We are Tius Shuaras now," he added hastily. "We would not kill. But Timas is different. Once we sent word to Timas and his brother that we wanted no more war. They would not listen."

"Timas' full sister is Shuunta's wife," Tucupe put in. "Will that stop him from killing Shuunta? I myself am brother to Cashijintu. We have different mothers but the same father. Does that mean anything? Is his anger to me not like a dog's?"

I let the subject drop.

The poor Atshuara! He can trust nobody. A relative—or supposed friend—may turn on him any time. From illness or accident comes suspicion that the unfortunate one has been cursed. Suspicion grows to hatred and hatred breeds killing. Nothing can end this vicious circle except the love of Christ.

Such were my thoughts as the motor hummed and the water slapped rhythmically between the two canoes. The scene looked so peaceful. Behind us the waves spread in a rippling V from the propeller to the banks where tangled vines made a solid wall.

About five o'clock, Tsantiacu ordered a stop. High up on a bank was a shelter he had built on a former trip. There we spent the night.

At noon next day as we were purring along, the Indians suddenly fell silent. They fixed their attention on a spot high up on the far bank. Ralph and I looked at each other. We couldn't see anything unusual. Tsantiacu, sensing our bewilderment, said,

"This is the place. It is from here that the trail leads back to the house of Timas."

All eyes remained fastened to it as we churned by. There were no canoes, no clearing, no life. It looked the same as the rest of the bank to me. But it told its story to the Indians.

Shuunta stood up and put his gun to his shoulder. I thought he saw something. Then, as he spoke, I realized he was acting out a drama.

"This is how they will be waiting for us when we return—ready to shoot from ambush," he predicted darkly.

"They would shoot, knowing white men are with you?" asked Wampiu.

"They would shoot," nodded Tucupe. "They fear no one."

"But we can trust in the Lord," Wampiu tried to assure them. "Remember, we pray to Him for protection and He promises to take care of His children."

The Indians grunted and nodded their agreement. We had passed the trail. As abruptly as it had ended, the busy conversation began again.

We were now in deep, smooth water. Turning the motor over to Ralph, I began to cast toward promising fishholes. Something grabbed; a splash and a swish left my line limp and minus the hook. Where there is one hungry fish there must be another. Putting on a new lure, I cast again. Another one bit. This one was smaller; I hauled him in without any trouble.

"Paani! Paani!" yelled the Indians, looking down at my catch which was flopping about in the bottom of the canoe. It had a big ugly mouth full of sharp-pointed teeth. I had never heard the name before, nor had I ever seen such a fish in the waters of the upper Macuma. Wampiu recognized it and explained to me that this was the dreaded man-eating piranha fish. Although it was smaller than my arm, I could easily see how a school of them could tear the flesh from a man's body.

Later in the day I couldn't help being impressed by the ferocity with which a piranha snapped in two a hard green banana and then some stout twigs. A man's finger would present no problem at all.

Shortly after, while I was casting, the canoe bumped into a log and threw me overboard. Visions of those sharp piranha teeth kept me from enjoying what might otherwise have been a pleasant swim. Ralph, shaking with laughter, said, "You came out of there so fast you hardly got wet."

Although the Indians claimed that piranha would attack a man only if he was bleeding, I had no desire to put their theory to the test. We were surprised, however, to find the fish tender and succulent when we roasted the white meat over the coals that night.

By mid-afternoon we had gone as far downriver as we intended. We set up headquarters in an abandoned hut. Aiju's house was two and a half hours inland. Tsantiacu sent some of his Indians to tell old Aiju we had come and to bring him the next day to barter for hides.

While we waited, I showed the chief one of the wordless booklets and taught him the meaning of the colored pages. He made me repeat it many times. He asked if he could take the book along with him. "It will help me explain God's way to my relatives."

"You may have it," I said. "But first tell me what it means to you so I will know you have learned it well."

He took the book tenderly in his big dirty hands. Page by page, he told the stories back to me—accurately and in much better Atshuara than I could have done.

That evening we gathered around the fire to sing hymns and talk of Christ's teachings to His disciples. Long before Tsantiacu and Shuunta grew tired of singing and listening, Ralph and I were yawning as we shifted our legs from one uncomfortable position to another on the hard bamboo racks.

Our Indian brothers weren't even aware of our weariness as they listened to our interpretation of the Scriptures. When we stopped they begged us for more. There were times when I wondered if their interest was not pretended to gain our favor. But if pretense it were, it was certainly consistent.

As Ralph and I moved away from the fire and stretched out for the night, I heard a sound which brought surprise, joy, and thanksgiving to my heart. It was the voice of Tsantiacu praying—as a son talking with his father. He reviewed the events of the day; then he prayed for the women and children left at home; for Aiju and his household; and for his people that he was going to visit. It had been well worth coming all this way just to hear Tsantiacu's spontaneous prayer.

Morning dawned on a scene of bustle and impatience. Tsantiacu was fidgety. He was anxious to meet with Aiju, sell his pigskins, and be off downriver. While we waited, we planned the return journey.

"Today," I began, "is Wednesday."

"Today," Tsantiacu repeated, turning down the little finger of his left hand, "we will go downstream to where the trail takes off to the right. Then, after walking all afternoon, we will be caught by the night. Next day we will walk all day without meeting anyone." He turned down the fourth finger. Touching the third finger, he continued, "From there we will walk fast and come to the place of my people before the sun is straight up over our heads." He turned down the middle finger and index finger. "These two days we will spend searching out the widows and children of the murdered one." He turned down his thumb. "The next day we will leave very early and start back with them." Switching to his right hand, he turned down the little finger and looked at me. "You sleep here and we will meet you before the next day. I will come upriver at night, so that if my enemies are watching they will never see me." He turned down his fourth finger. "On the next day we will start back together to my house."

I reminded him that we had already arranged for the plane to come for us on the eleventh day, which would be a Thursday. Tsantiacu assured me we would be back by then—if all went well.

Voices outside told us Aiju's men were approaching. They marched in with quiet assurance, holding their big Winchester .44's proudly over their shoulders. They were wearing striped skirts; fresh black and blue designs were painted across their bare chests and stomachs. Ralph and I moved quietly to one side as they sat down possessively on our bamboo racks. We were very conscious of our drabness in this colorful Atshuara world.

No one spoke. Then all four began to talk at once, so rapidly and with so many unfamiliar expressions that we could barely catch the gist of what they were saying. Suddenly a remark of one of Aiju's men seemed to cause Tsantiacu great agitation. His dark face flushed; his heavy brows knit together in a worried frown. He turned on me angrily.

"They are saying that Timas and Cashijintu have sworn to kill me if I ever come into their territory," he said excitedly. "Now they tell me we have already passed very near their main trails. This means they know I am here. Will they not be lying in wait for me on the return trip?"

He began to talk hard to me.

"I never should have come on this trip!" he shouted. "Why did you make me?"

It took all my patience to keep from reminding him that the trip had been his idea. Quietly I said to him,

"Have you forgotten how God answered our prayer years ago when the Copatasa Atshuaras started out to kill you and your family? Have you forgotten how, after we prayed, they went back home without ever coming near your house? I ask you, have there been any attacks on your place since you built the airstrip? God will never forsake you, Tsantiacu, no matter what happens. Trust in Him!"

Tsantiacu did not answer. He began to open his rolls of stinking, bristling pigskins. We heard the calls of Indians outside. The rest of Aiju's men were approaching from across the river. They were waiting for us to come and get them in the canoe.

One of the last to come gingerly down the bank was a short, stooped old man. His wizened face peered out at me from under a brown and yellow plastic cap and a thick mat of graying hair.

"Are you not the old and respected Aiju?" I asked.

"I am," he answered, straightening up proudly. "And are you not perhaps Panchu?"

"I am he," I said. "I have come to be your friend and to tell you about God."

"That is fine," he nodded approvingly. "I want to hear those beautiful words. Now let us cross to the other side."

The hut quickly overflowed with Indians, all bartering noisily for hides. Aiju, Tsantiacu, and Tucupe measured and counted and haggled. They might have gone on all day. But Tsantiacu, noticing the straight-up position of the sun, ordered his Indians to be on their way.

Tsantiacu and his men stepped into their canoe, and we towed them an hour's travel farther downstream.

"From here the river becomes too rocky for your engine," the chief said. "We go on by ourselves. Then we will hide our canoe and walk as far as we can before night falls."

We were ready to say good-by. As we sat in the two canoes, we all bowed our heads.

"Lord, give these men strength for their journey, and bring them back soon," I prayed. "May they help their relatives to know Thee and turn away from their terrible wars."

Tsantiacu, Shuunta, Tucupe, and the others poled away downstream. We waved to them until they were lost to sight. We turned our canoe back upstream.

Until Tsantiacu's return, we would stay in Aiju's house. But we arrived at the trail too late to walk there before nightfall; so we had to pass the night again in the hut along the river.

In the morning we took the greatest care to leave no sign. After hiding our motor and gasoline cans in the brush, we looked for a place to conceal the canoe.

"I can show you where I always hide my own canoe," said one of Aiju's Indians.

He took us to a stream well-hidden between high banks. No canoe was there.

"Where is yours now?" I demanded.

"Oh," said the Indian, "someone helped himself to it a few days ago without so much as asking. It was one of Timas' men."

This cast a chill over everybody.

"But what if he comes to return it and finds Tsantiacu's canoe? Won't he then go tell Timas and Cashijintu that Tsantiacu is nearby?"

The Indian had to admit that this was not impossible. All we could do was pray that Timas' Indian would not return the borrowed canoe until after Tsantiacu had made his way back upstream.

Our welcome at Aiju's house was quite different from that which we had received in other Indian houses. These people did not crowd around us like curious children, eager to handle our clothes and our belongings. Foreign visitors were no rarity, for Aiju's house was a key trading post. He gathered hides from widely scattered Indians. In the rainy season when the river was deep, traders came from far downstream to exchange the white man's goods for his wild pigskins.

That explained their indifference toward us. The few goods we had brought for trading were hardly worth their attention. They brightened up when they learned we had medicines, but lost interest when we told them medicines cost money.

Their trading visitors had never mentioned Jesus Christ. If He meant so much to the foreigners, why had none of them ever spoken of Him before? They could not grasp this as the real reason why we had come.

It did not seem likely that we would make much impact on this smug, materialistic household in our four-day visit.

An Indian with a hoary head such as Aiju's is rare among either the Atshuaras or the Jivaros. Most of them die of disease or in war

long before their hair turns white. But Aiju, as a valued middle
man, had achieved a kind of neutrality. He boasted, though, that in
his prime he had killed his four fists of enemies.

Aiju's house was not attractive. The thatched roof was alive with
cockroaches. They ate our bananas and cassava and crawled over us
when we tried to sleep.

Aiju spent most of his time hunched on his low *cutanga*, scratch-
ing or combing lice from his straggly hair. Seated at his feet were
two plump, comely young women. Now and then one helped
pick a thorn from the old man's leathery foot, while the other
helped him comb, occasionally killing a louse between her teeth.
A third, older woman served him his food from a steaming clay
pot. Although the young women looked contented with their job
of making the patriarch's last years as pleasant as possible, we knew
they served Aiju because there was no other choice.

One afternoon I asked Aiju to name me as many of his Atshuara
neighbors as he could, and to tell me where they lived. As I wrote
down their names I judged that including the children they must
number nearly four hundred. All were souls for whom Christ had
died; but they were cut off by geography, language, and custom
from knowing of Him. I felt ashamed for the weakness of our
missionary effort that had not made any headway in this area. The
thought made me determined to do all I could now to win these
people for Christ and to pray that someone would be able to work
among them soon.

We held services morning and evening. The first morning I
asked Wampiu to preach. He began with John 3:16:

"For God so loved the world," he repeated in Jivaro, "that He
gave His only begotten Son, that whosoever believeth in Him
should not perish, but have everlasting life."

I smiled to myself. Wampiu was beginning at the wrong place,
making the same mistake I had made the first time I preached to a
heathen people.

The result was discouraging. He was not holding their attention.
Some of the women who had sat obediently at their husbands'
feet during the singing got up and went to the other end of the
room to tend their fires. The sound of little children quarreling interrupted the words. The men yawned, swatted flies, or looked list-
lessly out into the jungle through the open walls.

Then came bored, cynical questions, along with a wearied shaking of heads:

"Just who is this God?"

"Is he a man like I am, with many wives?"

"How could He have a Son?"

"These are unknowable words. We have never heard them before. Therefore we cannot understand."

Then Wampiu behaved like a true Christian. Laughing at himself, he folded the little pieces of paper on which he had painstakingly written out some Scripture verses in Jivaro and put them away. He faced the crowd with humility.

"I am sorry," he said. "It is so long since I first heard these wonderful words that I have quite forgotten how little meaning they had for me then. If you will listen again, I will try to help you understand."

He began this time with the Biblical account of Creation, which captured their imaginations. He went on to the story of our first ancestors. Here they also listened intently, as ancestry is a subject of great importance to all Indians. He was doing better now. He held them until he tried to explain the present-day existence of sin. Once more he lost them. They began to get up, stretch, and walk about.

Undaunted, Wampiu tried again that night. He began where he had left off, with sin. His audience couldn't go out, since it was raining. They just sat there dully. Wampiu went on to the subject of eternal life. All of a sudden they sat up. They paid attention. They asked questions. Here was something they really wanted to know—how they could live forever.

At every service after that, they asked to hear the same message again. We were also heartened when the men came to our beds often and asked us to tell them more about God. But this was only a first step: we did not press them to become Christians before they fully understood.

During our visit we saw all around us the turmoil and misery common to polygamous households. If I only had the time to stay with these people—if I could teach them patiently—then I would see Christ change their lives as He had done with so many believers around Macuma.

But we were due to meet Tsantiacu by the river to start the

journey home. Aiju, with most of his men, insisted on going with us as far as the hut by the riverside. Tsantiacu was uppermost in our minds. We hoped that he would be there waiting for us.

But he wasn't.

When we went to get our canoe, we saw another lying along-side. But it was not the one Tsantiacu had taken downstream.

"That's the canoe Timas' Indian borrowed a few days ago!" said one of Aiju's men. "Now he has brought it back!"

This was not good. Timas' Indian had no doubt recognized the canoe as Tsantiacu's.

"The plot thickens," Ralph smiled wanly.

All that day we waited anxiously. As afternoon wore on, we kept telling each other the chief must be hiding through the day to travel upstream in the hours of darkness. We stayed the night in the hut, sharing the cramped sleeping quarters with old Aiju and one of his wives. I awoke at 3:00 A.M. No Tsantiacu. Rousing again at 4:30, I saw on one had arrived. Our lone canoe rocked gently on the waves nearby.

Dawn came. We expected Tsantiacu to show up any minute. After breakfast, we busied ourselves reloading the canoe. By mid-morning, we made up our minds to go downstream again to the point where he had said good-by. But there was no sign of Tsantiacu and his Indians.

On the way back to the hut, I tried without success to think of some plan. Then, at the moment of my despair, God's words came to me:

"Fret not thyself because of evildoers. . . . Commit thy way unto the Lord; trust also in Him; and He shall bring it to pass" (Ps. 37:1, 5).

Peace came to me. Here was a situation I could not control; this was the Lord's work; He would find a way to bring Tsantiacu back safely.

Time was running out. We could stay here no longer if we were to keep our date with the plane. Wampiu shoved a long pole into a sandbar opposite the place where we had left the chief. The end of the pole pointed upstream. This was his way of letting Tsantiacu know we had gone on.

Reluctantly, we buzzed the motor and started back. Swift currents slowed our progress. We wondered if we'd make it in time to meet the plane. We had been traveling quite a few hours when Wampiu again pointed out the trail that led to Timas' house. I could not cut the motor; we kept on; but our speed past that point was agonizingly slow.

One more day on the river and we reached the landing at Tsantiacu's from which we had started out. We only wished we had Tsantiacu with us instead of having to speculate on what had happened to him.

We pulled the tarpaulin over motor and gas cans, shouldered our other gear, and went off to the house. As we labored up the last rise, we saw the women come running out to meet us. Their faces were expectant; but when they saw we were alone, their expressions changed.

They set up a shrill, mournful wailing. It was a terrible sound to hear, but we could not quiet them. When they did not see their men, they believed the worst: they had been killed by enemies.

Then they accused me.

"Why did you leave them?"

"Why didn't you wait and bring them back with you?"

"If they have not already been killed, they surely will be."

"Now we are helpless. How we will suffer without our men!"

I had to wait until we were back at the house before I could persuade them to listen quietly. I asked them to trust in the Lord.

"Your men have many times returned safely from long trips even before they were Christians," I said. "Why should they not this time? Remember, God is with them. He has promised never to leave or forsake them. Even if they should die, they would go to be with Him forever. Now stop your crying and think about God and His power."

The wailing gave way to subdued sobbing. The women began to busy themselves with their children and tend their fires. I promised that after supper we would hold a prayer meeting for their husbands.

That night in the big, smoky Atshuara house, we sang and prayed together. The light from the fires flickered on moving lips and strained, intense faces. Their voices rose and fell. Formerly, it had been easy for them to say they trusted in God, but now they were in trouble. They were praying for something very dear—the safe return of their men. Only by such a trial as this could they really learn to trust God. It was a test of their faith. I could not believe God for them. They had to learn for themselves.

Next day the MAF plane, with a new pilot, Dan Derr, came to pick us up on the dot. I hated to leave without knowing what had happened to Tsantiacu.

Wonderful as it was to be back home in Macuma once more with Marie and the children, I could not get the chief out of my mind. After a week had gone by, Dan came to Macuma on his regular bi-monthly vegetable run. I asked him if he could spare the time to fly me back to Tsantiacu's to pick up the equipment we had left there. Happily he could.

As we flew again over the little clearing, I could hardly bear the suspense. I looked out of the plane, straining my eyes. Surely those figures streaming out of the house were men!

Tsantiacu himself stepped forward to meet me before the propeller had stopped turning. Foregoing the usual greetings, he put a hand upon my shoulder and said reproachfully,

"Why did you go away and leave us, Panchu? Why did you not wait a little longer?"

"I did wait longer than we promised," I answered. "When you did not appear, we had no way of knowing how much longer you would be delayed; and we had to be back to meet the plane. But," I added, "before we left, we went back downstream to try to find you. Did you not see the pole we planted in the sandbar?"

The fact that we had made this extra effort seemed to satisfy him.

"We missed you only by a little passing of the sun," the chief said, indicating the time by bending his finger.

He went on to describe the journey home. "Not having any motor the trip was slow. There were many in the canoe and it was hard poling against the strong current. When we came to enemy territory—his voice became matter-of-fact—"we—"

"Tell me!" I interrupted.

"Coming around a bend in the river, I saw a canoe, far ahead. Two men were in it, poling in our direction. As they came closer, I saw who they were—Timas and Cashijintu. They gave no sign they had seen us. We stopped, climbed quickly up the bank, and pulled our canoe after us. From behind jungle leaves we watched. Timas and Cashijintu passed quite close by. We had our guns cocked. We could have shot them. But remembering God's Word, we didn't. We are Tius Shuaras; we do not kill.

"We did not want to return by the river. They might have seen us. They are not Christians and would kill us. We fled through the jungle. There was no trail. The widows of my nephew we were bringing back with us—ran ahead. They carried the children on their backs. We did not eat. At night we ran. We did not sleep. We suffered much. But now we are here!"

"Praise the Lord!" I exclaimed. "Praise the Lord!"

The dignified chief looked at me in puzzlement.

"Why do you say that, Panchu? Did we not suffer much? Were we not in great danger? Did we not almost die?"

"I praise the Lord," I told him, "because now I know why He let me come up the river without you. He planned everything to work out just the way He wanted it. You see, He does not want you to put your trust only in me. He wanted to show you that He could take care of you without my help. Do you not understand? God kept your enemies from finding you. He brought you home safely. I cannot always be with you. God wants you to remember that He is always with you."

Slowly his grim expression relaxed in a smile. He put his arm around my shoulders and led me toward the house.

"So that is what God wants," the old chief said, nodding his head as we walked along. "So that is what God wants. Well . . . Fine. Fine. Fine."

CHAPTER 17

Special Days in Macuma

AT THE BEGINNING OF EVERY YEAR IN ECUADOR'S JUNGLES, the fruit of the *chonta* palm begins to ripen. For the Jivaros the *chonta* is the marker, the calendar by which they reckon their age and the passage of the years. Their New Year's celebration occurs when the fruit is ripe. At its close some of them still throw their spears into the door of the house, as their ancestors have done before them, to kill the spirit of the old *chonta* and so insure better fortune for the *chonta* to come.

For us, too, the New Year is a time of beginning—or reviewing those things which are behind "and reaching forth unto those things which are before," that we might better "press toward the mark for the prize of the high calling of God in Christ Jesus" (Phil. 3:13, 14).

As we look back over the year 1960, some days more than others stand out in our memories as having brought us farther along toward our goal of establishing the church of Jesus Christ among the Jivaros and the Atshuaras.

One such day was the time of the school examination in July, which marked the end of the second full nine-month term we had been able to hold in Macuma.

The yellow, blue, and red-striped Ecuadorian flag, carried proudly by the first Jivaro boy in a long line of sprucely-uniformed school children, rose and fell on the breeze. Together, boys and girls took their places; together they sang, to Marie's accompaniment on the accordion, the stirring national anthem of this Latin-American Republic.

The sound of the sweet childish voices, rising on the quiet jungle air as they gave back to us with assurance the difficult Spanish phrases, brought tears to our eyes. These were Jivaros; but they were also Ecuadorians. They were beginning to comprehend a culture of which they were a rightful part, and to feel a sense of belonging. We foreigners from a far northern land were thankful we could help them become Christians, and thus better citizens of their country.

The singing over, we entered the girls' wooden school building which had long since replaced the crude, open, thatch-and-palm-pole structure where the first handful of youngsters began their lessons.

The girls at their desks squirmed nervously, while teachers and parents, seated on their hard benches around the walls, also squirmed in sympathy. These round-faced, bright-eyed, smiling little children were proud of their neat white blouses and blue jumpers. But they grew self-conscious on finding themselves the objects of admiring eyes, pointing fingers, giggles, and whispered remarks. Even the familiar squeaks of their pets—tiny agouti, marmoset monkeys, toy-sized green-and-blue parrots—failed to divert them.

One Indian girl stood up to answer the questions put to her by the "Señorita Professora." She tried hard to concentrate on what the teacher was saying. But her mind was more than half on the people watching her. She was so afraid of making a mistake that her face reddened, her head drooped, and her fingers became as stiff as the chalk she held. But in spite of her shyness she read from primers in Spanish and Jivaro, recited the alphabet, and, with the others, counted in singsong fashion to a hundred.

When the girls finished we went to the boys' school. For these sons of the jungle, who are used to being the center of attention and are pleased to perform before an audience, examination day was a treat.

After the exercises I stepped to the front of the room to give a final word of exhortation and prayer.

I saw before me sixty-four little Indians, all with warm brown complexions, round cheeks, and high cheekbones, ranging in age from six to sixteen; sixty-four black "butch" cuts in various stages of growth; sixty-four pairs of black eyes, fixed intently on me, or wandering restlessly over walls and roofs in hopes of finding some interesting distraction; sixty-four pairs of bare feet shuffling on the board floor in a vain attempt to elude the stinging gnats and flies.

Thirteen years ago when I faced a similar group, they all looked alike to me, although there were only fifteen of them then. It was a long time before I could tell Wampiu's jet-black eyes from Tsamaraing's—Jimpicti's shaggy head from Icam's. Today, each one before me was a personality. I knew well their family groups, their backgrounds. Some were sons of witch doctors or warriors; some were orphans of men dead in battle or from disease; others were children of Christian Jivaros. Five of the youngest wigglers on the bench were sons of former schoolboys now grown to manhood and eager for their children to learn the Christian way of life.

After a treat of hard candies, we bade good-by to the noisy, lively children we had come to love. Some we would see again at Sunday services, some, not until the next school term, and some—never more.

A number were relieved to be free and ran happily away. Others cried and did not want to go. Our hearts went out to them, knowing that some must return not only to the physical darkness of their homes, but to the darkness of their parents' ways. Each was a personal involvement to us now.

Such a child was Tatsemai, small daughter of Catani. That vicious old warrior, having killed his last wife in a drunken brawl, had been taken away by the authorities and was now locked up in a white man's jail. Tatsemai was being brought up by an aunt who sent her to our school. She learned very slowly, but loved being with us. We were never able to win Catani, who remained a man of violence. But "no man's land" now bordered by Christian homes, was at last clear of his shadow so that Jivaros and Atshuaras could go freely back and forth. And we found joy and satisfaction in teaching Catani's daughter to know Christ.

Then there was Casent, oldest son of Uyungara, whose favorite wife, Masuinga, died some time ago. Casent, like his half-brother, Wachapa, would not be in school at all were it not for a freakish accident. This was one in a series of tragedies that befell Uyungara, but which failed to move his hard heart.

A gun fell from the wall in Uyungara's home one night, going off as it hit the ground. The bullet lodged in Casent's abdomen.

For months he was in the hospital at Shell Mera, where he underwent three major operations. There was little hope for his life. But he recovered and came to us. His treatment was very costly and Uyungara willingly let the boy go to school as his way of payment. We knew God had used these strong measures to give this boy a knowledge of salvation. Casent was not yet a Christian; but he had no wish to follow in the footsteps of his warrior father. We had faith that one day he would accept Christ.

A sad case was that of Ayuy, Pitur's son. Ayuy was the boy who had been badly burned when he rolled into the fire as a baby. He wore a cap at all times to cover his scarred head. A solitary introvert, he dreaded the jibes of other boys and often ran away from school. Although we knew God had saved Ayuy's life for His own purpose, it hurt us to see the boy so rebellious against his fate. We prayed that he would respond to God's love and mercy and find the strength to live at peace with his disfigurement.

Tserempu, a son of Big Saantu, the witch doctor, flashed us a confident smile as he departed. Although only recently a Christian, he delighted in leading chapel services in his hoarse and squeaky changing voice. Tserempu went back to a Christian home. His mother, two younger brothers, and older brother Icam all preached the Word in their house, despite the ridicule of their neighbors.

It was with mixed emotions that we watched these youngsters leave. Many faced a hard fight to keep from falling back into witchcraft, polygamy, and killing. Since we knew they would need God's power to sustain them, our prayers went with them.

But at the same time we were heartened to realize that in these straight and stalwart youngsters marching away down the path, we were seeing future soldiers of Christ who would be spreading the Word throughout the jungle, in years beyond this time.

Every day that gives us the opportunity to show God's love for the Indians is a special day at Macuma. This happens often in our medical work.

One day an Indian mother came running up the path to our new, freshly painted dispensary in the "pentagon" carrying her baby in a cloth sling on her back. The baby was burning with fever. The mother wore an anguished look on her face.

"Help me!" she implored. "My child can't get her breath. Oh, she is going to die! She will die the same way my last baby did. Don't you have some medicines that will make her well?"

We diagnosed her illness as near-pneumonia and administered antibiotics. The child lived—one of many who are saved every year from respiratory infections.

When the older Indian women count on their fingers the children they have had—which may be from five to ten—and then count the number still living, it is unlikely that they will turn down even half as many fingers. But the younger mothers, by contrast, will have lost at the most only one or two. As we look in our files of nearly a thousand names, we find that the infant mortality is being reduced from nearly fifty to less than ten per cent. We know that our medical ministry is worth while. One needs only to have heard the heartbreaking death wail of a mother holding the body of her dead child, to want to do everything possible to eliminate this sorrow from their lives.

Many of the babies saved by medicine have grown up to know Christ, just as many adults have found healing for their souls from coming first for treatment for their bodies.

Now we are training some of our leading Christian Jivaros to give shots and simple remedies to Indians in their own communities. They have been able to treat tubercular patients, among others, thus helping many who are unable to come to us. All of this adds to the growth and influence of the Christian churches among the Jivaros.

As news of our work grows, so the demand grows. It has been our hope and prayer that a full-time missionary nurse come to help us.

Many days in Macuma are spent with visitors, a marked contrast to our early years of isolation when we went for months on end without seeing a friend from outside the station. We always have a warm welcome for fellow missionaries, agricultural experts, or any who are sincerely interested in our work.

One day there came to see us a friend from student days in Minneapolis, the Rev. Murlin Hansel, now a pastor in a small town in Iowa. We welcomed him into our home. We were living in a comfortable frame building with an aluminum roof that had long since replaced our old bamboo basket.

We set out to tour the mission station—by jeep.

"But I flew over jungle all the way!" our guest exclaimed, looking at the vehicle. "I saw no roads. How did you get that thing in here?"

"The same way you came—by plane," I said, "and piece by piece. We even had to cut the frame apart and weld it together again."

The long church building with its thatched-leaf roof was our first stop.

"It doesn't look so beautiful from the outside, does it?" I asked. "But the Indians built it themselves and even cut boards for the floor. They conduct their own services. Here former head-hunters and witch doctors gather to preach and pray rather than to invoke demons to help them win victory over their enemies. So you can see that it is very precious to us."

Across the street was the shop, light plant, granary, and garage. After a look at the school building, we drove around the farm. We came first to a field with little green shoots growing in long, even rows, which I explained were soybeans.

"We have experimented with many types of crops, but these have been our most successful. For one thing, the plant stands straight up. When mature, it drops its leaves and the sun shines on it and the wind blows freely through the stalk; the pod dries easily—a great advantage in this wet country. Other crops, such as wax beans, that fall to the ground, often mold and rot. Another great thing about soybeans is that you can harvest three crops in a twelve-month period.

"Soybeans are high in protein. The Indians haven't much stamina for steady work or resistance to disease because their diet lacks protein. Once they learn to cultivate this crop, you'll see a stronger people. When the children eat less cassava and more high protein foods like soybeans, so many of them won't have distended abdomens."

I went on to show our visitor the other gardens with such crops as papaya, sugar cane, cassava, bananas, rice, and corn. The corn caught his eye.

"We have more corn now than ever before in the history of

the mission," I told him. "Last year we planted a new variety. It did so well that this year many Indians planted it too. They all harvested a good crop."

On the way back up the road we passed some of our big white gobblers in the grass. My visitor expressed his surprise.

"Where on earth did you get big birds like that?" he asked.

I told him the story.

"When I was home on furlough I preached one night at Worthington, Minnesota. There I met Bedford Ludlow who owns a big turkey farm. He offered me some birds. But when I saw the size of them, I couldn't imagine how I could ever get them down to Ecuador. So he kindly offered me some eggs.

"Several months later a pastor friend from Worthington arrived in Macuma, carrying eighty turkey eggs in an egg crate. He had brought them more than three thousand miles by car, transport plane, bus, and small plane. We put them in a kerosene incubator and out of those eighty eggs, eighteen hatched! From the eighteen poults have come a whole flock. With their white feathers they thrive under the jungle sun. They will prove all-important to the Indians; besides giving them food, they will be a source of cash income for medicines and clothes."

We passed the saw mill Mike Ficke had brought from Sucúa several months before. With only an old automobile engine as his power source, Mike had already cut more than two thousand pieces of lumber from raw, virgin timber. Thanks to his skill and industry we would soon have boards for a new boys' schoolhouse, teachers' house, and an additional building for the girls' school, all of which we badly needed. It would have taken years for us to saw this lumber if we'd done it by hand. It took five Indians with handsaws, axes, and machetes to keep up with Mike; the Indians nicknamed him "Shuni" after a jungle bug that eats wood.

Before returning to the house I brought my guest around to the cattle barn where there were six big brown Brahma calves. "I owe my thanks to Heifer Project, Inc., for those beautiful animals," I told him. "They were flown from Miami to Shell Mera in a big transport plane."

He looked toward our little airstrip and remarked,

"But surely the big transport plane didn't land here?"

"No," I said; "getting them over the last lap was a job. Each animal—weighing from three- to four-hundred pounds, mind you —was flown in one at a time in a small plane. We strapped them in tight and gave each one a shot of tranquilizer.

"Eleven Indians now have dairy cattle and they are beginning to understand what the animals can do for them. The other day I overheard two Indians discussing whether it was better to buy a shotgun or a cow. The one having bought a cow said, 'Will a shotgun have little shotguns?'

"These animals, besides supplying meat and milk, will give the Indians another source of cash once a market is established. That will mean building open roads, but it will be worth it."

My friend looked out over our wide jungle acres. I could see something was troubling him.

"Frank," he said at last, "I thought you and Marie were here to preach the Gospel. Why do you emphasize farming so much?"

This was a subject dear to my heart. I almost began to preach.

"It all started out of necessity," I told him. "In our first years we couldn't keep the children in school because we didn't have enough to feed them. I had to find better ways of increasing food production from the poor jungle soil. I obtained different kinds of seeds from an organization run jointly by the Ecuadorian and United States governments called the Co-operative on Agriculture. Christian farmers in the States have helped me also.

"As I had some success in increasing our food supply, I began to see that the benefits of better farming should be made available to all our Jivaros.

"It was clear to me that the Indians needed not only new spiritual values, but also practical help in raising their standards of living. They could never establish a lasting Christian community in the jungle without changing their method of gaining a livelihood.

"When we first came to Macuma, the Jivaro was a warrior and a hunter. He still lived as he had since time immemorial; the centuries had passed him by. Now his world was changing. The game was dying out. The wars were becoming a thing of the past. The day of the valiant Jivaro whose prowess was measured by the number of enemies he killed was gone, never to return. The day of the big raiding parties in search of the head of a distant foe for a *tsantsa* was gone. With it was gone the need for a big house in which to hold the victory feast.

"But stripped now of the incentive to become strong men and great fighters, the Jivaros could easily sink into a purposeless existence. If nothing was done, they would soon vanish into the past, remembered only for their folklore, their curious customs, and their grisly practice of shrinking heads. Christianity is providing a new motivation. Zeal to win their one-time enemies for Christ is replacing the goal of destroying them. More peaceable and less nomadic, it is possible for them to live in communities centered around their churches and schools. But since a diminishing jungle food supply and their primitive methods of farming cannot support community life, they need all the help we can give them with agriculture.

"Prestige is also at stake here. At first many of the Christians suffered shame and ridicule for turning their backs on wars and drunkenness. Other Indians taunted them. But now, through the enviable happiness in their Christian way of living and their success in progressive farming, they are regaining the respect of their fellows. Unbelieving Indians are listening to the Christians who have made a successful change-over from their old way of life.

"If I help the Indian become a better farmer, he not only wins the respect of others but is on the road to becoming self-supporting. In the early days he could earn money for his medicines and clothing only by working for the missionary. But we could not always support a growing community. We must help the Indian to help himself. We want him to support not only his family, but his church and school. Agriculture will help the Indian reach that goal. We teach them, as Paul the apostle told the early believers in Thessalonica: '. . . do your own business, . . . work with your own hands, . . . walk honestly . . . and have lack of nothing' (I Thess. 4:11, 12).

"Elsewhere, the white man's civilization is already coming close. The Indian is suspicious, and not without reason. The benefits it offers are not always happy ones. Unless the Indian can be shown a Christian way in which he can preserve his own pride and culture, then the only destiny for him is to become a shabby imitator of the white man's poorest ways. One story in particular among many that I heard, spurred my efforts to help the Indians raise their living standards in their own habitat.

"Some Indians from the north jungles, having learned Spanish in mission schools, were going to the coast to work on plantations where they could make more money. The stories have been many of homes broken because only the man went out, never to return, or perhaps to come back to die of white man's diseases.

"Would the same thing happen to the Indians we had trained in our schools? Would the very help we were giving turn out to be a curse? I was shaken one day when I heard that just such an experience had befallen one of our own schoolboys. His name was Cajecai.

"Cajecai was a jungle boy who loved to hunt and fish. He was an orphan and lived with his grandfather across the river. He came to our school when he was about ten years old. He had already learned some Spanish from Shell employees near where he lived, so studying was not hard for him. After a while he married and seemed happy with his young wife. But he had not become a Christian and was restless.

"Then one day a party of Indians came visiting from far away. They told Cajecai that he could make a lot of money working on the banana plantations out on the coast. With no language handicap, he could not resist the temptation. He left his wife and went.

"At first he found that what he had been told was true; he made five times the money he might have made back in his jungle home. He worked hard and saved to buy tools, blankets, and other things that he would need in the future. But loneliness soon became too much for him. He spent his evenings and his money carousing. Why worry, when more could be earned so easily?

"It wasn't long before he fell sick. He packed his few belongings and hopped a bus for home. His faithful wife, who was still there waiting for him, surprised him with a son born during his absence.

"He stayed at home for a while. But the taste of high living left him dissatisfied with the humdrum jungle. Again he left his wife and boy and went back to the white man's country. He was full of good resolves; but a recurrence of his illness made him too weak to work. There was no one to extend a helping hand. His money gone, his health gone, in despair he headed back once more to the jungle. This time he went to other relatives and took a different wife. But he was no happier than before. He became an outcast, a wanderer, drifting helplessly back and forth between two worlds until all trace of him was lost."

My guest was disturbed, as I had been, at hearing this story. Now he was beginning to understand the place of farming in our missionary work.

But there was one more thing I wanted him to know.

"Our Indians," I went on, "have heard about others, living closer to civilization, who have lost their land to white settlers. When such stories reach them they say, 'Sooner or later the white man will come and take our land away from us. So why work hard for somebody else? Why not work just a little, get drunk, and live for today?'

"When I became aware of that attitude, I went up to Quito and began the process of getting titles to their land. This involved a lot of paper work. The great distance between capital city offices and jungle land further complicated matters.

"Today some thirty-five Jivaros own a hundred acres apiece. At first they were suspicious of me. A hundred acres didn't seem very much when they'd had the whole jungle for themselves. They felt they were being fenced in.

"But gradually they came to understand this land will be theirs for years to come, and that they will be assured of liberty and security for themselves and their children. They can hold up their heads and be proud before other Indians.

"So," I concluded, "I hope I've made it clear to you that agriculture isn't just a waste of time for missionaries, but a necessary foundation for our church development."

Many of our days are spent just sitting with the Indians, listening to their troubles and counseling them. Murders and plots for revenge are no longer the chief subjects of their talk. Rarely do they come seeking our help in their wars as in years gone by. Now, when they turn down their fingers, they are not counting the members of their families who have been killed since we last met, but rather those who have become Tius Shuaras. And they tell us of their victories and their defeats in trying to live for Christ. Although they are no longer likely to be overcome by the temptation to kill, they still fear the witch doctor.

Such a person is Canusa, who came to us one day and frankly discussed his problem. My heart went out to him as I listened to his story, typical of many others:

"Long ago my wife became a Tius Shuara, when Turuti [Dorothy Walker] was here. Then my little boy was saved and talked to me about God. I had known for a long time that I should become a Christian too, but I couldn't do it. Is my father a Christian? Did he teach us about God when we were young? Did he send me to school? I was already married and too old when you missionaries started the first schools here in Macuma. How could I become God's child? But after listening to God's Word from the preachers, as well as from my own wife and son, I finally became a Christian, too."

Canusa stopped, overcome with emotion at what he was about to tell me. I knew he had wanted to become baptized but had not been. Now perhaps I would learn why.

"There is an old witch doctor that used to treat our family," he continued. "Before I became a Christian I went to him, he didn't help me. Then I went to your woman. She gave me injections and I got some better. But after I became a Christian I got worse instead of well. I couldn't understand why. So I didn't pray to God; I went back to the witch doctor again.

" 'Why have you cursed me rather than helped me?' I asked angrily.

" 'It was not I who cursed you, but another witch—a young one living on the lower Macuma—he has done it,' the old one said.

"Since the old witch told me those things, I cannot pray, I cannot trust in God. Am I not getting sicker all the time?

"The evil spirits follow me and are always talking to me. I hear them in the voice of the owl when I go hunting partridges in the evening. I hear them talking through the *pangu* bird when I walk through the forest in the daytime. Even in my sleep the demons come to me and tell me I am going to die. Then I lie awake on my bed and think about how to get rid of that witch. And my head aches all the time.

"Lately I dreamed a herd of angry bulls was after me. They were going to kill me. Then a man came and said, 'I am Christ. Give me your hand and believe in me.' I know God was talking to me, but I cannot talk to Him so long as that witch is cursing me. If I were really God's child I would not be cursed. But because I am still sick, I wonder if God has saved me. Maybe He has forgotten me. My wife prays for me, but I cannot pray. When

I try to trust in God then I get sicker and I know I am cursed."
He looked at me appealingly.

"We must get rid of that witch doctor who is cursing me. Is not Catani in jail? Can you not put our enemy witch doctor there too?"

"You don't need to do anything to that witch doctor," I told him. "Lots of Tius Shuaras get sick, but that doesn't mean the witch doctors are more powerful than God. God can heal you, but He wants you to love and trust in Him even while you are sick. That is a better way to overcome the evil spirits and all the bad words they are sending you than even getting well would be."

Canusa's eyes rested on mine.

"Pray for me, Panchu," he pleaded.

Canusa went home, still wavering between faith in God and fear of the witch doctor. We felt sorry for him in his misery, but proud for him that he was waging the struggle. Before the Gospel came to these people, shuartica always won. Now we could see evidence of God's power at work. We prayed that He would win in this man.

Every year, there is a series of very special days between the closing of school and the beginning of the next term. This is the time when Jivaro believers from all seven churches in the Macuma-Cangaimi-Cumai area gather together. Among them are Indians from far places, once separated not only by distance but fierce family hatreds, now coming together in the love of God.

They come, not to indulge in the drunken orgy of the tsantsa feast as in days gone by, not to recount to one another all the horrible details and frightful experiences of their latest killing raids —but to attend what they call "a great feast of the Lord"—the regional Bible Conference.

To us these conferences are always amazing—the fulfillment of our dreams during the years when we were struggling to learn the language and itinerating through the jungle in the face of open hostility and threats of bodily harm.

The 1960 conference was held in the long bamboo church at the outstation of Cumai on the banks of the wide Pastaza River. More than a hundred and twenty Jivaros had trudged from their homes many long weary hours over muddy jungle trails to get there. Marie, Barb, and I had gone to Cumai ahead of time and were on hand for the thrilling moment when they began to arrive.

Marie later wrote of it to friends:

"I was standing on the riverbank with several Cumai Jivaros, watching Frank shuttle the Indians across in his outboard-driven canoe. Wichur, the leading believer at Cumai, was helping him. A toothless old Jivaro woman at my side was shaking her head in disbelief.

" 'Are all of those truly God's Indians?' she asked me. I nodded.

" 'When I was a girl,' she said, 'so many Indians would have crossed the river at once for a war or a *tsantsa* feast. Nothing else would have brought them.' "

"She laughed hoarsely and spat upon the rocks."

That night in the big Jivaro-style church, more than two hundred Indians, including the hosts from Cumai, overflowed the crude log benches and aisles and filled the open space around the platform.

On the wall behind the pulpit hung a large sign written in Jivaro: "WILL I RETURN THE SAME?"

Just before the service one proud old Jivaro warrior stalked in, glared at the sign, and, turning around, addressed those just beginning to fill the benches:

"Are not many of these arriving Indians old enemies of mine? If Tsantiacu comes, could I stand the sight of him? No. We have tried to kill each other too many times. Would we sit peaceably together now? No. I cannot change. I go—I shall return the same."

Shouldering his gun, he stamped off into the night. The other Jivaros looked after him curiously, wishing he would change his mind. But no one tried to restrain him and no one cared to follow him.

Just as their fathers had worked for a year to have plenty of food for a *tsantsa* feast, so these Christian Jivaros at Cumai had enlarged their gardens to raise quantities of cassava, plantain, rice, and beans. They had also killed many pigs which were to be the supreme delicacy.

It gladdened our hearts, therefore, to hear the Indians declare during the period of testimony:

"We did not come here to fill our stomachs with the Cumai

Jivaros' good pig meat. Since we are 'born-again-ones' we have come to feed our souls on God's Word so we can return home better Christians."

Each morning as the rising sun turned the blackness of the jungle to green gold, Wichur blew a blast on his cow horn to summon all to prayer. We all sang a hymn, then divided into four groups for the morning prayer hour—one group sitting together on the steep rocky bank of the Pastaza, one in the church, one in the yard, and another in the nearby cook shack. Afterward, everyone came together for Bible studies and reports from the different churches.

This year there were not only reports from Macuma, Cangaimi, and Cumai, where we missionaries had concentrated our efforts, but from four other groups of believers that had sprung up mainly as a result of the Indians' own evangelistic efforts. News of the changed lives of the Tius Shuaras had spread through the jungle.

"These Christians don't kill any more," the other Indians were saying. "They don't get drunk and they don't talk bad. They are living happy, peaceful lives. It would be nice to be like them."

One of our schoolboys who had come to Macuma from along the Cusutca River went back home and repeated the Gospel until, one by one, his relatives, including "Big Eyes'" mother, became Christians. They threw away their *chicha* pots and forgot their old hatreds. Soon they built their own church and began holding regular Sunday and Wednesday services.

One of the boy's uncles learned to do some preaching, too. Wherever he went visiting, he told of salvation. One day, while calling on some of *his* relatives who lived far downstream on a tributary of the Cusutca called the Yuwientsa, he found that they, too, wanted to become Christians. Another former Macuma schoolboy lived there and had already told something of the Bible. The uncle led them to become Christians and to build a church of their own. Two churches sprang up at about the same time, also through the efforts of our schoolboys—one between Macuma and Cumai, and the other between Macuma and Cangaimi. These indigenous churches were following Macuma's example in organization and practice.

We were impressed during these report sessions by the way the Jivaros discussed questions with reason and calmness. They respected one another's opinions. No one became angry any more. They no longer insisted on outtalking one another.

A recurrent problem discussed at the conference was how to encourage more of the believers to become baptized. Formerly, many had wanted to do so before they understood its meaning. Therefore, the first Bible Conference had set up these prerequisites for baptism:

1. Make an open profession of faith in Christ. (This to the talkative Jivaros meant not just with one's mouth but with all one's heart.)

2. Leave witchcraft. (To these jungle Christians, witchcraft represented the power of the Devil, and could not be endorsed along with faith in God.)

3. Give an active witness to those Indians who are not Christians, (Any Jivaro too ashamed of God to tell others about Him must not be a true Christian.)

4. Be consistent in attending church services. (This, their main source of Bible instruction, they dared not neglect.)

5. Leave drinking habit completely. (Since drunkenness resulted in so much misery, it could not be tolerated.)

6. Return thanks to God before meals. (Don't be like a dog and steal your food from God.)

7. Tell no lies or untrue stories. Do no tale-bearing. (Lying is of the Devil; a Christian should be different.)

8. Do not take multiple wives after becoming a Christian. (If you had more than one wife when you became a Christian, don't throw the others away and make harlots out of them. But if you have only one, then don't make more homes full of jealousy and misery.)

The decision as to whether to baptize a man who had become a Christian after marrying more than one wife was a particularly complicated one. A committee of nine Indians from widely separated groups set the standards for themselves, agreeing that no man having more than one wife could be baptized. Although the missionaries were not all agreed on this subject, we respected the Indians' right to decide what was best for their own people.

Wichur's situation was a case in point. When he first professed his faith in Christ, he was living with two wives. A year or so later a young nephew of his secretly wooed his second wife and ran off with her. When Wichur discovered this he flew into a rage and vowed he would never rest until he had killed his nephew.

When word spread that he was organizing a manhunt, a group of Macuma believers went to call on him. They pointed out that perhaps God had a purpose in allowing this unhappy thing to happen to him. They asked him if he had prayed to God for guidance and he admitted he had not. They prayed with him, pointing out the wickedness of his plan. Finally, Wichur bowed his head and agreed that this might be God's way of keeping him from living with two wives. He promised to call off the manhunt. Eventually, Wichur was baptized and became a leader of the Cumai church.

A sad note was the absence of any Atshuara Christians. None had yet come to any conference. There was no Christian church established among them.

We listened hopefully to Wampiu as he gave a report on one of his recent visits to them. He had spent most of his time at Tucupe's house.

"Tucupe is my friend," he smiled. "Although he has killed more than twenty men, including some of my relatives, he is like a brother to me now. Christ has changed his heart just as he has changed mine."

His report on Tsantiacu was not so favorable.

"Tsantiacu and Shuunta are not following God as Tucupe is. They are not happy because they sent other Atshuaras to avenge the death of their nephew. They did not kill him themselves but they ordered others to do it. They have disobeyed God and they know it. Many in Tsantiacu's house prayed and confessed their sins, but those two men sat on their *cutangas* and said nothing. They looked at the ground. We did not talk angry with them; we only felt sorry for them. You must remember they are weak because they have no church like we do."

Affirmative nods and grunts came from the audience. Marie and I agreed with them that, lacking regular Bible teaching and constant church fellowship, it is very hard for converts to become strong Christians.

Our first reaction was one of regret that we had been unable so far to succeed with the Atshuaras as we had with the Jivaros.

Then I thought back to that night around the campfire when Keith and I had made our first exploratory trip. How unlikely it had seemed then that Jivaros would ever be visiting Atshuaras in Christian fellowship. And yet it had happened, as Wampiu just described. Was the establishment of a strong church in the future any more impossible?

With God's help, we reaffirmed our purpose and set our hearts on this goal with new resolve.

In the course of the conference we also had a look at the future. The greatest need in all churches was for fuller knowledge of the Bible and ability to read it. Slowly, painfully, this work was going forward. Dorothy Walker, with Bill and Gladis Gibson, had recently established a Jivaro Bible training center at Sucúa. Several of the believers from our area had attended and were looking forward to more. Our work in translating was progressing.

We were also able to disclose to the Indians our most exciting plan for the future. This was to place a hundred transistor radios in Jivaro homes. A vision of several years was about to be fulfilled. We were still awaiting government permission to broadcast from Macuma. But in the meantime, our good friends at HCJB had offered to carry our taped programs for half an hour each day. This would be a great step forward in taking the Gospel regularly to Indians beyond the reach of weekly church services.

The crowning blessing of the conference came as we gathered together with our Indian brothers and sisters to celebrate the Lord's Supper. The elements in this jungle setting were simply tomato juice and pieces of steamed cassava; but humble as they were, their representation of the broken body and shed blood of our Lord was clear and precious to all of us.

A hush fell over the congregation as leaders from the different churches stepped to the platform. Here was evidence that the Holy Spirit of God could lead even illiterate jungle savages to know Him and to preach His truths. Ramon, head elder of the Macuma church, took his place behind the small table.

We wished the stouthearted missionaries who had gone before us could be with us now to see their long patient work over the years bearing fruit.

Ramon had lived through it all. He had seen the first gleam of the Gospel penetrate the jungle darkness and spread out over the towering hills and across raging rivers to change the lives of many of his people. He had gone to Mrs. Olson's school when that courageous lady was living to serve the Lord in a simple, Indian-style hut. As guide and carrier, he had tramped the trail with Ernest Johnson while that missionary itinerated ceaselessly, unmindful of danger and hardship, to spread the Word. He had helped Ernest clear the land and hew the first timbers for the Macuma Mission. He knew from his own experience what it was to carve a station out of solid jungle, and how a missionary must face down the hostility and ridicule of those who do not know the Lord. Later, when Christ had changed his own heart and given him eternal life, he understood why those early missionaries had kept on through the seemingly unrewarding years in which no churches were established.

As we watched Ramon pour the red juice into the crude pottery cups and listened to his prayer of thanksgiving for Christ's shed blood, we were moved by the consciousness of God's immediate presence. It was He who had changed the hearts and lives of these former head-hunters, and established His church among them. It was He who had brought us to take part in this work.

Happily, we thought of all we had seen and heard during these days. Much had been accomplished in our area, but it was only a small beginning compared to the task still remaining.

Far out beyond the few thousands who had been brought within reach of the Gospel—far down the rivers and the tangled forests, beyond the most distant points reached by our Jivaro believers—countless fearful, death-doomed Jivaros and Atshuaras still lived in the evil grip of *shuartica*. These, too, must be set free. Our work was not done.

All the problems we faced had not been solved: some we had overcome; others had only changed. Just as we were able to build on the efforts of all who had gone before us, we looked forward to the coming of other missionaries to help in completing the tasks begun. The age-old spiritual struggle would not end until the Day of Jesus Christ.

"Lord, we see Thyself in the lives of these Christian Jivaros. We love and adore Thee and give ourselves anew to the work which is before us."

Glossary

Aiju (*ah*-ee-hyoo) neutral Atshuara, trader of pigskins

Ambato (ahm-*bah*-toh) mountain town in central Ecuador

Antri (ahn-*dree*) a young Atshuara widow protected by Tsantiacu

Atshuara (aht-*shwah*-rah) Indian tribe living in southeastern Ecuador, speaking a dialect of Jivaro; enemies of the Jivaros

Auca (*ah*-oo-cah) tribe of savage Indians living in north Ecuador's jungle that killed the five missionaries at "Palm Beach"

Big Saantu (*sahn*-doo) witch doctor living across the river from Macuma mission; brother of Capitu

Cajecai (cah-*he*-cah-ee) former Macuma schoolboy, who, lured by easy money, ran away to the coast and disappeared

Cangaimi (cahng-*ahee*-me) mission station about fifteen miles south of Macuma on Cangaimi River

Canusa (cah-*noo*-sah) Jivaro from Macuma, wavering between witchcraft and Christianity

Capitu (cah-*pee*-tyu) Jivaro chief living across river from Macuma; brother of Big Saantu

Casent (cah-*sent*) son of Uyungara; survivor of freakish accident

Cashijinto (cahsh-i-*hin*-too) Atshuara killer, brother of Timas

Catani (cah-*tah*-nee) Jivaro chief and witch doctor; principal enemy of Tsantiacu

Chiip (cheep) Atshuara living near Tsantiacu

chicha (*chee*-chah) Spanish word for a Jivaro household drink, made from fermented cassava

Chingasu (cheeng-*yah*-soo) effective teacher of Gospel to women; wife of Chumpi; mother of Wampiu

Chiriapa (chee-ree-*ah*-pah) Atshuara whose head was taken and shrunk by Jivaros on a killing raid

Chumpi (chuum-*bee*) Chingasu's young husband

Copataza (co-pah-*tah*-sa) river north and east of Macuma flowing into the Pastaza

Cumai (cuu-*mah*-ee) first of the mission outstations, ten miles north of Macuma

Curaray   (coo-rah-*ray*)   river on whose banks the five missionaries were killed by Aucas

Cusutca   (coo-*soot*-cah)   church built by Indians of Cusutca River area

cutanga   (coo-*tahng*-ah)   carved, two-legged stool, used by Jivaro and Atshuara men; most important piece of household furniture

Cutucu Mountains   (coo-too-*coo*)   range of mountains east of the Andes; clearly seen from Macuma

ekenta   (e-*ken*-dah)   women's section of the Jivaro house

Icam   (*ee*-kyam)   Jivaro who became a Christian; son of Big Saantu

Itipi   (ee-*tee*-pee)   wrap-around skirt worn by Jivaro men

Jeencham   (*heen*-jahm)   Jivaro for "bat"; name of Indian who explained witchcraft, went along on first trip to Atshuaras; father of Tsapacu

Jimpicti   (heem-*beec*-tee)   one of the first five Jivaro converts; son of Washieta

Jintachi   (*heen*-dah-chee)   Cangaimi Jivaro who opposed building the airstrip

Jisma   (*hees*-mah)   Cangaimi Jivaro injured by falling tree

Jivaro   (*hee*-vah-roh)   tribe of Indians living in eastern Ecuador; enemies of the Atshuaras; Jivaro is Spanish name for them; they call themselves Shuaras

Jua   (hoo-*ah*)   schoolboy who married Tsapacu, Jeencham's daughter

Juani   (hwah-*nee*)   young Jivaro girl whose baby was delivered in Macuma dispensary

Juang   (hoo-*ahng*)   brother-in-law of Nawich; killed by Uyungara

Huasaga   (wah-*sah*-gah)   river running through Atshuara country

Little Saantu   (*sahn*-doo)   Jivaro who went on first trip to Atshuaras; no relation to Big Saantu

Macas   (*mah*-cahs)   provincial capital in Ecuador's jungle

Macuma   (mah-*coo*-mah)   jungle mission station on banks of Macuma River; later base for other mission outstations

maicua   (*mah*-ee-kyoo-ah)   drug drunk by witch doctors to induce visions; similar to belladonna

Mamaisa   (mah-*mah*-ee-sah)   one of the first Jivaro girls to be baptized; daughter of Puanshira

Mamatu   (ma-*mah*-too)   first Atshuara believer

Mangash   (*mahng*-ash)   Macuma Jivaro, wounded by Tsantiacu

Masuinga   (mah-*sweeng*-ya)   sick wife of Uyungara who became a Christian before dying

Mayacu   (*may*-ye-coo)   Christian Jivaro from Cangaimi

Mayapruwa   (may-*ye*-proo-wah)   young son of Tucupe, the Atshuara who became a Christian

Mura Shura (*moo*-rah *shwah*-rah)   literally, the hill people; Jivaros from around the Cutucus

Naicta (*nah*-eec-tah)   Macuma Jivaro who related story of the last killing raid and head-hunt in the Macuma area, in which he took part

nantar (*nahn*-dar)   good-luck stone placed in Jivaro gardens to make crops grow

natema (nah-*te*-mah)   narcotic drink used by witch doctors to induce visions

Nawich (*nah*-weech)   Jivaro who plotted and executed the death of his own son-in-law

Oriente (oh-ree-*en*-te)   jungles of eastern Ecuador

paani (*pahn*-ee)   piranha fish, sometimes called the man-eating fish

Panchu (*pan*-choo)   name given Frank Drown by the Jivaros

pangu (*pahn*-goo)   small jungle bird which makes a peculiar sound disagreeable to the Jivaros

Pastaza (pah-*stah*-sa)   large river flowing from Shell Mera southeast past Cumai

pinta (*peen*-tah)   disease that causes discoloration of the skin

Pitur (*pee*-tyoor)   Jivaro who took missionaries on first trip to the Atshuaras

Puanshira (poo-*ahn*-chee-rah)   father of Mamaisa

Quichua (*kee*-choo-ah)   large tribe of Indians living in the high Andes and northern jungles of Ecuador

Ramon (rah-*mon*)   head elder of the church at Macuma

Shuara (*shwah*-rah)   Indians; people; Jivaro name for themselves

shuartica (*schwar*-tee-kyah)   ancient Jivaro custom which rigidly guided everything they did until they became Christians

shuni (*shoo*-nee)   bug that eats wood

Shuunta (*shoon*-dah)   nephew of Tsantiacu; young warrior and witch doctor

sua (*soo*-ah)   jungle tree whose fruit gives a stain used as a black body paint, camouflage for hunting or war parties

Sucúa (soo-*coo*-ah)   jungle town south of Macas where first mission to the Jivaros was established many years ago

Tatsemai (tah-*tse*-mah-ee)   young daughter of Catani, in school at Macuma

Tucupe (too-*coo*-pe)   father of Mayapruwa; member of Tsantiacu's household

Taisha (*tah*-ee-shah)   Jivaro chief living on border of "no-man's land"

Tangamash (tahn-gah-*mash*)   men's section of the Jivaro house; also, name of Jivaro who went on first trip to Atshuaras

Tayujinta (tah-yoo-*heen*-dya)   Atshuara living with Tsantiacu

tikishmamtaicawaru (tee-*keesh*-mahm-*tay*-ii-kyah-wah-roo)   literally a "bowed-the-knee-one"; Atshuara expression for one who has become a Christian

Timas (tee-*myas*) hostile Atshuara chief who planned to kill missionaries

Tirisa (tee-*ree*-syah) young schoolgirl among the first to be baptized

Tius Shuara (*tyoos* shwah-rah) a Christian; one who had become God's Indian

Tius shuartica (*tyoos* shwar-tee-kyah) Christian customs

Tiwi (*tee*-vee) schoolboy who deceived Ernest Johnson and helped kill Nawich's son-in-law.

tsaangu (*tsahng*-oo) a brew of tobacco leaves drunk by witch doctors to induce visions

Tsamaraing (tsah-mah-*rah*-eeng) young Jivaro preacher who was bitten by a snake and recovered; son of Chief Washicta

Tsantiacu (*tsahn*-dyah-coo) Atshuara chief; long-time enemy of Catani; reached by Christianity, but wavering

tsantsa (*tsahn*-tsah) shrunken head of an enemy which becomes a talisman of power and strength to the possessor

Tsapacu (tash-pah-coo) Macuma schoolgirl and bride of Jua; daughter of Jeencham

Tserempu (*tse*-rem-boo) Macuma schoolboy who became a Christian

Tsetsempu (tse-*tsem*-boo) mother of "Big Eyes"

Tsungi (*tsoong*-ee) young Jivaro who became a Christian; husband of Juani

Tuitsa (*twee*-tsah) Jivaro host on first visit of missionaries to Cangaimi

Upano River (oo-*pah*-noh) large river starting in eastern Andes and flowing past Macas and Sucua

Uyungara (oo-*yoon*-gah-rah) Jivaro killer from the upper Macuma, who cared faithfully for his wife until her death; husband of Masuinga; father of Casent and Wachapa

Wampiu (wahm-*byoo*) brightest boy at Macuma school who became a preacher; son of Chingasu by an earlier marriage

Wachapa (wah-chah-*pah*) young son of Uyungara who attended mission school

Washicta (wah-*sheek*-tyah) patriarchal chief who had nine sons, among them Tsamaraing and Jimpicti

Wichur (vee-*choor*) Cumai Jivaro from Macuma who became a preacher there

Yuwientsa (yoo-*vee*-en-tsah) church between Macuma and Cangaimi on the Uwientsa River